Instant *Excel 2000* Answers ...

Toolbar Button	Shortcut	Function	First Click Menu	Then Choose Option	Next
Σ		Add obvious group of numbers			
		Apply border to selected cells	Format	Cells	Border
≡		Apply center alignment	Format	Cells	Alignment
🎨 ▾		Apply color background to selected cells	Format	Cells	Patterns
A ▾		Apply color to selected text	Format	Cells	Font
,		Apply comma format to numbers	Format	Cells	Number
$		Apply currency format to numbers	Format	Cells	Number
	CTRL-1	Apply formatting to selected cells	Format	Cells	Select type of formatting
≡		Apply left alignment	Format	Cells	Alignment
%		Apply percentage format to numbers	Format	Cells	Number
≡		Apply right alignment	Format	Cells	Alignment
		Apply style to selected text	Format	Style	Select type of style
		Center heading over selected columns	Format	Cells	Alignment
B	CTRL-B	Change selected items to/from bold	Format	Cells	Font
I	CTRL-I	Change selected items to/from italic	Format	Cells	Font
U	CTRL-U	Change selected items to/from underlined	Format	Cells	Font
100% ▾		Change size of screen display	View	Zoom	Select magnification
ABC ✓	F7	Check spelling	Tools	Spelling	
		Choose to have errors corrected automatically	Tools	AutoCorrect	
10 ▾		Choose type size	Format	Cells	Font
Arial ▾		Choose typeface	Format	Cells	Font
	ALT-F4	Close application	File	Exit	
	CTRL-F4	Close current document	File	Close	
	CTRL-V	Copy clipboard contents	Edit	Paste	
		Copy format of selected character(s)	Edit	Paste Special	Format
	CTRL-C	Copy selected item to clipboard	Edit	Copy	

Instant *Excel 2000* Answers ...

Toolbar Button	Shortcut	Function	First Click Menu	Then Choose Option	Next
		Create and insert chart	Insert	Chart	Use wizard
		Create and insert map	Insert	Map	
	CTRL-N	Create new document	File	New	
		Decrease decimal places	Format	Cells	Numbers
	DELETE	Delete selection	Edit	Clear	Select what to clear
		Display hidden row/column/sheet	Format	Row/Column/Sheet	Unhide
		E-mail	File	Send to	Choose recipient
	CTRL-D	Fill cells below	Edit	Fill	Down
	CTRL-F	Find text or number in document or file	Edit	Find	
	F1	Get Help	Help	Microsoft Excel Help	
	CTRL-G	Go to new location	Edit	Go To	Indicate location
		Increase decimal places	Format	Cells	Numbers
		Indent/decrease indent one tab setting	Format	Cells	Alignment
		Insert function at cellpointer	Insert	Function	
	CTRL-K	Insert hyperlink to URL/document	Insert	Hyperlink	
	CTRL-O	Open existing document	File	Open	
		Preview file before printing	File	Print Preview	
	CTRL-P	Print selected pages/area	File	Print	
	CTRL-X	Remove selected item to clipboard	Edit	Cut	
	CTRL-Y	Reverse Undo command	Edit	Redo	
	CTRL-Z	Undo last action	Edit	Undo	
	CTRL-S	Save current document	File	Save	
		Sort selected or obvious data	Data	Sort	
	ALT-TAB	Switch to different open document	Window	Document name	
		Toggle Drawing toolbar	View	Toolbars	Drawing

Excel 2000

Answers!

Gail Perry

Osborne/**McGraw-Hill**

Berkeley • New York • St. Louis • San Francisco
Auckland • Bogotá • Hamburg • London
Madrid • Mexico City • Milan • Montreal
New Delhi • Panama City • Paris • São Paulo
Singapore • Sydney • Tokyo • Toronto

Osborne **McGraw-Hill**
2600 Tenth Street
Berkeley, California 94710
U.S.A.

For information on translations or book distributors outside the U.S.A., or to arrange bulk purchase discounts for sales promotions, premiums, or fund-raisers, please contact Osborne/**McGraw-Hill** at the above address.

Excel 2000 Answers!

1234567890 AGM AGM 90198765432109

ISBN 0-07-211883-0

Publisher
Brandon A. Nordin

**Associate Publisher and
Editor in Chief**
Scott Rogers

Acquisitions Editor
Megg Bonar

Project Editor
Jennifer Wenzel

Editorial Assistant
Stephane Thomas

Technical Editor
Bryan Seningen

Copy Editor
Sally Engelfried

Proofreader
Rhonda Holmes

Indexer
David Heiret

Computer Designer
Roberta Steele
Gary Corrigan
Jean Butterfield

Illustrator
Robert Hansen
Beth Young

Series Design
Mickey Galicia

To Katherine and Georgia,

Excel users themselves,
who love to pick up one of
mom's books in a bookstore
and find their names inside!

Contents @ a Glance

Contents

Acknowledgments

I'm always amazed at the enormous team effort that goes into the production of a computer reference book. If you imagine that one person sits at a computer and writes the book, then ships it off to be printed, you couldn't be more wrong. This book began with an idea, a joint effort between Osborne/McGraw-Hill publishers and Stream Tech Support, to produce a definitive reference that would be able to take the place of thousands of the tech support calls that Stream fields on a regular basis. Why not consolidate the most commonly asked questions in a single resource so that, for the price of a tech-support session, the reader can have the benefit answers to questions asked by users from all over the world?

The people at Osborne who made this project possible include Megg Bonar, who hired me to write my first book many years ago, and who found me again for this book; Stephane Thomas, who provided the guiding beacon that kept this book on track; Jennifer Wenzel, who oversaw the extensive review that made sure the material in this book is accurate; Ron Hull, the alternate project editor; Sally Englefried, the copy editor; and Bryan Seningen, the technical editor.

Meanwhile, Mike Blake, Joe Monte, Pat Nadeau, Bonnie Brown, and Howard Lotis from Stream provided input and technical advice for this book, as well as the top ten FAQs you see listed in Chapter 1.

These names are only a small handful of the force behind producing the book you hold in your hand. From acquisition, to edit, through design, layout, printing, indexing, binding— the list of people who helped make this book possible is enormous, and I am grateful to them all.

On a personal note, I want to thank my family for their constant support as they witness me moving through what seems to be an endless assortment of deadlines; they keep their distance when time starts running out on a project, yet they're always there to help me cheer when the mail carrier delivers the advance copy of a new book I've completed.

xi

Introduction

Every year or two, new versions of all the major software programs seep out into the market, trying to claim their share of users. The new versions strive to provide that "something extra" that will attract new users to consider the program and encourage existing users to upgrade to the latest fashion. There are those who would argue we've gone well past the need for new versions—doesn't one spreadsheet add a column of numbers just as well as the next? How can basic tasks be improved upon?

The improvement, if you will, in many of the latest versions of software programs, occurs in the areas of expediency, ease of use, shortcuts, options for dressing up data, and plenty of new features like art files and music clips, all of which adds up to a program that is more and more complicated and confusing. Thus, the overwhelming need for having questions answered.

If you're trying to keep up with the latest technology—a never-ending task, I might add—you probably find yourself asking lots of questions about how features work and how you can take advantage of the capabilities of your program. This book is designed in a question-and-answer format, with questions grouped into logical topics that make up the areas where most people have problems when they use Excel.

Excel 2000 Answers! is divided into 17 chapters, each covering a major topic about using Excel. Within each chapter are subtopics, and questions users have about these topics. You can explore this book by topic, or you can flip to the back and find all the topics listed alphabetically in the index.

Besides the questions and answers, there are tips that call attention to particularly important Excel features. Sprinkled throughout the book are cautionary notes that point out areas of the program where users experience problems.

Start with Chapter 1, "Top Ten FAQs," for the ten most frequently asked questions about Excel. Then dig in, thinking of this book as your own personal technical support guru.

Chapters 2–17 focus on specific topics within Excel, offering answers to the common questions that arise among typical users. At the beginning of each chapter, you'll find a listing of the topics covered there. The "Answer Topics" section is followed by an "@ a Glance" section, where you can read a summary of the information covered in the chapter. The chapters are filled with questions and answers relating to the topics described at the front of each chapter.

At the front of the book is a handy command reference that lists common menu commands, buttons, and shortcuts. There is an extensive and thorough index in the back of the book as well, where you can search for key words to help you find the answers to your questions.

CONVENTIONS USED IN THIS BOOK

Excel 2000 Answers! uses several conventions designed to make the book easier for you to follow. These conventions include the following:

- **Bold type** is used for text that you are to type from the keyboard.

- *Italic type* is used for terms and phrases that deserve special emphasis. Italic type is also sometimes used for labels and names of fields and controls that appear on screen, particularly when the capitalization of the labels and names makes them difficult to distinguish from regular text.

- Small capital letters are used for keys on the keyboard such as ENTER and SHIFT.

When you are expected to enter a command, you are told to press the key(s). If you are to enter text or numbers, you are told to type them.

Chapter 1

Top Ten Questions

Answer Topics!

Excel Top Ten Questions @ a Glance

- Sharing Excel 2000 files with users of other Excel versions
- Turning off the Office Assistant
- Controlling menu display
- Displaying the Euro currency format
- Entering dates for the year 2000
- Working with files that have been converted to HTML format
- Using the new Office 2000 intelligent menus
- Creating pivot tables without the wizard
- Importing table data from a Web page
- New features when selecting cells

1. If I give/send an Excel 2000 file to someone who has Office 97, will that person be able to open it?

Yes, Office 2000 is backward compatible with Office 97. The two programs use the same file structure. However, any features *new* to Excel 2000 will not be available when you open that file in Excel 97. Also, if you send an Office 2000 file to someone with a version lower than 97, the file won't open. As an alternative, remember that you can always save a file in an earlier format by choosing File | Save As and indicating an earlier version of Excel under Files of Type.

2. How do I turn off the Office Assistant?

In Office 97, you could disable the assistant, but hitting F1 or using Help would bring it back unless you emptied out the actors folder. In Office 2000, you can right-click on the Office Assistant and choose Options. On the Options tab, uncheck the Use Office Assistant option. From this point forward, the Office Assistant will not come on when you use Help unless you go to help and tell it show the Office Assistant.

3. How do I get Excel to show my menus the way they were in earlier versions?

To set the menus to the Office 95/97 view, go to Tools | Customize | Options and uncheck the Menus show recently used commands first checkbox. Click the Close button. From this point forward, Excel will display full menus and the order of items on the menus will remain stable.

Note that making this selection while in Excel (or any Office 2000 program) affects the display of menus in all Office 2000 programs.

4. Does Excel support the new Euro currency format?

Excel 2000 supports the new Euro currency as a new currency format. It can display both the three-letter ISO code (EUR) and the Euro symbol. The symbol can be formatted in the front of the amount or after the amount. To insert the symbol, select the cell(s) on the spreadsheet and then, from the Format menu, select Currency and use the drop-down box to select the format.

5. How can I enter year 2000 dates?

Excel 2000 has added additional date formats to make displaying four-digit years easier. Excel 2000 now has two administrator settings to make the transition to year 2000 easier. With the first setting, users can set their own rules for what century a two-digit year falls under. The second setting allows a user to enter a date with a full four-digit year and format the cell(s) to show all four digits of the year. You can access this setting through the System Policy Editor of the Microsoft Office Resource Kit.

The Office Resource Kit is a collection of tools for use in customizing your Office programs. Download the Office Resource Kit from the Microsoft Web Site, at http://www.microsoft.com/office/ork/default.htm. When the Kit has been downloaded, an executable file, ORKTools.exe, will be placed on your computer. To install the Office Resource Kit, double-click on this file name (you can find the

file name by finding the folder into which the file was downloaded in your My Computer window) and the program files will be extracted.

Once the Office Resource Kit has been installed, click the Start button, point to Programs, point to Microsoft Office Tools, and then point to Microsoft Office 2000 Resource Kit Tools or Microsoft Office 2000 Resource Kit Documents. Look for references to date settings to take advantage of the new year 2000 options.

6. Will I be able to work on my Excel files in Excel after they have been converted to HTML format?

Yes. Excel 2000 makes this easy because it preserves the rich features of the original spreadsheet when converting a document to HTML. This allows users to reopen an HTML file in Excel and receive the same functionality, formatting, and edit state as when the spreadsheet was originally created. This makes HTML documents easily accessible through a browser, while maintaining the original edit state of the documents.

7. The menus in all the Office 2000 applications are changing themselves on me! What's going on?

The Office programs now use intelligent menu technology, a feature Microsoft calls Personalized Menus, which moves the most recently used command from each menu list to the top of the menu. This feature can be disabled. In any of the Office 2000 programs, go to View | Toolbars | Customize, go to the Options tab and remove the checkmark from the Menus show recently used commands first option. This will turn off the feature in all of the menus.

8. When making a pivot table, I no longer see all the steps to drag and drop the items in the wizard.

Excel 2000 has you drag and drop the fields on the actual sheet where your pivot table will be. This way you can see how your data will come out, and you can change it instantly instead of having to go through the wizard again.

 ## 9. What is the easiest way to bring in table data from a Web page?

Use drag and drop. Tabular information on a Web page can be copied from the browser directly into Excel with excellent results. You can select the information and copy it, then paste the information into Excel, or you can select the information and drag and drop it. It's the easy, fast way to transfer and manipulate any Web-based table data.

 ## 10. Am I selecting cells properly? They don't highlight like they used to.

Excel 2000 has changed how cells look when selected. Instead of displaying in reverse video (where the normal cells have a black background and white letters), it uses a feature called *see-through cell selection*. Now when you select cells, they are highlighted with shading which enables you to see the contents much more easily than before.

Chapter 2

Excel Worksheets

Answer Topics!

Excel Worksheets @ a Glance

Overview. Getting comfortable with Excel means getting used to the day-to-day operation of the program—file management, getting from here to there on your worksheet, selecting areas of the worksheet, copying information from one place to another, and moving data from one part of a worksheet to a new location. As you become more comfortable with Excel and begin storing your financial information on worksheets, you may find a need to protect sensitive data. All of these features are covered in depth in this chapter.

Opening, Saving, and Closing Files. Data is stored in files, and it is imperative that you know how to save your data and retrieve it at a later time. Excel has its own ideas about where it wants to put your files, and you can let Excel have its way, or choose your own locations for file storage. When you are finished working in Excel, there is a variety of ways to save your files and close the program.

Moving Around the Worksheet. Use the keyboard, use your mouse—one way or another, you will find the best way to get from place to place on your worksheets.

Selecting Cells. There are lots of shortcuts for selecting cells—both with your mouse and from the keyboard. Select cells in your worksheet in order to use them in formulas, or select cells in order to change their appearance and formatting.

Copying and Moving Cell Contents. You don't have to reenter information that has already been entered in another cell. Use copying, moving, and pasting techniques to copy or move data from one place to another. Copy formulas and copy the contents of cells with the AutoFill feature, and create links with information in another file that will update as the original data in the other file changes.

Security. You should be able to feel that your data is safe. Use passwords to keep unauthorized users from viewing sensitive information. Use techniques for hiding portions of your worksheet so that only the information you want others to see will be viewed.

OPENING, SAVING, AND CLOSING FILES

 When I try to open a file, Excel always looks in the My Documents folder. How do I find a file located in another folder?

Choose File | Open and Excel presents you with a dialog box that lists all the Excel files that are in the My Documents folder. To look in a different folder for files, click the down arrow in the upper-right corner of the Look in list box, and a miniature directory tree will appear (see Figure 2-1). If the folder in which you wish to look is shown on this tree, click that folder name. If you don't see the folder you are searching for, click on the drive letter that contains the folder you wish to view. All the folders located on the first level of that drive will appear. Double-click a folder name to view its contents.

Click here to display the directory tree for your computer

Click here to examine the contents of the folder one level up from the current folder

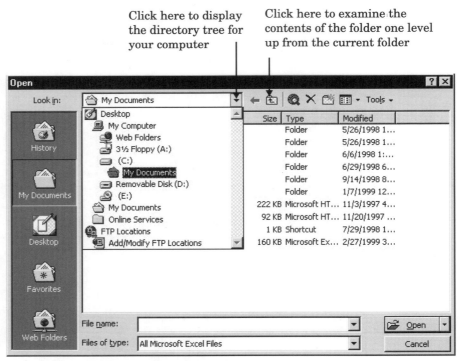

Figure 2-1 Search for a folder in the directory tree

Subfolders and any Excel files that are in the folder will be displayed. Continue double-clicking on subfolders to view their contents.

Each time you double-click on a folder name, you advance down one level in the directory tree. Clicking on the folder icon to the right of the Look in list box returns you up one folder level at a time.

As long as you don't close the Excel program, the next time you choose File | Open or File | Close, you will return to the folder whose contents you last viewed. Once you close Excel and reopen the program, the My Documents folder is once again the default location for files.

Can I change the default folder Excel uses when opening files?

If you want to change the default directory so that files are automatically saved to a directory of your choice and the contents of your chosen directory appears when you issue the File | Open command, follow these steps:

1. Choose Tools | Options. The Options dialog box will appear.

2. Click the General tab. The window shown in Figure 2-1 will appear.

3. In the Default file location text box, enter the drive and folder (and, if applicable, subfolder) that you want to use as your default location for saving and retrieving files.

4. Click the OK button to save your changes.

My co-workers have created spreadsheet files using software programs other than Excel. How do I use Excel to open these files?

The first step in opening a spreadsheet file not originally created in Excel is to choose File | Open and locate the file you wish to open. Excel automatically looks in your default folder (My Documents, unless you have changed the default as described in the above answer) and searches for Excel

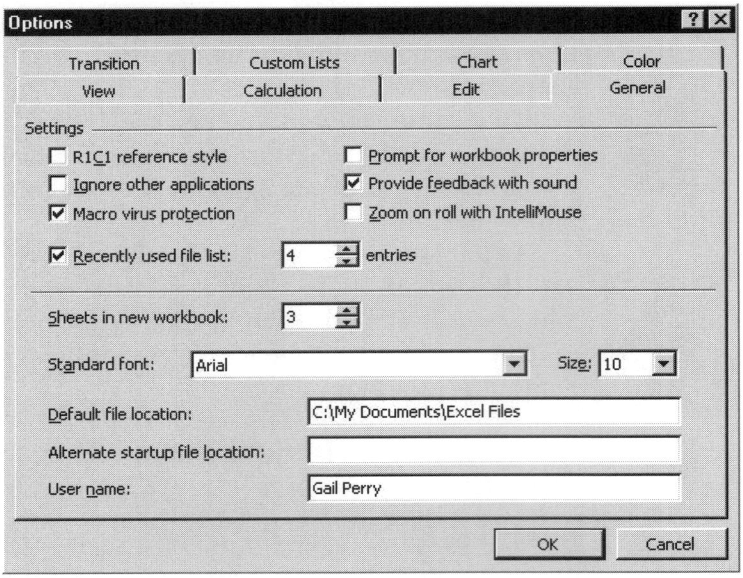

Figure 2-2   The General options. Change the default file location to the folder of your choice

files. If necessary, change the folder shown in the *Look in* list box to the folder that contains the file you wish to open.

Next, click the arrow in the Files of type list box at the bottom of the window. From the list that appears (see Figure 2-3), choose the file type that most closely matches the description of the file you wish to open. For example, if you want to open a file created in any version of Lotus 1-2-3, choose Lotus 1-2-3 Files as the file type. Files that match the type you have selected will appear in the file list. If no files appear, double-check the file location (in the Look in list box) that you indicated, or change the Files of type description to All Files.

***

Note: *The instructions here indicate that you should change the folder in the* Look in *list box, then change the file type in the Files of type list box. It doesn't matter in which order you perform these steps. You can change the file type first and then change to the directory containing files of that type, if you prefer.*

Click on the name of the file that you wish to open, then click Open to open the file in Excel. Excel will convert the

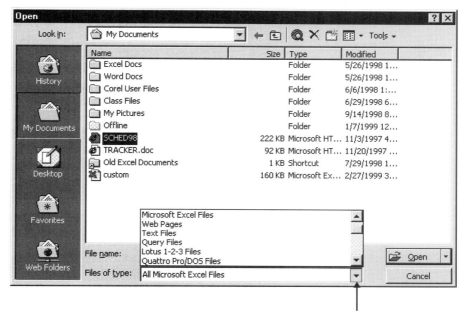

Click here to change the file type

Figure 2-3 Open a file not created in Excel

file as necessary so that it will appear on your Excel worksheet screen.

There are some file formats that Excel cannot read. If Excel cannot read the file, go back to the program in which the file was created (or have the coworker who created the file do this), open the file in program that created it, and save the file as an Excel file by choosing File | Save. In the window that appears, change the file type to Excel.

 I want to be able to open my Excel file in a different spreadsheet program. How do I save the file so it can be read in another program?

When you are ready to save the file, choose File | Save As. The Save As dialog box will appear. At the bottom of the dialog box, click the arrow in the Save as type list box and choose the type of file you prefer. Enter the file name and location in the appropriate boxes, then click the Save button.

Excel will save the file as the type indicated, and you will be able to open the file in the designated program.

 ### I saved an Excel file and now I can't remember where it is located. Is there a way to search for lost files in Excel?

Search for files that are hiding on your computer by following these steps.

1. Choose File | Open. The Open dialog box will appear.

2. Enter the name of the file for which you are searching in the File Name box. You can use wild cards (for example, typing **Sales*** would produce a list of all file names beginning with "Sales").

3. Click the Find Now button to begin the search. Excel will search through the folder designated in the Look in list box for files that match the description you entered. Files that match your description will be displayed in the file list.

You can extend your search to include subfolders by clicking the Advanced button, clicking the Search subfolders check box, and clicking the Find Now button.

In addition to searching for filenames, you can search for files containing particular text. After choosing File | Open, enter text in the Text or property box, then click Find Now. Excel will return a list of all files in the designated folder (and subfolders, if the appropriate box is checked in the Advanced area) that include the text you entered.

 Tip: *An alternative way to search for files, without using the Excel menus, is to click the Start button on your taskbar, choose Find, and then click on Files or Folders. In the Named area, enter the name of a file for which you are searching or, in the Containing text area, enter specific text (or a string of numbers) that is contained in the missing file. Click the Find Now button to begin the search. A list of all files matching the chosen criteria will appear.*

Is there a way to create an automatic backup while I'm working in Excel so that I won't lose all of my unsaved work in the event of a power failure?

By default, Excel does not automatically save worksheets while you work. This feature has been available in word processing programs for years but is not a part of the standard Excel program. There is, however, an add-in program available with Excel called AutoSave that will perform this task for you.

First, check to see if the AutoSave program is loaded on your computer. Click the Tools menu. If AutoSave is on the Tools menu, the add-in program has already been loaded. If AutoSave is not on the menu, choose Add-Ins from the Tools menu, select AutoSave, and click the OK button. The program may load automatically, or you may be prompted to insert the disk or CD that you used when you installed Excel.

When AutoSave has been loaded, you will see the AutoSave command on your Excel Tools menu. To activate AutoSave, choose Tools | AutoSave. The AutoSave window will appear (see Figure 2-4). Choose from the following options:

- Automatic Save Every xx Minutes. Fill in the number of minutes you wish to elapse between AutoSaves and check the box to activate this feature. The default time is to save every ten minutes.

- Save Active Workbook Only or Save All Open Workbooks. The active workbook is the one that is on top of your Excel screen. Choosing all open workbooks will create an AutoSave for any workbook that is open if Excel is shut down unnaturally.

- Prompt Before Saving. If this box is checked, you will have to respond to an onscreen message each time Excel attempts to AutoSave your workbook.

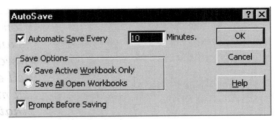

Figure 2-4 Use the AutoSave feature to protect your data from power failures and computer shutdowns

> *Caution:* *The AutoSave feature only saves your file—it does not create a separate backup file as the AutoRecover feature in Word does. Be careful when using AutoSave that you don't save temporary changes to a file that you wanted to keep intact. If you use AutoSave and want to keep your original file intact while making some temporary changes in the worksheet, save a working copy of the file in addition to the original, and make your changes in the working file.*

I notice I have the choice of saving my workbook or saving my workspace. What's the difference between the two save options?

When you choose File | Save or File | Save As, you are requesting Excel to save your active workbook file. The active file is the one that is currently on top—the one that is in view on your Excel screen. Any other open workbooks are not saved when you select one of these commands.

When you choose File | Save Workspace, Excel asks you for a name for your workspace. The name you choose encompasses all open files and the save process saves not the files, but the layout of the files (which files are open, which file is active). In addition, you will be given the option of saving any changes that have been made to the files, but this is not mandatory. In the future, when you open Excel, you can choose to open a workspace, just as you would open a file by choosing File | Open and selecting the name you gave to the workspace. Excel will open all files that are associated with the workspace you saved and will place the same file in the active position. Your cellpointer will be located in the same cell as it was when you saved the workspace.

Tip: *The Save As Workspace option is useful for opening a group of files at once, but it also has another interesting use. You can set up a spreadsheet to be used by another person and position the cellpointer in the cell exactly where the other person should start. Or you can open multiple workbooks and arrange your screen in such a way that pertinent areas of the various files are visible at once. Saving your workspace in these circumstances can make your Excel worksheets more accessible to other users and can also be a time-saver when several files are needed in conjunction with each other.*

What is the quickest way to close all the files I have open in Excel without closing my Excel program?

When closing multiple files, if you click the File menu and choose Close, Excel thinks you are only closing one file at a time—the active file. However, if you hold down the SHIFT key before clicking the File menu, the Close command changes to a Close All command. Choosing this command produces the box shown in Figure 2-5.

When you choose Close All, Excel picks one of your open files and asks if you want to save the changes you have made to the file. Your options are as follows:

● Choose Yes to save the changes you made to the particular file. Excel will save the changes, close the file, and display the same box, listing the name of another open file. This process will repeat for each open file in which unsaved changes have been made.

● Choose Yes to All to save the changes in all open files and close all open files at once.

● Choose No to close the selected file without saving changes. Excel will close the file and display the same box, listing the name of another open file. This process will repeat for each open file in which there are unsaved changes.

● Choose Cancel to close this box without saving changes to any files, leave all files open, and continue working.

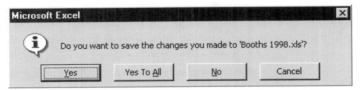

Figure 2-5 You can use the Close All command by pressing SHIFT before opening the File menu. A box like this will appear when you choose Close All

MOVING AROUND THE WORKSHEET

How can I move around quickly to different areas of my worksheet using the mouse?

There are several techniques for moving from one place to another on a worksheet while using the mouse:

● Use the mouse to click in any visible cell. That cell becomes the active cell—the cell in which your data will appear when you begin typing.

● Click on the arrows at the ends of either scroll bar to advance the worksheet one cell at a time in the chosen direction.

● Click in the gray area on either side of the box that appears in the scroll bar to advance the worksheet one screen at a time in the chosen direction (see Figure 2-6).

● Drag the box that appears in the scroll bar to slide the worksheet in the chosen direction.

● Click on the Sheet tabs at the bottom of the screen to change from one sheet to another.

Are there shortcuts for moving around the worksheet using the keyboard?

There are several keyboard shortcuts for getting from here to there in Excel:

● The RIGHT, LEFT, UP, and DOWN ARROW keys on the keyboard advance your worksheet and your active cell one cell at a time in the chosen direction.

	D	E	F	G	H		I	J	K	L		M	N	
36	55,967.38		29	640			29	41.32	815.68	88,942.47		350	143.20	7
37	55,812.14		30	640			30	41.69	815.31	88,900.77		350	147.72	7(
38	55,655.73		31	640			31	42.08	814.92	88,858.70		350	152.29	7(
39	55,498.15		32	640			32	42.46	814.54	88,816.24		350	156.89	7(
40	55,339.38		33	640			33	42.85	814.15	88,773.38		350	161.54	6(
41	55,179.43		34	640			34	43.24	813.76	88,730.14		350	166.22	6(
42	55,018.27		35	640			35	43.64	813.36	88,686.50		350	170.96	6(
43	54,855.91		36	640			36	44.04	812.96	88,642.46		350	175.73	6(
44	54,692.33		37	640			37	44.44	812.56	88,598.02		350	180.55	6;
45	54,527.52		38	640			38	44.85	812.15	88,553.16		350	185.42	6;
46	54,361.48		39	640			39	45.26	811.74	88,507.90		350	190.32	6(
47	54,194.19		40	640			40	45.68	811.32	88,462.22		350	195.28	6(
48	54,025.65		41	640			41	46.10	810.90	88,416.13		350	200.27	6!
49	53,855.84		42	640			42	46.52	810.48	88,369.61		350	205.32	6!
50	53,684.76		43	640			43	46.95	810.05	88,322.66		350	210.41	6.
51	53,512.39		44	640			44	47.38	809.62	88,275.29		350	215.55	6.
52	53,338.74		45	640			45	47.81	809.19	88,227.48		350	220.73	6;
53	53,163.78						46	48.25	808.75	88,179.23			225.96	6;
54	52,987.50			28800			47	48.69	808.31	88,130.54			228.03	6;
55	52,809.91						48	49.14	807.86	88,081.40			230.12	6;
56	52,630.99						49	49.59	807.41	88,031.82			232.23	6;
57	52,450.72						50	50.04	806.96	87,981.77			234.36	6;

Click in these areas to advance or
move back one screen at a time

Figure 2-6 Clicking around the worksheet

- HOME changes the active cell to the cell in column A of the current row.

- CTRL-HOME makes cell A1 the active cell.

- CTRL-END changes the active cell to the cell that is the farthest down and to the right of all the cells that have been used in your worksheet.

- PAGE UP and PAGE DOWN advance the worksheet and the active cell up and down, respectively, one screen at a time.

- ALT-PAGE UP and ALT-PAGE DOWN advance the worksheet and the active cell left and right, respectively, one screen at a time.

- CTRL-PAGE UP and CTRL-PAGE DOWN change the view to the next sheet and previous sheet, respectively.

● CTRL-ARROW key (or END key followed by an ARROW key) moves the cellpointer in the direction of the arrow pressed. The cellpointer goes to the first occupied cell if you are starting from a blank cell, or it goes to the last occupied cell if you are starting in an area where the cells are occupied.

● To advance to a particular cell, press the F5 function key, enter the cell reference, and press ENTER.

Tip: *To move quickly through a range of occupied cells, use this quick mouse trick. Place your mouse pointer on the edge of an occupied cell, choosing the edge that corresponds to the direction in which you want to move. If you want to move down, place your mouse pointer on the bottom edge of a cell; if you want to move right, place your mouse pointer on the right edge of the cell, and so on. The mouse pointer will resemble a white arrow. Double-click on the edge of the selected cell, and Excel will relocate your mouse pointer to the farthest occupied cell in the chosen direction.*

Is there a way to use the Name Box to move to another cell in the worksheet?

Click once in the Name Box at the upper-left corner of the worksheet—the box that shows the address of the active cell—and enter the cell address of the cell that you wish to make active (see Figure 2-7). Then press ENTER. Your cellpointer and your view of the worksheet will be changed to the cell you entered in the Name Box.

SELECTING CELLS

How do I select an entire row or column without having to drag the mouse pointer through every cell in the row or column?

Click the row number of the row you wish to select (or click one cell in the row and press SHIFT-SPACE), or click the column letter of the column you wish to select (or click one cell in the column and press CTRL-SPACE). The entire row or column will be selected at once.

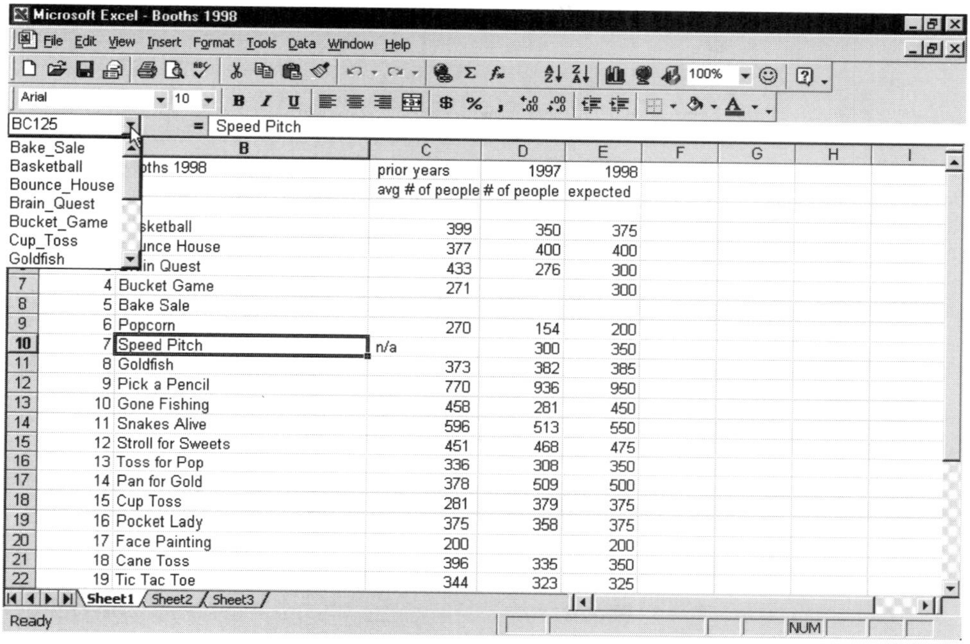

Figure 2-7 Enter a cell reference, then press the ENTER key to move to the selected cell

Select multiple rows that are adjacent to one another by dragging the mouse pointer through several row numbers. Select multiple adjacent columns by dragging the mouse pointer through several column letters.

Select multiple rows and/or columns that are not adjacent to one another by holding down the CTRL key while you click on various row numbers and/or column letters.

Turn off the selection of any area by clicking once anywhere on the worksheet.

Sometimes I like to apply the same formatting to different areas of the worksheet. Is there a way to select nonadjacent areas of the worksheet and apply the formatting commands to all selected areas at once?

You can select nonadjacent areas of your worksheet by holding down the CTRL key, then clicking on or dragging through the different areas of the worksheet. Each area you

select will be added to the entire selection area, and any formatting changes you make will affect all selected cells.

You can select multiple columns and rows with this technique as well. For example, you can change the width of several columns at once by selecting all the columns you want to change, then changing the width of a single column. All the other columns will follow the example.

Turn off the selection area by clicking in any cell on the worksheet.

Can you tell me about shortcuts for selecting cells with the mouse?

Using the mouse to select cells is often considered a shortcut in itself, but I know of at least one slick mouse shortcut for selecting cells. Follow these steps to select a range of cells that are already occupied:

1. Click on one cell in the range. The cell you selected becomes the active cell.

2. Hold down the SHIFT key and place the mouse pointer on any edge of the selected cell. The mouse pointer will change shape so that it appears to be a white arrow instead of a white cross.

3. Continue pressing the SHIFT key and double-click on any side of the active cell. Depending on which side of the cell your cellpointer is pointing to (top, bottom, right, left), the occupied cells from the selected cell to the end of the occupied area will be selected (see Figure 2-8).

Is it possible to use the keyboard to select cells in a worksheet?

When you hold down the SHIFT key, you can use the arrow keys on your keyboard to select cells on the worksheet. Use the following key combinations to select areas of the worksheet:

● SHIFT-ARROW selects an area that starts with the active cell and continues in the direction(s) of the arrow key(s) you press.

Press SHIFT and double-click
here to select this cell and all
occupied cells to the right

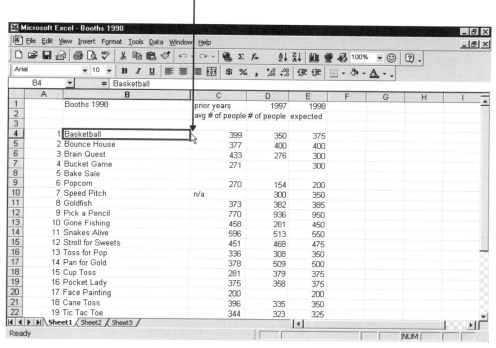

Figure 2-8 Double-click the outer edge of a cell while pressing the SHIFT
key to select all occupied cells in the chosen direction

- SHIFT-HOME selects an area from the active cell to Column
  A in the current row.

- SHIFT-CTRL-HOME selects an area from the active cell to
  cell A1.

- SHIFT-CTRL-END selects an area from the active cell to the
  lower-right corner of the cells used in the current worksheet.

- SHIFT-SPACEBAR selects the current row.

- CTRL-SPACEBAR selects the current column.

- SHIFT-END-ARROW selects the area from the active cell to the
  last occupied cell in the direction of the arrow key you press.

- CTRL-A selects the entire worksheet.

 Is there a way to make global changes (changes that will affect all the cells in the worksheet at once) in Excel?

You can make a change that will affect all the cells in the worksheet, such as changing the number format for the cells, changing the typeface, or changing the column width. To make a global change, click the Select All button in the upper left corner of the worksheet or press CTRL-A (see Figure 2-9). The entire worksheet will be selected. Any changes you make will affect every cell in the worksheet. The changes are for the current worksheet only and will not affect other worksheets or files.

Select All button

	A	B	C	D	E	F	G	H	I
1		Booths 1998	prior years	1997	1998				
2			avg # of people	# of people	expected				
3									
4		1 Basketball	399	350	375				
5		2 Bounce House	377	400	400				
6		3 Brain Quest	433	276	300				
7		4 Bucket Game	271		300				
8		5 Bake Sale							
9		6 Popcorn	270	154	200				
10		7 Speed Pitch	n/a	300	350				
11		8 Goldfish	373	382	385				
12		9 Pick a Pencil	770	936	950				
13		10 Gone Fishing	458	281	450				
14		11 Snakes Alive	596	513	550				
15		12 Stroll for Sweets	451	468	475				
16		13 Toss for Pop	336	308	350				
17		14 Pan for Gold	378	509	500				
18		15 Cup Toss	281	379	375				
19		16 Pocket Lady	375	358	375				
20		17 Face Painting	200		200				
21		18 Cane Toss	396	335	350				
22		19 Tic Tac Toe	344	323	325				

Figure 2-9 Clicking the Select All button selects all the cells in the worksheet

COPYING AND MOVING CELL CONTENTS

How do I copy the contents of one cell or a group of cells to another location?

Copying cells within a spreadsheet is quick and easy. Follow these steps, but check out the shortcuts that come next, too.

1. Click on the cell (or cells) you wish to copy.

2. Click the Copy button on the Standard toolbar. The contents of the cell(s) will be copied to the Windows clipboard.

3. Click in the upper-leftmost cell in which you wish to place the copied information. Note that the target location for the copied information can be a location in the current worksheet, in another worksheet of the same file (click on the appropriate Sheet tab, then click in the location where you want to paste the information), or a location in a different file altogether (open the other file—this can be a file in a program other than Excel—then click in the location where you want to paste the information).

4. Click on the Paste button. The information you copied will be pasted to the new location.

5. You can continue to click on other locations and paste the copied information again and again.

6. Turn off the Copy/Paste activity by pressing the ESC key.

 Tip: *If you plan to copy the contents of a cell to several different cells within the same file, hold down the CTRL key while you click on and select each of the target cells, then click the Paste button. The copied cell contents will be pasted to all selected cells at once.*

Shortcuts for copying and pasting:

● Copy selected cells by pressing CTRL-INSERT or CTRL-C, or by choosing Edit | Copy.

● Paste to a new location by pressing SHIFT-INSERT or CTRL-V, or by choosing Edit | Paste.

How does the AutoFill feature work for copying cells?

The AutoFill feature is activated by dragging the little square that appears in the lower-right corner of the active cell. Here are the options for copying with AutoFill:

● If the cell contains a formula, dragging the AutoFill box will copy the formula to all cells over which you drag. The formula will be updated to logically respond to the information in the cells to which you copy. In other words, using AutoFill to copy formula =A1+A2 one cell to the right would result in the formula =B1+B2.

● If the cell contains text, dragging the AutoFill box will copy the text to the cells over which you drag. If the text is contained in a custom list (custom lists can be viewed at Tools | Options | Custom Lists), dragging the AutoFill box will result in filling the adjacent cells with entries from the custom list.

● If the cell contains a number, dragging the AutoFill box will copy the number to all cells over which you drag.

● If the cell contains a number, holding down the CTRL key while dragging the AutoFill box will increment the number by one in each of the cells over which you drag.

Tip: *If you double-click on the AutoFill box of an active cell, the cell contents will be copied vertically if there is an obvious vertical location. For example, in Figure 2-10, if you double-click the AutoFill box of cell F4, the formula in cell F4 will be copied down through column F. This is a great way to copy formulas. If you have several formulas in columns and need to copy them all down x rows, you can select all the formulas and double-click the AutoFill pointer to copy them down as far as the other data.*

The mouse pointer changes to a plus sign when you point to the AutoFill box

			1995	1996	1997	Total
	1	Basketball	399	350	375	1,124
	2	Bounce House	377	400	400	
	3	Brain Quest	433	276	300	
	4	Bucket Game	271		300	
	5	Bake Sale	325	317	368	
	6	Popcorn	270	154	200	
	7	Speed Pitch	n/a	300	350	
	8	Goldfish	373	382	385	
	9	Pick a Pencil	770	936	950	
	10	Gone Fishing	458	281	450	
	11	Snakes Alive	596	513	550	
	12	Stroll for Sweets	451	468	475	
	13	Toss for Pop	336	308	350	
	14	Pan for Gold	378	509	500	
	15	Cup Toss	281	379	375	
	16	Pocket Lady	375	358	375	
	17	Face Painting	200		200	
	18	Cane Toss	396	335	350	
	19	Tic Tac Toe	344	323	325	
	20	Staff Sensation	385	532	550	
	21	Cotton Candy	621	438	600	
	22	Sno Shak		355	350	
	23	Bingo	284	205	300	

Figure 2-10 Double-click the AutoFill box of a cell at the top of a column to copy the cell contents down through the column

How do I move the contents of one cell or a group of cells to another location?

Much like copying, *moving* cell contents involves using the Windows clipboard. Move cell contents by first selecting the cells whose contents you wish to move, then clicking on the upper-left-most target cell and clicking the Paste button. You can only paste information that has been moved once. After you paste the information, the clipboard is emptied and you must select the information again if you wish to paste it to a different location.

Shortcuts for moving and pasting:

- Move selected cells by pressing CTRL-X, or by choosing Edit | Cut.
- Paste to a new location by pressing SHIFT-INSERT or CTRL-V, or by choosing Edit | Paste.

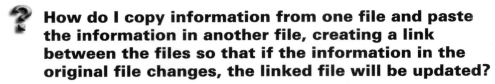

How do I copy information from one file and paste the information in another file, creating a link between the files so that if the information in the original file changes, the linked file will be updated?

To create a dynamic link between files so that pasted information is updated when the information in the original file changes, first select the information to copy. Click the Copy button. Open the file with which you wish to create a link. Paste the information in the file by choosing Edit | Paste Special. When the Paste Special window appears, click the Paste Link button, then click OK. The copied information will appear in the new file.

Tip: *When closing files that are dynamically linked, you should make a habit of closing the file containing the original information first, then closing the linked file. This ensures that a name is assigned to the original file and that the next time you open the linked file it will retrieve the updated information from the original file.*

SECURITY

Is there a way to use passwords to protect the information in my files from prying eyes?

You can assign two passwords to a file, one that prevents a file from being opened and one that prevents an opened file from being changed.

Apply password protection to your files by following these steps:

1. Choose File | Save As. The Save As box will appear.

2. Enter the correct file name and location for the file you wish to save and protect.

3. Click the Tools button at the top of the window, then choose General Options. The Save Options window will appear (see Figure 2-11).

4. To require a password to open the file, enter the password in the Password to open box. To require a password to change the file, enter the password in the Password to modify box. These two passwords do not have to be the same. You don't need to use both password options—you can choose the one that fits your needs.

5. Click OK to save your password(s). You will be asked to reenter each password. Click OK after reentering one or both. The Save Options box will close.

6. Click the Save button. Your file will be saved, along with its password(s).

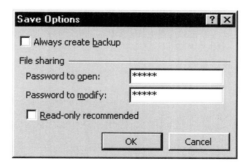

Figure 2-11   Enter your password twice—and don't forget what you entered!

In the future, to open the file, a user will have to enter any applicable passwords. Incorrect passwords will result in an error message requesting the user to try again. Users who attempt to open a file that has been saved with a password to modify have the option of not entering the password and opening the file as a read-only file.

I would like to hide from view certain areas of the worksheet without having to actually delete information. How can this be accomplished?

Choose a column or a row (or a range of columns or rows) by clicking on the letter or number of the column or row, right-click on the selected area, and choose Hide. The selected area is now hidden from view. Column letters and row numbers do not change to accommodate hidden information, so you will notice that the columns and/or rows are out of sequence when information has been hidden.

Return hidden areas to view by selecting the surrounding columns or rows (for example, select columns D and F when E is hidden), right-clicking on the selected area, and choosing Unhide.

Note: *Hidden information reappears if the hidden information is copied to another area. For example, assume Column D is hidden and you copy the contents of cells C5 and E5 by selecting the two cells and clicking the Copy button. The contents of cell D5 will appear when you paste the information to a new area of the worksheet.*

I move my arrow keys, but the cellpointer seems locked and won't move to another cell. What's happening?

Excel probably thinks you are editing or attempting to change the information in the cell in which your cellpointer is locked. If your cursor is blinking in a particular cell and none of your arrow keys seem to move you out of the cell, press the ESC key. That should free your arrow keys to move to another cell.

Check to see if your arrow keys are moving you across the menu bar instead of through the worksheet. If this is the case, press the ESC key once or twice to return to regular worksheet operation.

Chapter 3

Data Entry

Answer Topics!

Data Entry @ a Glance

- **Text and Numerical Entry.** You can enter text, numbers, or formulas into cells. Excel has special default settings for text and for numerical/formula entries. When entering information in cells, there are techniques and shortcuts for moving out of one cell and into another.

- **Editing Data.** After information has been entered in a cell, or while you are in the process of entering the information, you can make changes to the data. There are shortcuts for moving around in the cell, and you have control over whether the information you enter is to be treated as numerical information or as text.

- **Number Formatting.** Enter a number in a cell, and Excel displays the number, just as you entered it. Right? Not necessarily. You can control the way numbers appear (with or without dollar signs, decimal places, commas), and you can create your own formats for numbers. Choose a number format for certain cells (or your entire worksheet) before you begin entering numbers, and all the numbers you enter will follow that format. In addition, Excel offers special options for applying underlining to numbers.

- **Entering Dates.** There are many styles for entering dates in Excel, and you can choose the one that best suits your needs. Dates can appear in any cell on a worksheet, in a header, or in a footer. You can perform mathematical operations using dates, and there are shortcuts for entering dates

TEXT AND NUMERICAL ENTRY

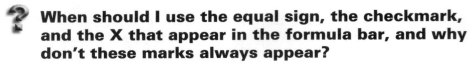

When should I use the equal sign, the checkmark, and the X that appear in the formula bar, and why don't these marks always appear?

The symbols in the formula bar appear when you begin entering information in a worksheet cell. The checkmark acts the same as the ENTER key. After you finish entering information in a cell, you can click on the checkmark, and the information is entered as if you pressed the ENTER key.

The X has the same effect as pressing the ESC key. If you click on the X after you begin entering information in a cell, the information you entered will be cancelled and the cell will be left as it was originally.

The equal sign opens an area called the Formula Palette. This area appears right beneath the formula bar and provides an ongoing calculation while you create your formula. In addition, you can access Excel's built-in functions from a drop-down list that appears in the Formula Palette (see Figure 3-1).

Every time I press ENTER, my cellpointer moves down one cell. Is there a way to make the cellpointer remain in the active cell when I press ENTER?

To prevent the ENTER key from moving your cellpointer down one cell, choose Tools | Options, and click on the Edit tab. Uncheck the Move selection after Enter box. Then click the OK button to close the Options window. From now on, every time you press ENTER, the cellpointer will remain in the cell in which you are working.

To go back to having your ENTER key move the cellpointer down a cell each time you press it, return to Tools | Options | Edit, and check the box that you previously unchecked. Make sure the Direction indicator that follows this box reads Down (alternative directions are Up, Right, and Left). Click OK to save your changes.

This, as with any of the changes you make in the Tools | Options window, is a default change that will remain in effect in your Excel program until you change the option again.

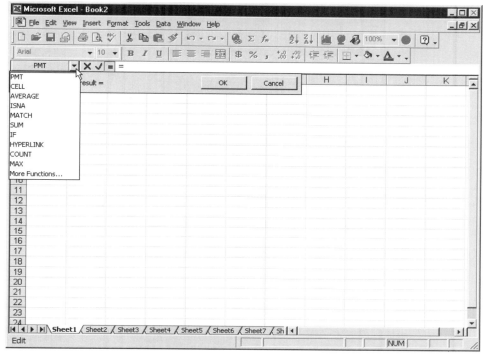

Figure 3-1 The Formula Palette appears when you click the equal sign. Click the drop-down arrow next to the function name to display a list of available functions. Notice that the result of your formula calculation appears in the Formula Palette

 I have information that has to be entered across several columns in my spreadsheet. Is there a way I can make the cellpointer move from the bottom of one column to the top of the next column without having to use my arrow keys?

When you enter information in your worksheet that will fill several columns, you can first select all the cells that you wish to fill by dragging your mouse over the whole area. Then, as you begin entering information in the highlighted cells, each time you press ENTER, the cellpointer will move down one cell through the highlighted block until it reaches the bottom row of the block (see Figure 3-2).

When you reach the bottom row of the block and press ENTER, the cellpointer will move to the top of the next column

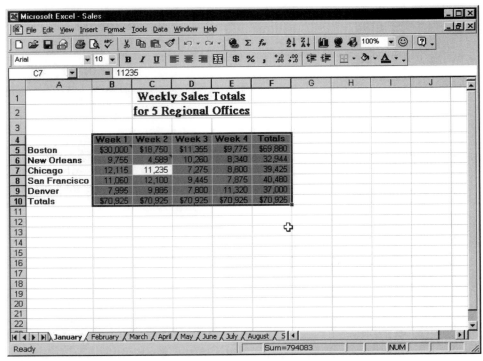

Figure 3-2 Each time you press ENTER, your cellpointer will move one cell at a time through the highlighted block, snaking from one column to the next

in the selected block. Each time you press ENTER, the cellpointer will advance one cell down in the selected area, then advance to the top of the next column, and so on. The cellpointer will continue snaking through the highlighted block of cells in this manner until you turn off the highlighting by clicking somewhere outside the highlighted block or you use your arrow key to move the cellpointer.

If you prefer to move your cellpointer from left to right instead of from top to bottom of the columns within the highlighted block, use the TAB key instead of the ENTER key after you enter the contents of each cell. To move backwards through a highlighted block, press SHIFT-ENTER (or TAB) each time you move from a highlighted cell.

Is there a way to enter a number or a formula in a cell and have it treated as text?

Before you begin typing the number or formula, enter the apostrophe (single quote mark) character. It will not appear in your cell, nor will it print. You will, however, see the apostrophe in the formula bar when you examine the contents of the cell. Entering the apostrophe causes Excel to treat the contents of the cell as text.

If you enter the apostrophe before entering a formula, the actual formula will appear in the cell instead of the results of the calculation. When an apostrophe preceding a number is entered in a cell, the number will be left-justified in the cell, just as text would be.

Be careful! Numbers that are entered in cells as text can be used in some calculations, but not all. Excel won't calculate a text number in a function such as SUM or MAX, but a formula that refers to a cell containing a text number (such as =A23+A24) will calculate properly.

EDITING DATA

When I enter information in a cell and realize I've made an error, do I have to start over or can I correct it while I'm typing?

You can use the BACKSPACE key to edit cell contents while you type. If you try to use the arrow keys to move your cursor, however, the cell entry process will terminate and your cellpointer will move to the next cell in the direction of the arrow key you pressed.

Tip: *Pressing the* F2 *key while entering information into a cell will automatically take you into Edit mode. When Edit mode is turned on, you can move around in the cell with the right and left arrow keys to make editing changes.*

What different ways are available for editing cell information without reentering the entire cell contents?

There are three ways to initiate an edit of a cell:

- Click once in the formula bar to edit the active cell in the formula bar.
- Click twice in tahe cell to edit the active cell in the cell itself.
- Click in the cell and press the F2 key to edit the active cell in the cell itself.

After you have made changes in the cell contents, press ENTER or click the checkmark in the formula bar to save your changes, replacing the original cell contents. Alternatively, press ESC or click the X in the formula bar to end the edit session, discard your changes, and return the cell to its original contents.

Are there shortcuts available for moving my cursor while editing a cell, or am I limited to one character at a time with the arrow keys?

After initiating an edit (see previous question), click your mouse on the area of the cell contents where you wish to edit, or use the following keystrokes as shortcuts for moving the cursor:

- **HOME** Moves the cursor to the beginning of the cell contents. An exception to this occurs when the cell contents wrap to multiple lines. Pressing HOME while editing moves the cursor to the beginning of the current line.
- **END** Moves the cursor to the end of the cell contents (or the end of a line when multiple lines exist).
- **CTRL-LEFT ARROW and CTRL-RIGHT ARROW** Move the cursor one word at a time left or right through the cell contents. When editing formulas, each number or cell

reference is considered a word for purposes of this type of cursor movement.

When the cursor is placed where you want to edit, you can press BACKSPACE or DELETE to remove characters. You can select a quantity of characters to delete or replace by dragging the mouse pointer over the characters or using a combination of SHIFT and the RIGHT or LEFT ARROW keys. If you begin typing, your characters will be inserted at the cursor location.

 Are there shortcuts available for selecting text that I want to replace or delete while editing a cell?

Here are some shortcuts for selecting text (or numbers) while in Edit mode:

- Drag through the text to select it.
- Double-click on a single word to select the word.
- To select everything from the first click to the last, click at the beginning of the characters you want to select, press SHIFT, and click at the end of the set of characters.
- Hold down the SHIFT key, then use the RIGHT or LEFT ARROW keys to select characters to the right or left of the cursor.
- Press SHIFT-CTRL, then use your RIGHT or LEFT ARROW keys to select one word at a time to the right or left of the cursor.

NUMBER FORMATTING

 I've heard the number format buttons on the toolbar referred to as accounting formats. What does this mean?

There are two number formats on the Formatting toolbar that are called accounting formats: the Currency format and the Comma format. The Currency format inserts a dollar sign at the left side of the formatted cell and inserts comma separators and two decimal places. The Comma format inserts comma separators and two decimal places. Both of

these formats have the effect of nudging the formatted numbers a bit to the left within the cell (so there is room for a parenthesis symbol on the right side of the number, in case you are displaying negative numbers).

Select the cells to which you wish to apply one of these formats, then click the appropriate button to format the selected cells.

 Note: *Cells that are formatted with an accounting format receive special treatment when it comes to underlining (see question about underlining formats later in this chapter).*

 ## What additional number formats are available and how do I apply a number format that is not found on the toolbar?

You may notice that there is no button on the toolbar to remove an accounting format once it's applied. You may also find that the accounting number formats are too limiting for your needs.

If you've formatted cells with an accounting format and choose to return to the General format (the Excel default format for numbers, meaning no dollar sign, no comma separators, and no automatic decimal places), you must follow these steps:

1. Select the cells whose format you wish to change.
2. Choose Format | Cells (or right-click on the selected area and choose Format Cells).
3. Click the Number tab in the Format Cells dialog box.
4. Choose General.
5. Click OK to apply your changes.

 Note: *Another technique for returning your numbers to a general format is to choose Edit | Clear | Formats. Be careful, though, as this command will reset all of the formats in your worksheet to the defaults, not just the number formats.*

Other number formats available from the Format Cells dialog box are displayed in Table 3-1.

Number Format	Description
General	Numbers have no comma separators, no automatic decimal places (however, digits appear after a decimal place if you enter the decimal and the digits).
Number	Choose the number of decimal places you wish to display or if you want to display comma separators; indicate a preference for the appearance of negative numbers.
Currency	Same options as the Number format with the addition of a currency symbol. This format is not to be confused with the Accounting currency format, which lines up the currency symbol on the left side of the cells.
Accounting	Choose the number of decimal places you wish to display and whether you wish to display the currency symbol; negative numbers are shown in parentheses.
Date	Choose from a variety of date formats that display the current month and/or the day, year, and time.
Time	Choose from a variety of time formats, some of which display the date.
Percentage	Indicate the desired number of decimal places. Negative numbers are displayed with a minus sign. The percent symbol appears.
Fraction	Display cell contents in fraction form; you control the degree of accuracy in the fraction.
Scientific	Displays a number followed by the letter E and another number which identifies how many spaces to the right (positive number) or left (negative number) the decimal place will have to move to display the entire number.
Text	Treats the cell contents as text even if the cell contains a number.
Special	Accommodates five- and nine-digit zip codes, seven- and ten-digit telephone numbers, and social security numbers.
Custom	Lets you create your own number format.

Table 3-1   Excel Number Formats

 ## How can I customize number formats to accommodate special needs that I have in my worksheet?

The number formats provided by Excel meet most, but not all, worksheet needs. You can start with an existing number format (or start with no format at all), and customize the number format so that your numbers will appear in a manner appropriate to your worksheet needs. Choose Format | Cells and, in the Format Cells dialog box, click on the Number tab. Use the Custom number format option (see Figure 3-3) and the codes described in Table 3-2, to create your own number format. It will then be saved with your worksheet (but will not be readily available to other worksheets).

Tip: *You can use the Format Painter to copy the customized format of a cell from one worksheet to another. Display both worksheets (open both worksheets, then use Window | Display All to display them simultaneously), click on the cell containing the customized format, click the Format Painter button, click on the other worksheet, then click the cell(s) on the worksheet to which you want to apply the format. When you save the worksheet, the format is saved with it and becomes part of the custom format list.*

Number Format Code	Description
#	Displays significant digits. A code of ####.# would display the number 0789.0 as 789.
0	Displays insignificant zeros as well as other digits. A code of 0000.0 would display the number 789.0 as 0789.0.
?	Displays a space for insignificant zeros. Can be used on the right side of the decimal so that numbers with varying decimal digits will align. Can also be used to enable the display of fractions with varying numbers of digits. A format of # ???/??? would display the numbers 5 8/13 and 4/9 with aligned division symbols.
*	Followed by a character (can be a space), will use the character to fill the cell to the width of the column. A format of $*.###.## will display the number 2549.2 as $·······2549.2 with the dollar sign at the left side of the cell and the dots filling the spaces up to the number which is right-justified in the cell.
_	Leaves a space the width of the character that follows this symbol. Most often used with parentheses, the combination _(#,###.##_) leaves a space in the cell for the right and left parentheses when those characters aren't in use in the cell. The above code will display the numbers 3596.25 and −4765.33 as 3,596.25 and (4,765.33) with the digits and the decimal places lined up.

Table 3-2   Codes for Customizing Number Formats

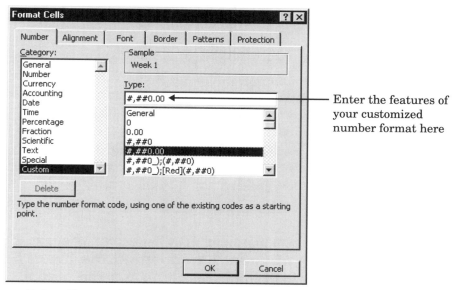

Figure 3-3 Choose Custom as a starting place for creating a customized number format

What's the easiest way to set a global number format (a number format that will apply to all cells) in a worksheet?

Click the Select All button (the blank button in the upper-left part of your worksheet) to select all cells in the worksheet. With all cells selected, apply the number format you wish to affect all cells. Click once anywhere in the worksheet to turn off the Select All feature.

Excel uses the General number format by default. Is there a way to change this default to the number format I prefer to use?

To set a default number format in Excel, follow these steps:

1. Open a new worksheet (File | New, and click OK, or click the New button on the Standard toolbar). A new blank worksheet will appear onscreen.

2. Click the Select All box. All cells in the worksheet will be selected.

3. Choose the number format you wish to use as the default format.

4. (Optional) Make any other changes to the worksheet that you wish to apply to all future new worksheets.

5. Choose File | Save As. The Save As dialog box will appear.

6. Enter **Book** as the File name. Change the location folder to XLStart, a folder located under the Excel folder. In the Save as Type box indicate that the file type is Template.

7. Click OK to save this file. All future new worksheets will contain the features saved with this worksheet.

Is there a quicker way to enter the symbol for British pounds than opening the Insert Symbol dialog box and searching for the symbol?

You can enter symbols in your worksheet directly from the keyboard if you know the ASCII codes for the symbols. Enter an ASCII code by holding down the ALT key on your keyboard while you type the code using the keys on the number pad of your computer. Release the ALT key after you have entered the numerical code.

Codes for common currency symbols are listed here:

Currency Type	ASCII Code
Cents: ¢	155
British pound: £	156
Japanese Yen: ¥	157

I'm confused about the way numbers are underlined in Excel. How do I control the width of the underlining in my worksheets?

The width of an underline in Excel depends on two factors: the width of the item being underlined and the format of the item being underlined.

When you underline a number that has been formatted with an accounting format (either Currency or Comma), the accounting underline is automatically applied. The resulting underline is separated slightly from the bottom of the number, and the width of the underline is uniform throughout the column. In fact, the width of the accounting underline is dependent on the width of the column and stretches from the left side of the column where a dollar sign would appear (even if such a character is not in use), to the right side of the column where a parentheses indicating a negative number would appear (even if such a character is not in use). If you widen the column, the underline will widen as well.

The standard underline that applies to cells that have not been formatted with an accounting number format hugs the bottom of the cell contents more closely than does the accounting underline. It stretches only to the width of the characters being underlined.

Another option for underlining is to use the Border option. Either click the Border button on the Formatting toolbar or go to Format | Cells, and click the Borders tab to place a border along the bottom of the cell. The border serves as an underline which covers the entire width of the cell. Cells in adjacent columns underlined in this way will appear to have a continuous underline across all the affected columns.

ENTERING DATES

 What year will Excel think I am referring to if I enter the year as 00?

The newest version of Excel defaults to the year 2000 when you enter **00**. For example, if you enter a date as **4/15/00**, Excel will display it as 4/15/2000. If you want Excel to use 1900, 1800, or some other year ending in two zeros, you should enter all four digits of the year with your date, like this: **4/15/1900**.

 When I enter the date 8/15/98, Excel displays 8/15/1998 in the cell. I can change the format of the cell to show the date as I typed it, but is there a way to change the default so that the date style will be 8/15/98 for future dates that I enter?

The way that Excel is displaying your date is actually controlled outside of Excel; in the Windows Control Panel. Click the Start button on your taskbar, then choose Settings | Control Panel. Double-click the Regional Settings icon to display the Regional Settings Properties box.

Click the Date tab and you will see an indicator for Short date style. This is where Excel is getting its standard setting for displaying the date. You will also see a Long date style in this window which, by default, would enter your date as Saturday, August 15, 1998.

You can change these default styles if you want to see a different style in your worksheets. The change you make will only affect future worksheets, not those already created.

 What's the best way to enter a date and time in the same cell?

You can enter a date and time directly in a cell by typing the information and then revising the cell format to match your desired display. For example, if you enter the date and time in your cell as 8/15/98, 3:06 AM, Excel will change the cell to display 8/15/1998 3:06.

Change the format of the cell by choosing Format | Cells, and clicking the Number tab. Choose Date or Time, then select the style you prefer.

Alternatively, enter an apostrophe before you begin typing the cell contents, and Excel will display the characters exactly as you enter them.

A quick way to enter the current date and time in a cell is to use the function **=NOW()**. Type the function (beginning with the equal sign and ending with an open and a closed parentheses with no space between them), press ENTER, and Excel will display the current date (in the default short date format), and the current time (using the 24-hour clock, so that 3:06 AM will appear as 15:06).

There are date buttons available in the header and footer windows. How do these buttons work?

Choose File | Page Setup, and the Page Setup dialog box will appear. Click the Header/Footer tab. Click the Custom Header or Custom Footer button. In the window that appears, click in the Left, Center, or Right area to choose the place on the page where you want the date to appear (see Figure 3-4).

  There is a Date button and a Time button in Excel's header and footer feature. Clicking the Date button inserts a code in the header or footer (&[Date]) that represents the current date. Clicking the Time button inserts a code in the header or footer ([&Time]) that represents the current time.

These codes cause the date and time to be constantly updated. Each time you reopen the file, or even each time you

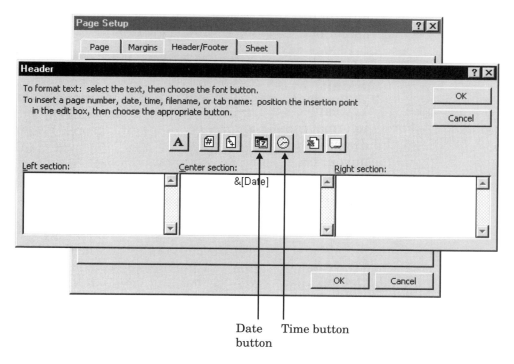

Date   Time button
button

Figure 3-4   Click in the area where you want the date to appear, then click the little calendar button to place the date in the header or footer

view the header or footer, the date and time are updated to the current date and time. If you want the date and time to be fixed rather than to update, simply type the date and time in the header or footer, instead of using the codes.

Tip: *Some shortcuts for entering the date or time in a cell are to press CTRL+; to enter today's date or to press CTRL-SHIFT+: to enter the current time.*

I understand that Excel views all dates as serial numbers. What is a serial number?

Dates are actually stored in Excel with a numerical value, which makes it possible to perform calculations with dates. When you enter a date, such as 4/15/1999, the date appears on your worksheet in the format in which you enter it, in this case with slashes separating the day, month, and year. Excel thinks of this date as a serial number that represents the number of days since 1/1/1900 (1/1/1900 is day number 1, 1/2/1900 is day number 2, 4/15/1999 is 36265, and so on).

To view the date as its number equivalent, change the format of the cell containing the date to a General format. You can do this by selecting the cell containing the date, then choosing Format | Cells | Number | General. Or, a quick way to change the format of a cell to the General format without going through the menus is to click on a blank cell that you have not formatted (when you open a new worksheet, all of the cells contain the General format), then click the Format Painter button, and click on the cell containing the date.

Another quick way to view a date as its numerical equivalent is to select the cell containing the date, then click on the Comma button on the Formatting toolbar. Excel will apply the comma number format to the selected cell.

How can I find the date that is represented by a particular serial number?

When you enter a date on your worksheet, such as 6/6/44, Excel automatically changes the format of the cell to a date-type format, so that your date appears as 6/6/1944. Once your cell contains this date format, you can enter a positive integer in the cell and Excel will automatically transform that number into a date.

For example, enter a date in a cell and press ENTER to have Excel apply the date format to the cell. Return to the cell and enter a number (such as 100000) and Excel will display the date represented by calculating the number of days since 1/1/1900 (day 100000 is 10/14/2173).

Is it possible to perform mathematical operations with dates in Excel?

Because Excel thinks of dates as numbers, you can perform mathematical calculations on cells containing dates. For example, to find a date that is 150 days after 5/26/2000, enter 5/26/2000 in cell A1, then enter =A1+150 in cell A2.

If you want to perform a calculation on dates that results in a number (such as how many days are between date one and date two), you don't need to change the appearance of the cells containing dates to their serial number equivalent. However, you do have to change the cell containing the date function so that it displays the results of the function in a number rather than a date format.

For example, if you have dates in cells A1 and A2, and you want to know the number of days that separate the two dates, enter the formula =A2-A1 in cell A3. Excel will display the answer as the date represented by the serial number that is the result of the formula. Change the format of the formula cell to a general format (or a numerical format such as the comma format, which appears as a button on the Formatting toolbar), and Excel will display the number of days separating the two dates.

How does the AutoFill feature work with dates?

Dates that appear in a date format will be incremented by one if you drag the AutoFill button from a date cell to adjacent cells. Dragging the AutoFill button from a cell containing the date 1/1/2000 will produce 1/2/2000, 1/3/2000, 1/4/2000, and so on in adjacent cells.

To produce an increment of greater than one, enter two dates representing the desired increment in adjacent cells, then select both cells, and drag the AutoFill button. For example, if you want dates to increase by 30 days for purposes of creating an aging schedule of accounts that are 30, 60, 90, 120, 150 days overdue, enter the first two dates (such as 10/5/1999, 11/4/1999) in two adjacent cells. Select both cells, then drag the AutoFill button to additional cells. This will produce 12/4/1999, 1/3/2000, 2/2/2000, 3/3/2000, and so on in the cells to which you dragged the AutoFill button.

Be careful, though, when the dates in the two examples are the same. Entering like dates in two cells, such as 10/5/1999 and 11/5/1999, selecting the two cells, and dragging the AutoFill button to additional cells will produce 12/5/1999, 1/5/2000, 2/5/2000, and so on.

Holding down the CTRL button when you drag the AutoFill from a cell containing a date will duplicate the same date in the cells over which you drag.

Chapter 4

Formulas and Functions

Answer Topics!

Formulas and Functions @ a Glance

Performing Calculations with Mathematical Formulas. Use Excel to perform mathematical calculations and display the results in a professional-looking worksheet. Use the quick Auto-Sum feature for nearly any type of addition, write simple and complex mathematical formulas with ease, use Excel's formulas to combine text on your worksheet, and manipulate formulas so that the display is exactly the way you want it to be. You can use your mouse pointer to help you select information for your formulas. Also, Excel gives you the ability to display your actual formulas in your worksheets.

Excel's Built-in Functions. Have you forgotten how to compute factorials, or how to convert degrees of a circle to radians? You don't have to dig through boxes in the attic to find your old high school math books. Excel provides over a hundred built-in functions that will take the drudgery out of writing formulas. And there is a Function Wizard that shows you how the functions work. Functions work with numbers, dates, and text, to make complex computations seem like child's play.

Troubleshooting. Even a powerful program like Excel has its limits. Excel provides you with standard error messages that explain why the results you see are not the results you expect. Sometimes a simple act like changing the number of decimal places that display can alter the results of your formulas. Excel has a function that may solve this problem.

PERFORMING CALCULATIONS WITH MATHEMATICAL FORMULAS

 **I want to add cells that aren't next to each other on my worksheet. Does AutoSum only work when adding adjacent cells?**

You can use AutoSum to perform any addition operation on your worksheet. The most frequent use of AutoSum is to add a vertical column of numbers. Place the cellpointer in a blank cell at the bottom of the column, click the AutoSum button twice, and the answer appears in the cell.

To use AutoSum for adding cells that are aligned horizontally across several columns, place the cellpointer in a blank cell at the right edge of the row of numbers, click the AutoSum button twice, and the answer appears. However, if there are occupied cells above the cell in which you want your horizontal sum to appear, AutoSum will try to add vertically if it can. If at least two cells above the current cell contain numbers, double-clicking the AutoSum button will result in the sum of the cells above the current cell (see Figure 4-1).

 Tip: *To add a horizontal column of numbers using the AutoSum button, first select the cells containing the numbers you wish to add (and, if you wish, extend your selection area to include the blank cell to the right of the row of numbers). Double-click the AutoSum button, and the sum of the selected cells will appear to the right of the row of numbers.*

If you want to add numbers that are not adjacent to each other, you can still use the AutoSum button to perform the addition. Follow these steps to add nonadjacent cells using AutoSum:

1. Click in the cell where you want the answer to appear, making that the active cell.

2. Click *once* on the AutoSum button rather than twice. You may see a moving marquee surrounding some cells on the worksheet; you can ignore this.

Microsoft Excel - Book1

File Edit View Insert Format Tools Data Window Help

Arial   ▼ 10 ▼   **B** *I* <u>U</u> ≡ ≡ ≡ 🔲 $ %

E5   ▼   =

	A	B	C	D	E	F
1	First Quarter Sales					
2		January	February	March	Total	
3	Spencer	25486	26455	24568	76509	
4	Marlowe	31556	23845	37222	92623	
5	Spade	31287	37526	19552		
6	Poirot	43215	15899	34583		
7	Wimsey	39677	19887	28435		
8						
9						
10						
11						

Figure 4-1   Double-clicking AutoSum at cell E5 will result in the sum of cells E3 and E4 instead of cells B5 through D5

3. Click on the first cell you want to add. While holding down the CTRL key, click on other cells or drag through ranges of other cells that you wish to include in your sum.

4. When all the cells you wish to add are selected (the cell borders of all selected cells will appear to be moving), release the CTRL key, and click the AutoSum button again or press ENTER. The moving cell borders will return to solid borders and the sum will appear on your worksheet (see Figure 4-2).

It's been a while since I took a math class. What order of operation does Excel follow when performing mathematical calculations?

When creating a formula in Excel, you must keep in mind the order in which math operations are executed. Placing parentheses around any operations can supersede the standard order. The order in which mathematical operations are performed is:

● Parentheses

● Exponents

● Multiplication and division from left to right

● Addition and subtraction from left to right

In one of her math classes, my daughter learned a little trick for remembering this order. She uses the phrase, **P**lease **E**xcuse **M**y **D**ear **A**unt **S**ally to help her remember **P**arentheses, **E**xponents, **M**ultiplication, **D**ivision, **A**ddition, and **S**ubtraction.

For an example of how the order can affect an operation, look at the difference parentheses make in the following formulas:

$$48+8/2*4-1=63$$

$$(48+8)/2*4-1=111$$

$$48+8/2*(4-1)=60$$

$$(48+8)/2*(4-1)=84$$

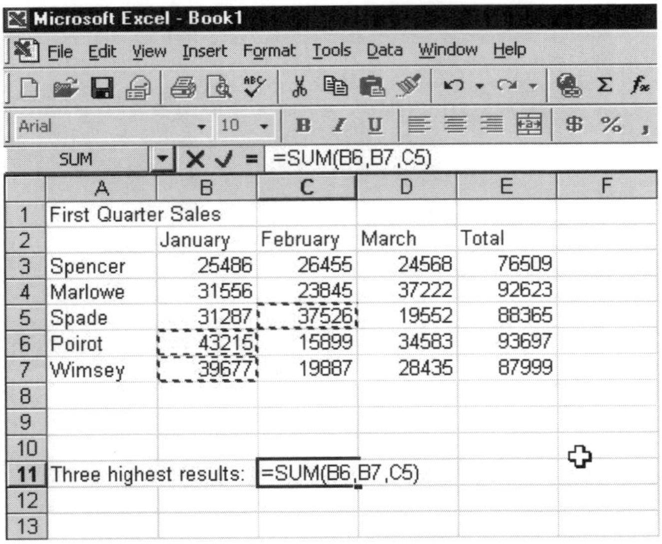

Figure 4-2 Using AutoSum with CTRL-click enables you to add nonadjacent cells

? How do the comparative operators (less than and greater than) work in formulas?

In addition to the mathematical operators mentioned previously, you can also use the less than and greater than symbols to generate formulas that will return a result of TRUE or FALSE. If the formula meets the comparative criteria, the cell will reflect that situation by displaying the word TRUE. If the formula fails the comparative test, you will see FALSE in the cell containing the formula.

For example, the following formulas will produce the result of TRUE when the contents of cell A1 are greater than the contents of cell B1:

- =A1>B1 (read: A1 is greater than B1)
- =B1<A1 (read: B1 is less than A1)
- =A1<>B1 (read: A1 is not equal to B1)

? My worksheet displays first names in one column and last names in another column. Is there a way I can combine the contents of the two columns to display a full name in a cell?

Use the concatenation symbol, &, to combine the contents of two cells (see Figure 4-3). This feature works for combining cells containing numbers as well as cells containing text.

To combine the contents of column A (first names) and column B (last names) into column C (combined first and last names), use the following formula in column C, across from the first item in the list. Then copy the formula down as far as you need to in column C:

= A1&" "&B1

Make sure to include a space in quotation marks to separate the names.

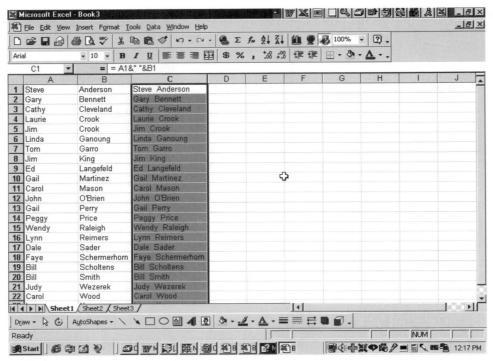

Figure 4-3 Combine first and last names to form a one-column list of full names

---

Caution: *If A & B cannot be deleted or names will not stay, copy C then Edit, Paste Special, Values. Now columns A & B can be removed.*

Is there an easy way to include a cell reference in my formula without having to type the cell reference?

You can save yourself keystrokes when creating formulas by using either the mouse or an arrow key to reference a cell in a formula. For example, to place the formula, =D3–D4, in cell F9, begin by clicking on cell F9 and entering the = sign. Then click on D3, enter the minus sign, click on D4, press ENTER (or click the green check mark in the formula bar), and the formula is completed.

Alternatively, to enter the formula, =D3–D4, in cell D5, begin by clicking on cell D5 and entering the = sign. Then press the UP ARROW key twice to move the cellpointer to cell D3. Enter the minus sign, then press the UP ARROW once to cell D4. Press the ENTER key, and the formula is completed.

Generally speaking, you will save time by using the arrow keys to point to adjacent or nearby cells and using the mouse to click on cells while creating a formula.

Is there a way to instruct Excel to present my formulas in the worksheet so that I can print a copy of the worksheet that will display the formulas?

You can change a worksheet view so that all of the formulas actually display right on the worksheet. One use of this type of display is to print one copy of the worksheet with its formulas showing and one copy with the completed calculations, so that someone without a computer can analyze your calculation methods.

To turn on the display of all formulas in your worksheet, follow these steps:

1. Choose Tools | Options. The Options dialog box will appear.

2. Click the View tab.

3. In the Window options section, click to place a check in the box next to Formulas.

4. Click OK to save your changes. The Options box will close, and your worksheet will display formulas instead of results in all cells containing formulas.

To return to a normal view of your worksheet, repeat the above steps, but in step 3, uncheck the box next to Formulas.

Tip: *A shortcut for changing a worksheet view so that all formulas actually display on the worksheet is to use the keystroke combination of CTRL+- (both keys at the same time). Some computers may not respond to this shortcut—on some machines, this shortcut expands and contracts column widths instead of showing formulas. You can also use "paste special" to paste the entire worksheet onto a new sheet, choosing formulas when you execute the paste.*

 I would like to change some of the calculations in my worksheet to the actual values, removing the formulas. How can I do this?

Excel has a feature that enables you to change the nature of a cell from a formula to the results of that formula. When you apply this feature, the formula that created the cell's contents disappears and cannot be retrieved (except with the Undo command).

Change the contents of a cell from a formula to its value by clicking on the cell you want to change, then clicking the Copy button on the toolbar. Choose Edit | Paste | Special, and when the dialog box appears, click to check the Values box, then click OK. Press ENTER (or ESC) to turn off the copy marquee.

The cell contents on the worksheet will appear to be the same as it was before. However, if you click on the cell and look in the formula bar, you will see that the formula is gone and only the cell value remains.

Be aware that if the information in the cell is a result of calculations involving other cells on the worksheet and those other cells change in value at some point in the future, the cell whose formula you have replaced with a value will not change.

 I use extremely large, complex worksheets, and Excel seems to take forever to recalculate. Is there any way around this problem?

Excel recalculates the entire workbook each time you make a change on any sheet. With a large workbook, in particular one that uses many sheets, you may find this recalculation process takes a measurable amount of time. This can be frustrating. You can turn off this recalculation feature while you work, then turn it back on again (or not, if you prefer to leave it off) when you have finished making changes to the workbook.

To turn off Excel's recalculation feature, choose Tools | Options, and click the Calculation tab. Choose from Automatic (constant recalculation after every change), Automatic except tables (constant recalculation after every change except for calculations within data tables), and Manual (recalculation occurs only when you press the F9 key). If you choose Manual, you have the option of checking the Recalculate before Save box.

Checking this box will force Excel to recalculate your entire workbook whenever you execute a Save command.

If you have turned off the recalculation feature, you can quickly recalculate your worksheets at any time by pressing the F9 function key. Alternatively, you can recalculate only one sheet at a time by choosing Tools | Options, and clicking the Calc Sheet button on the Calculation tab.

EXCEL'S BUILT-IN FUNCTIONS

Excel comes with a large quantity of mathematical formulas, statistical formulas, financial formulas, and more. These formulas have been created for you and saved as functions. You could create these functions yourself, but Excel gives you the timesaving option of letting you choose from among several of these formulas already packaged for your use.

 Do I have to use the Paste Function feature in order to use Excel's built-in functions?

The Paste Function dialog box is provided as an aide to entering function information in cells, but you are not obligated to use this feature. The Paste Function (formerly called the Function Wizard) is a short-cut feature that describes a function to the user and then walks the user through the creation of a function on a step-by-step basis. By using the Paste Function feature, you can watch the results of the function form while you create the function, and you can make sure you provide all the necessary information for the execution of the function, in the order needed.

The Paste Function feature includes definitions of all the functions in Excel, as well as descriptive information about how the functions should be created. It's interesting to spend a little time just poking around in the Paste Function window and learning about what all these functions can do by clicking on function names and reading the definition of them. For more detailed descriptions of how functions operate and how they can be used in your worksheets, look up the particular function in the Excel Help index. The Help screens provide more information than the Paste Function window.

To use the Paste Function feature, click the Paste Function button on the standard toolbar. The Paste Function window will

appear. On the left side of this screen is a list of function categories. The first category is Most Recently Used. Initially, when you install Excel, the Most Recently Used function list includes the functions Microsoft thinks you will use most frequently. Once you begin using functions of your own, the functions you use will replace those on this list.

The next category is All, and if you choose this category you will display a list of all of the functions available in Excel. When you scroll through this list of functions you can see just how many functions there are in this program. You may never use more than a few of them, but one could certainly argue that there is something for everyone on this list.

When you find a function that you want to use, click on the function name once. Descriptive information about how the function works and what it does will appear at the bottom of the window.

Once you have chosen the function you want to use and have clicked once on it, click on the OK button in the Paste Function window. On the screen that appears you will see text boxes for each argument or piece of information that Excel needs to complete the function. Some of these arguments may appear dimmed; these are considered optional to the proper execution of the function.

Click in the space where you plan to enter a piece of information and enter it. As you enter the information, a preliminary calculation of the function will occur, and you will see the result within the Paste Function box. If, when filling in information for an argument of the function, you need to highlight cells on the worksheet or refer back to the worksheet for information, click the little box containing a red arrow, and the Paste Function box will slide out of the way on your worksheet. It won't be completely out of sight, however—you'll see it lurking somewhere near the top of your worksheet with its red button displayed. Highlight the cell(s) you wish to use for the particular argument of the function, then click the red button, and the Paste Function window will return, entering your highlighted cell reference(s) in the appropriate field. When all of the arguments for the particular function have been entered, click the OK button. The Paste Function window will close, the function will execute, and the results of the function will be placed in the current cell.

> *Tip:* *When entering information in the Paste Function window, you can click the little red arrow box to move the Paste Function window out of the way and then easily select a cell or cells from your worksheet. You may find it easier, however, to simply drag the Paste Function window out of the way, thus making the cells in your worksheet visible and accessible, rather than clicking on those little red arrow boxes.*

If you do not wish to use the Paste Function feature, and you know how a function is to be presented in the cell, you may enter the function itself. You can bypass the dialog box by entering the = sign, then the function name, and the arguments of the function separated by commas and enclosed in parentheses. There can be no spaces in a function.

 ## My mailing list contains first and last names within the same cell. How can I sort this list by last name?

From time to time you may want to separate text in your worksheet. You can separate a column of first and last names so that you will be able to sort by the last name instead of the first name (see Figure 4-4).

Using the following formulas, you can separate the full names in column A into a column (B) of first names and a column (C) of last names:

The formula for Column B: =LEFT(A1,FIND(" ",A1))

The formula for Column C: =RIGHT(A1,LEN(A1)-FIND(" ",A1))

The results for Row 1:

Column A	Column B	Column C
Gail Perry	Gail	Perry

> *Caution:* *This sorting technique will only work if none of the names have middle initials.*

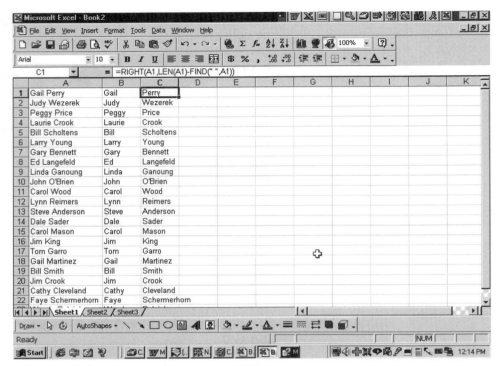

Figure 4-4 Use the RIGHT and LEFT functions coupled with the FIND
function to separate a list at the space between the first and
last name

 My worksheet contains several range names. Can these names be used in functions?

Use a range name whenever possible in a worksheet. You can
enter the named range in place of any cell reference you might
otherwise enter. One benefit of using a range name in a
function is that it may make the function more understandable
to a user of the worksheet who doesn't yet know exactly what
functions do. If you created the worksheet, named ranges can
also serve to remind you what the functions do if you've forgotten.

Another benefit of using a range name as a function
parameter is that range names are automatically absolute.
So, if you create a formula where an absolute reference is
required, you can use a range name instead of a cell reference

and save yourself the step of having to assign an absolute reference to the cell(s) being referenced in the formula.

Is there a quick way to enter today's date into my worksheet?

Enter the function =TODAY() (with nothing between the parentheses) into a cell and Excel returns today's date. To display the current time along with today's date, enter =NOW() into a cell. These functions automatically update as time passes. In an active worksheet, pressing the F9 key will cause Excel to update the time to the current up-to-the-minute time. Open a worksheet that contains these functions and Excel will present the current date and time (not the date on which the worksheet was created).

My worksheet contains several dates. Is there a way to determine in which quarter a particular date falls?

If your dates are in column A, beginning at cell A1, you can create a formula using the IF, AND, and MONTH functions to indicate in which quarter a date falls. Place the following formula in cell B1 to determine what the quarter would be.

=IF(AND(MONTH(A1)>=1,MONTH(A1)<=3),"First Quarter",IF(AND(MONTH(A1)>=4,MONTH(A1)<=6), "Second Quarter",IF(AND(MONTH(A1)>=7,MONTH(A1)<=9), "Third Quarter","Fourth Quarter")))

Can I create a formula in which I choose numbers from a range that meet particular criteria, then sum those numbers?

There are many functions that enable you to indicate particular criteria that the contents of certain cells should meet. Once you've determined which cells meet the criteria, you can perform mathematical operations on those cells. We'll use the LARGE function to choose the three largest numbers from a range (A1:A10) and, at the same time, determine a sum for those numbers.

To accomplish this task, click in the cell in which you wish to place the answer to the calculation, then enter a formula such as this one:

=LARGE(A1:A10,1)+ LARGE(A1:A10,2)+ LARGE(A1:A10,3)

The sum will appear in the selected cell.

How can I find the square root of a number on my worksheet?

Use the built-in function, =SQRT(*cell reference*) to find the square root of any number. For example, if cell A1 contains the number 5625, placing the formula =SQRT(A1) in cell A2 will return the amount 75 in cell A2.

The SQRT function only works for positive numbers. You'll get an error message (#NUM!) if the number for which you are trying to find a square root is negative.

Tip: *Another way to write the square root function is like this: =A1^(1/2). It would then follow that you can compute the cube root of a number in this manner: =A1^(1/3), and other roots can be calculated by changing the 1/3 to 1/4, 1/5, and so on.*

How can I use an Excel function to average a collection of numbers which are not located in contiguous cells on my worksheet?

The AVERAGE function returns the average of any cells identified as arguments of the function. Use a colon to identify a range of contiguous cells, use commas to indicate individual cells, as shown below:

=AVERAGE(A1:A3) returns the average of cells A1, A2, and A3

=AVERAGE(A1,A3) returns the average of cells A1 and A3

=AVERAGE(A1:A3,A5,A7,A9) returns the average of cells A1, A2, A3, A5, A7 and A9

You don't have to type the colons and commas when identifying cells to Excel for use in this function. Use the Paste Function feature and click on each line of the argument, then click on the cell or cells to which this function should apply. Or, enter the function, =AVERAGE, on your worksheet, enter the left parentheses, then click on each cell or range of cells to be included in the function, pressing the CTRL key to select more than one group of cells or non-contiguous cells.

I need to enter data in Roman numerals. Can I use Excel to change my numbers to Roman numerals?

Use =ROMAN(*cell reference*) to convert existing numbers to Roman numerals. This function works for positive numbers from 1 to 3999. If cell A1 contains the number 2563, the formula =ROMAN(A1) returns MMDLXIII.

Is there a quick way to switch text on my worksheet to all upper case?

Use the =UPPER(*cell reference*) function to switch cells (identified by the *cell reference* to upper case). For example, if you want to change the column headings in row 2 of your worksheet to upper case, here's a quick way to make the switch.

Insert a blank row under the row of existing column headings. In the blank cell (B3), beneath the first heading in cell B2, enter the formula =UPPER(B2). Copy this formula to all cells in row three that correspond to a title in row two. When all headings have been converted, select the new, capitalized headings. Choose Edit, Copy, then, while the headings are still selected, choose Edit, Paste Special, Values, OK. You can now delete the row containing the non-capitalized titles.

I entered a list of cities in lowercase and then realized I needed to switch the first letter of each city name to uppercase. Is there a quick way to make this switch?

In word processing programs such as Microsoft Word, there is an easy-to-access keystroke command for switching from lowercase to uppercase and vice versa (SHIFT-F3). In Excel, you can switch your lowercase city names so that the first

letter is in uppercase by using a formula that examines the text (the city name, in this example), extracts the first letter and capitalizes it, then extracts the remaining text and concatenates the text to the first letter. This formula only works for one-word names (but see below).

Place the formula in a cell other than the cell containing the original text. For example, if your city name is in cell A1, place the formula in cell B1, and the revised city name will appear next to the original name (see Figure 4-5). Here's an example of a formula that will accomplish the capitalization task:

=UPPER(LEFT(A1,1))&RIGHT(A1,LEN(A1)-1)

There is another Excel formula that can accomplish this task as well, the =PROPER() formula. For a name appearing

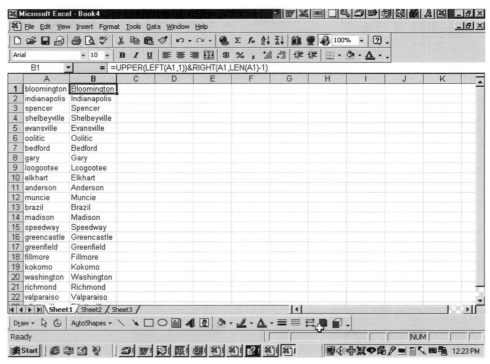

Figure 4-5 The city names in column A will be capitalized and the results will appear in column B

in cell A1 which you wish to capitalize, enter the formula in a blank cell (B1, for example), as follows:

=PROPER(A1)

Excel will place the capitalized name in cell B1. This function works well for names containing more than one word. If cell A1 contains the name "san jose," the result of the formula in cell B1 will be "San Jose."

My mailing list in Excel contains a column for zip codes, and many of the zip codes appear more than once. I want to create a column that will display each unique zip code.

Before creating a column to identify the unique zip codes, sort your list by zip code. This way all the duplicate zip codes will be grouped together. Choose the column or insert a new blank column where you want the unique zip codes to appear. Assuming the zip codes are in column A, beginning in cell A1, and the blank column you will be using is column B, enter the following formula in cell B1:

=A1

Tip: *Make sure the column containing zip codes is formatted for zip codes, otherwise Excel will drop the leading zero(s) from zip codes that begin with a zero. Select the column, choose Format, Cells, Number, Special, Zip Code, then click OK.*

In cell B2, enter the following formula, then copy this formula down through column B for the length of the entire list of zip codes:

=IF(A2–A1=0,"",A2)

This formula tests to see if the zip code in column A matches the zip code above it. If the zip code is the same as the one above it, the adjacent cell in column B will be left blank (the quotation marks containing nothing in the formula above signify a blank). If the zip code is different from the one above it, the new zip code will be entered in column B. Ultimately, column B will be

filled with many blank cells, and one cell will be filled for each unique zip code.

To sort the resulting list of unique zip codes so that you can remove the spaces, first change the formulas in column B to values. The process used to do this is described earlier in this chapter. Then, select the cells in column B, and click on one of the sort buttons on the standard toolbar. The zip codes will be sorted and grouped together, no longer separated by spaces.

I need to borrow some money. How can Excel help me calculate the amount of my loan payments?

Use Excel's financial functions to help with all aspects of analyzing your loan options. To calculate the amount of your loan payments, you can use the PMT function, which requires that you provide the interest rate (Rate), the number of payments you will be required to make (Nper), and the amount of the loan (PV). The formula is constructed like this:

=PMT(Rate,Nper,PV)

Use a worksheet like that pictured in Figure 4-6 to calculate the loan payment. Once you have created such a worksheet, you can experiment with different scenarios, changing the amount of the loan, the interest rate, or the number of payments you will make.

	A	B
1	Loan Amount	10000
2	Interest Rate	8%
3	Number of Payments	48
4	Payment Amount	($244.13)

B4 = =PMT(B2/12,B3,B1)

Figure 4-6 Fill in the principal amount you intend to borrow, the interest rate, and the number of payments you will make

 Caution: *If you enter an annual interest rate and your payments are to be made monthly, the formula should be adjusted to: =PMT(Rate / 12,Nper,PV).*

TROUBLESHOOTING

Sometimes formulas in spreadsheets don't produce the results you're expecting. There are limitations to what formulas in Excel can do. Also, mistakes can happen. The following points cover some of the more frequently encountered situations in which problems can arise.

 It seems my formula is too big to fit in the cell. Does Excel impose a limit on the size of a formula?

You are limited to a certain number of characters in any cell in an Excel worksheet, and cells containing formulas are no exception. Text cells can include up to 32,000 characters, but cells containing formulas are much more severely limited.

A cell containing an Excel formula can accommodate a maximum of 1,024 characters. Every keyboard character counts towards this total, including commas, parentheses, and math operators. If your formulas are so lengthy that they exceed this character limit, you can circumvent the problem by entering as much of the formula as possible in one cell, then, before you run out of characters, include a reference to another cell where you can continue creating the formula.

 I write IF functions that include other IF functions. I haven't exceeded the character limit in my cells, but I'm still getting error messages on some of my larger nested functions. How can this problem be avoided?

Aside from the cell character limits mentioned in the previous topic, Excel also imposes a limit on the number of functions that can be nested within one another. According to the Excel rules, you are limited to seven levels of function nesting. A nested function contains another function as one of its parameters. For example, if a parameter of an IF function contains another IF function, there are two IF functions present, and one is nested

in the other; therefore, you have exercised one level of nesting. If a parameter of a nested IF function contains another IF function, you have proceeded to the second level of nesting.

You can overcome the limitation of seven levels by including a reference to another worksheet cell in your last allowed nested IF function. The cell to which you refer can contain additional IF functions, nested for another seven levels, and so on.

 ## What can I do to correct the appearance of formulas not calculating correctly due to rounding of decimal places?

It may be that you've limited your spreadsheet to displaying x number of decimal places. Calculations performed in the worksheet may result in numbers that, formatted differently, would extend beyond x numbers of decimal places. Due to the number format inherent in the worksheet, Excel is being forced to round these calculations to x number of decimal places.

Occasionally a situation occurs where numbers don't appear to calculate correctly on your worksheet because of this rounding. Consider the following example:

14.62	15
14.62	15
29.24	29

The first group of numbers (14.62 and 14.62) is added, and the proper sum appears beneath the numbers. In the second column, the numbers 14.62 and 14.62 have been rounded to 15 and 15 to remove the display of decimal places. When the second group of numbers is added, the resulting sum is 29. The result is correct when you consider the true nature of the numbers, but because they have been rounded, the result appears to be in error.

If you create a worksheet that is subject to this kind of problem, consider using the ROUND function to actually round the numbers to a particular quantity of decimal places before the calculation occurs.

Considering the above calculation with the first column of numbers appearing in cells A1, A2, and A3, apply the following formula in column B, which will round the 14.62 to zero decimal places, or to 15:

=ROUND(A1,0)

Copying this formula down to cell B2 will result in the following calculation in column B:

15

15

30

What is a circular reference?

A circular reference is a formula that uses itself in a calculation. For example, if the active cell is A3, and in cell A3 you create a formula that reads: =A1+A2+A3, you have created a circular reference. The formula results in an infinite calculation because the answer is being added to itself, so the answer is constantly changing.

Rather than attempting to calculate to infinity, Excel will stop the calculation as soon as it detects the circular reference. A window will appear onscreen providing you with information about the circular reference, and then the Circular Reference toolbar will appear (see Figure 4-7) to help you resolve your circular reference(s).

While this toolbar is open, click the down arrow in the Navigate Circular Reference field (the left field of the toolbar), and all cells containing circular references will appear. Click on the reference to the cell you wish to analyze, then click the Trace Dependents button to display which cells in the worksheet are dependent on the selected cell. Click the Trace Precedents button to display which cells in the worksheet are used in computing the result in the selected cell. You can click the Remove All Arrows button at any time to remove the tracing lines Excel has placed on your worksheet.

Excel's Error Messages

Excel has its own language when it comes to telling you something is wrong on your worksheet. The following error values may appear in your cells. Use this table to help interpret these messages.

If you see:	This has happened:
#####	The column is not wide enough to display the numerical value required in this cell. Widening the column should cause Excel to replace the pound signs with the actual number.
#VALUE!	Text has been entered in a cell where Excel was expecting a numerical value. This may be the result of a calculation that refers to other cells which contain text instead of a value. Check all cells that ultimately feed into this cell for the source of the problem.
#DIV/0!	A calculation has occurred in which Excel is expected to divide by zero or a blank cell. Check the formula and the contents of the cells to which the formula refers.
#NAME?	The information Excel is attempting to display in this cell refers to a named range that does not exist. Check the names that have been assigned in this worksheet, check the spelling of the range name, and check any references to other worksheets or files that are supposed to contain the range name.
#N/A	A function or formula is attempting to refer to a cell that does not contain the required information. This can occur when the formula has been entered before all the related cells have been filled in. Check all cells to which the formula refers.
#REF!	A function or formula is attempting to refer to a cell that is not valid. This message can appear when a cell to which a formula or function refers is deleted or another cell is moved into the location of the cell to which a formula or function refers
#NUM!	A function or formula requiring a numerical value is receiving unacceptable information, such as a non-numerical argument, or a number too large or too small for the function or formula to calculate.
#NULL!	An incorrect range has been specified in a formula. This can occur when a comma has been omitted in a formula that refers to more than one range.

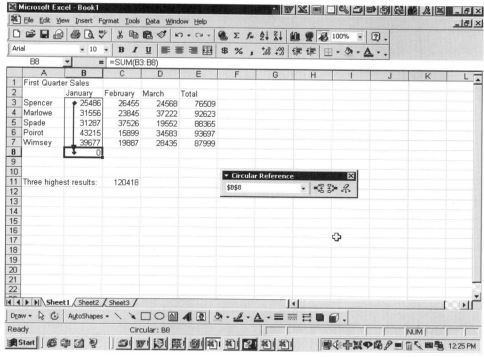

Figure 4-7   Use the Circular Reference toolbar to display the location of a circular reference

Resolve the problem by changing the formula containing the circular reference.

Note: *Excel comes with an analysis tool pack add-in which contains many higher-end functions. Choose Tools | Add-Ins, and pick Analysis ToolPak and click OK to gain access to additional functions.*

Chapter 5

Worksheet Design

Answer Topics!

Worksheet Design @ a Glance

Worksheet Appearance. You don't have to settle for a plain worksheet. You can create centered headings, assign formats that will apply to the entire worksheet at once, control page breaks, hide information that is not for prying eyes, and hold your titles in place while you roam the rest of the screen.

Fonts. Dress up your worksheets with Excel's selection of fonts. Choose from a large gallery of font styles and sizes. You can even change the font or the appearance of individual letters and numbers within a cell. Experiment with various options for borders and shading. There are tools for formatting numbers, and you can choose from an array of colors that can be displayed on your screen and printed to a color printer.

Enhancements. Don't feel confined to the traditional spreadsheet look. Dress up your work with AutoFormats. Excel's underlining capabilities have evolved over the years. You can use single underline, double underline, use an accounting format for your underline which gives the underline a fixed width, and even create your underline in color.

Using Styles. Once you settle on a style you like, you can save the style and re-use it on other worksheets. Or if there is a style you like that someone else created, copy the style for your own use.

Troubleshooting. Find out what causes column letters to appear as numbers, and how to make this happen if you want to use this feature.

WORKSHEET APPEARANCE

 ## Is there a way to turn off the Merge and Center feature after I've centered headings over several columns?

If you would like your text to adjust as the width of the columns changes or as new columns are inserted, begin by entering the text in one of the cells above the range of columns over which you want the heading centered. For example, if you want to center text over columns A, B, C, and D, enter the text in column A, B, C, or D.

Next, select the all cells in the row containing your heading that cover the columns over which you want to center. In our example, to center text over columns A–D, select all the cells in the row containing the heading from column A to D. If your heading is in row 1, select cells A1, B1, C1, and D1.

 Now click the Merge and Center button on the formatting toolbar. You can only center text over columns, one row at a time. If there are two or more lines of heading, you will have to center each line individually.

What happens if you center text over columns and decide you no longer want it centered? It is not as easy to turn off the Merge and Center feature as it is to turn it on. One fairly simple way, however, is to use the Format Painter and paint the format of a normal cell onto the cell that has been merged and centered over several columns. For example, if you center a heading in row 1 over columns A–D and you want to turn off the centering feature, click on a cell that contains no unusual formatting, click once on the format painter button, and click on cell A1 (see Figure 5-1). That will turn off the Merge and Center feature.

 Tip: *Another way to turn off the Merge and Center feature is to select the merged cell, choose Format | Cells, click the Alignment tab, and uncheck the Merge Cells check box. The text will still be centered in the first cell, but you can change the alignment to Left if you prefer.*

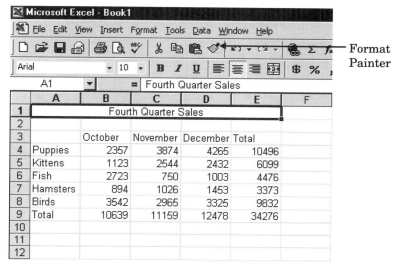

Figure 5-1   Click on a normal cell, click on Format Painter, then click on
your centered heading to turn off the centering format

 **I want to apply certain format commands to every
cell in my worksheet. In Lotus this is called a global
format. How is this type of formatting accomplished
in Excel?**

There will be times when you want to make a formatting
change that affects all the cells of your worksheet. For example,
you may want to change the column width for all the columns
of the worksheet, or you may want to set a number format or
choose a typeface that will apply to all cells in the worksheet.

To make any kind of global change, you can click the
Select All button, which is located to the left of the column
letters and above the row numbers, in the upper left corner
of your worksheet. Clicking on this button selects every cell
in the worksheet, as shown in Figure 5-2. Alternatively you
can press CTRL-A. Then any formatting change that you make
affects all the cells of the worksheet. Click once anywhere on
the worksheet to turn off the Select All feature.

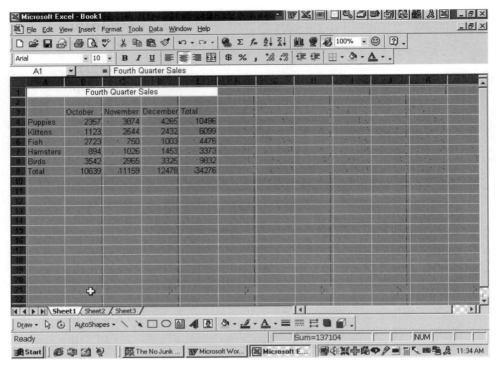

Figure 5-2 Clicking the Select All button highlights every cell on your worksheet

Tip: *Clicking the Select All cell to initiate a global change in a worksheet affects only the current worksheet. To change multiple worksheets in your workbook, select all the worksheets you wish to change by holding down SHIFT while clicking the first and last tabs of the sheets you wish to select, and then click the Select All box. All cells on all selected worksheets will be affected by the global change.*

Note: *Applying formatting changes to every cell in your worksheet can have the effect of dramatically increasing the size of your file.*

 ## The page isn't breaking at a convenient location in my worksheet. How can I control the page breaks?

When you enter information in your worksheet, Excel automatically creates page breaks at appropriate places based on the length of paper you select and the amount of information that you enter. Sometimes, however, the page breaks created by Excel don't correlate with where you actually want pages to stop and new pages to begin. You can insert your own page breaks by selecting the row or column where you want a break to occur, then choosing Insert | Page Break. A vertical page break will occur immediately above a row that you select; a horizontal page break will occur immediately to the left of a selected column. Clicking an individual cell, then choosing Insert | Page Break, will result in a vertical and horizontal break being placed above and to the left of the active cell. A dashed line appears on your worksheet to indicate where the manual page break that you inserted will appear.

You can remove a manual page break by placing your cellpointer anywhere along the lower or right edge of an existing page break. Choose Insert | Remove Page Break to remove the break.

Caution: *Inserting a manual page break will not work if you have selected the fit to x number of pages option under File, Page Setup.*

 ## I've hidden a column—now how do I get it back?

You can hide a column in one of two ways. Click anywhere in the column you wish to hide, then choose Format | Column | Hide. Or, resize a column to zero width by dragging the right border of the column to the left until it closes all the way to a width of zero. Either way, the results are the same.

The contents of a hidden column do not show on your worksheet, and a hidden column won't print. You can tell that a column is hidden if you look at the sequence of letters across the

top of your columns because there will be missing letters where there are hidden columns. For example, if you hide column C, columns A, B, and D are displayed, but column C, of course, will not be displayed.

You can restore a hidden column by selecting cells in the columns on either side of the hidden column, then choosing Format | Column | Unhide. The Unhide command applies only to the hidden columns that have been selected. Other hidden columns on your worksheet will remain hidden.

 Tip: *Here's a shortcut for restoring a hidden column: Place your mouse pointer on the line separating the column letters—the line separating columns B and D, for example, if column C is hidden. Slide your mouse pointer carefully to the right until it appears, not as a single vertical bar with an arrow on each side, but as a double vertical bar with an arrow on each side. When you see this double-vertical bar, you can drag the mouse and thereby open the hidden column.*

Another way to restore a hidden column is by selecting the entire columns on either side of a hidden column—for example, if column C is hidden, press the Shift key and select columns B and D—then resizing any of the selected columns. All selected columns will be resized, including any hidden columns.

These procedures apply to hiding rows as well.

 How do I freeze titles on one part of the screen so the titles won't scroll off the screen when I view the rest of my data?

There may be times when you have spreadsheets that extend beyond the borders of your screen. As you scroll through a spreadsheet like this, the titles at the top will scroll out of view; or, if you are scrolling from left to right, the titles on the left side may scroll out of view.

You can lock in these titles by placing your cellpointer where you want the area of your spreadsheet to freeze, then choosing Window | Freeze Panes.

● Clicking anywhere in column A, then choosing Window | Freeze Panes, will freeze the rows above the cell in which you clicked.

- Clicking anywhere in row 1, then choosing Window | Freeze Panes, will freeze the columns to the left of the cell in which you clicked.

- Clicking anywhere on the worksheet other than in column A and row 1, and then choosing Window | Freeze Panes, will freeze all rows above and all columns to the left of the cell in which you clicked.

Unfreeze all frozen panes by choosing Window | Unfreeze Panes from any point in the worksheet.

An alternative to freezing panes is separating the worksheet into multiple scrollable sections. Create two scrollable sections, one above the other, by dragging the split box that appears on the top of the vertical scroll bar. Or, create two scrollable side-by-side sections by dragging the split box that appears at the right edge of the horizontal scroll bar. Using this technique, you can view and scroll through different areas of your worksheet simultaneously, even if those areas are not located near each other.

Move a split bar by dragging it, or remove a split bar by double-clicking on the bar. Also, you can choose Remove Split from the Window menu.

The use of the split bars or the frozen panes does not affect the way in which the worksheet prints.

 I would like to apply a solid border around a selected area of my worksheet so that the area will stand out from the rest. How do I apply a border to selected cells?

Select the cells to which you wish to apply a border. Choose Format, Cells. The Format Cells window will appear. Click on the Border tab to view your border options. Follow these steps to choose and apply a border to the selected cells:

1. First, choose the style of border you wish to apply from the Style selection box at the right of the border window.

2. Choose the color for your border from the Color drop-down list in the Border window.

3. From the Preset selections, choose from the following options: None applies no border or removes any existing

border; Outline applies a border to the outside edge of the entire selected area; Inside applies border lines to the internal grid lines of the entire selected area. You can choose both Inside and Outline to apply a border to both the outside and internal gridlines of the selected area. You will see a sample of the border choices you make in the Border area of the window.

4. To apply individual borders to sides, top, bottom, grids, or diagonals of selected cells, choose your border style and color by following steps one and two above, then click on the individual pieces of the border, as shown in Figure 5-3, below.

Click here to remove a border from the selected cells.

Click here to place an outside border around the entire selected area.

Click here to place border lines on the internal gridlines of the selected area.

This is a sample of how your border will appear.

Choose from a variety of styles for your border.

Click here to change the color of your border (the default is black).

Click on these buttons to make individual border choices in the selected area.

Figure 5-3   Customize a border by choosing Format, Cells, Border, then making specific selections in this window

Click OK when you have made your selections. The Format Cells window will close and your border will be applied to the selected cells.

FONT SELECTION

 I need to switch the case of my titles from proper case to upper case. Do I have to retype the titles?

If you want to change the case of text you've entered in a worksheet, you can use the UPPER, LOWER, or PROPER (where the first letter of each word is capitalized) function in a blank area of the worksheet, then copy the results to the cells containing the original text, as shown in Figure 5-4. Follow these steps to execute a change in case:

1. Choose a blank area of the worksheet for making the case conversion. Ideally, this should be an area that is similar to the area containing the cells you want to change. For example, if you want to change the case of titles to uppercase in column A, rows 4 through 9, you might choose to work in column G, rows 4 through 9.

Microsoft Excel - Book1

File Edit View Insert Format Tools Data Window Help

Arial   10   **B** *I* U

G4   =   =UPPER(A4)

	A	B	C	D	E	F	G	H
1		Fourth Quarter Sales						
2								
3		October	November	December	Total			
4	Puppies	2357	3874	4265	10496		PUPPIES	
5	Kittens	1123	2544	2432	6099		KITTENS	
6	Fish	2723	750	1003	4476		FISH	
7	Hamsters	894	1026	1453	3373		HAMSTERS	
8	Birds	3542	2965	3325	9832		BIRDS	
9	Total	10639	11159	12478	34276		TOTAL	
10								
11								

Figure 5-4   Use a formula to change the case of your text

2. In the first cell of the blank work area, enter the formula that will convert the case. In this example, enter =UPPER(A4) in cell G4. The text from cell A4 will appear in cell G4, with all letters in uppercase.

3. Copy the formula down to all cells in the range you wish to capitalize. In this example, copy the formula from cell G4 to cells G5 through G9.

4. Highlight the cells containing the correct case (in this example, cells G4 through G9), and click the Copy button on the toolbar, or choose Edit | Copy.

5. Click on the first cell in the original range (A1), then choose Edit | Paste Special. The Paste Special window will appear; select the Values option.

6. Click OK in the Paste Special window. The converted text will appear in place of the original text.

7. Select the text in the work area (in our example, cells G4 through G9), and press Delete, or choose Edit | Clear | All, to remove the extraneous text.

❓ Is there an easy way to insert a checkmark into a cell?

Here's a quick trick for inserting a checkmark:

1. Select the cells in which you would like a checkmark to appear.

2. Choose Format | Cells, and click on the Font tab.

3. Select the Monotype Sorts font, then click on OK.

4. In each of the selected cells, enter the number 3 or 4. A checkmark will appear in each cell, as shown in Figure 5-5.

 Tip: *The Monotype Sorts font provides you with a checkmark when you enter the number 3 or 4 after changing to this font. If you don't have the Monotype Sorts font on your computer, take a few minutes to examine your other fonts, and you may find a checkmark symbol that you can enter in a similar fashion.*

	A	B	C	D	E	F	G
1		Fourth Quarter Sales					
2							
3		October	November	December	Total	Bestsellers	
4	PUPPIES	2357	3874	4265	10496	✓	
5	KITTENS	1123	2544	2432	6099		
6	FISH	2723	750	1003	4476		
7	HAMSTERS	894	1026	1453	3373		
8	BIRDS	3542	2965	3325	9832	✓	
9	TOTAL	10639	11159	12478	34276		
10							
11							

Figure 5-5 Change the font to Monotype Sorts and type the number 3 or 4 to enter checkmarks

How can cells containing zero values be formatted so that they appear blank?

There are two ways to change zero value cells so that they appear blank. The first way is a default change that will affect your entire worksheet and all other worksheets that you use. Only use this method if you want all zero values suppressed on all sheets in all workbooks. Choose Tools | Options | View. Uncheck the box labeled Zero Values, then click the OK button. To view zero values in the future you will have to return to this window and check the Zero Values check box.

Tip: *To show zero value cells as blanks in your entire worksheet without making a change to the default that would affect other worksheets, click the Select All button at the upper left corner of your worksheet, then follow the steps given here for hiding zero values in particular cells.*

You can hide zero values in particular cells by first selecting the cells to which you want to apply the change, then following these steps:

1. Choose Format | Cells, and click the Number tab.

2. In the Category list, click on Custom.

3. In the Type box, enter: **0;-0;@**

4. Click the OK button to apply this format to the selected cells.

The zero will still appear in the formula bar for cells with a zero value, even though the cell appears blank.

To remove the formatting that changes zeros to blanks, select the affected cells and choose Format | Cells | Number, and select a different number format such as General. Or, use the Format Painter to copy a number format from other cells to the range of cells that you formatted for blanks.

If I want certain words in a title to appear in bold and others to appear without the bold, must I enter the two parts of the title in separate cells?

You can change the format of particular words or characters within a cell without affecting the format of the rest of the cell's contents (see Figure 5-6). Edit the cell containing the text you wish to change by double-clicking on the cell, or pressing the F2 key. Select the characters you wish to affect by dragging over them or holding down the SHIFT key while using your arrow keys. With the text selected, apply your formatting changes, such as bold or italics or a font size change. Press ENTER to finalize your changes, or press ESC if you change your mind and wish to return to the original text formatting.

My font size selection offers 12 point and 14 point. What if I need a 13-point font?

The list of sizes that appears with your font selections is not all inclusive. The numbers on the font size list give you a guideline and a general list of choices, but you are not limited to only the numbers on this list. Scalable fonts can be resized to fit your worksheet needs. To choose the font size you want, even if it is not on the list of font sizes, select the area where you want to apply the font (or select the entire worksheet).

	A	B	C	D	E	F	G
1		Fourth Quarter Sales					
2							
3		October	November	December	Total	Bestsellers	
4	PUPPIES	2357	3874	4265	10496	✓	
5	KITTENS	1123	2544	2432	6099		
6	FISH	2723	750	1003	4476		
7	HAMSTERS	894	1026	1453	3373		
8	BIRDS	3542	2965	3325	9832	✓	
9	TOTAL	10639	11159	12478	34276		
10							
11							

Figure 5-6 Format a portion of a cell while in Edit mode

Click on the font size button on the formatting toolbar, and enter the number of the size font you want.

Some fonts are not scalable. You can tell which ones they are because they will only have one or two size choices. In most cases, however, you can enter any font size you wish and the size you enter will be applied to the selected area on your worksheet.

ENHANCEMENTS

Is it possible to apply more than one AutoFormat to a group of cells?

You can combine two AutoFormat designs in the same group of cells on your worksheet, if you choose the formats in the correct order.

To apply two AutoFormat designs to an area on your worksheet, first select the area you wish to format (but see the following Note). Choose Format | AutoFormat, and the AutoFormat selection window will appear. For this example, choose a number format, such as one of the Accounting formats, then click OK to apply that format to your cells.

Return to the AutoFormat window and choose a colorful format. The colorful format will apply in addition to the numerical format you already chose.

Note: *When choosing cells for AutoFormat, the selection process is optional. If the area to be formatted is obvious, for example if there are no blank sections, you don't need to select the cells first. Excel will figure out which area you plan to format.*

If you try to choose a colorful format first, however, and then go back to the AutoFormat window and choose a numerical format, the second format you choose will take the place of the first format, removing the color scheme.

 ### How can I make my underline appear in a different color from the information I am underlining?

The regular underline tool on the formatting toolbar produces an underline that is the same color as the text in the cell. To underline in a different color, you must use the line drawing underline tool to create your line, and then apply a color to the line.

Click the line drawing tool, which appears on the Drawing toolbar, then draw the line in your cell. For a better view while drawing, increase your Zoom factor to 150% or 200%. When your line is completed, make sure the line is still selected (click on it if it's not), then click the Line Color button on the Drawing toolbar and choose a color.

Tip: *Having trouble making your line straight? When using the line drawing tool, you can force a line to be straight by holding down the SHIFT key while you draw.*

To produce duplicate lines elsewhere in your worksheet with the same width and line color, select the line, then use the Copy and Paste features to replicate the line in other cells.

Tip: As an alternative to drawing lines with the line drawing tool, you can use the Border option to apply a lower border line that will span the width of the cell. You can choose a different color for your border line as well. Select the cell(s) to which the border will apply. Choose Format | Cells, then click the Border tab. Click on the style of line, choose a color, and then click in the sample Border box to indicate where you wish the border to appear in the selected cell(s).

What's the difference between regular and accounting underlines?

There are two styles of underlines in Excel, regular and accounting. These underlines come in both single and double. Accounting underlines apply to numbers that have been formatted with an accounting format, that is, either a comma or currency format. An accounting underline is one that stretches a particular length based on the width of the cell rather than the width of the characters being underlined. As your cell width increases, the accounting underline width will increase. Alternatively, a regular underline is only as wide as the characters being underlined. To apply an accounting underline, format your numbers with an accounting format and then apply a regular underline by clicking on the underline button on the Formatting Toolbar. You don't have to go to the Format Cells window to choose a single accounting underline. An accounting underline will automatically appear if you click the underline button in a cell containing numbers formatted with an accounting format.

How do you get a double underline on a worksheet?

The Underline button on the Formatting toobar provides you with a single underline. To apply a double underline, click in the cell that deserves the underline, then choose Format, Cells, Font. Click the drop-down arrow in the Underline field, then choose between a regular or accounting Double underline (you will automatically receive an Accounting Double underline if the cell has been formatted in an accounting number format).

 Tip: *If you use double underlines frequently, consider customizing your toolbar to include a button for double underline. Do this by choosing View | Toolbars | Customize (or right-clicking on a toolbar and choosing Customize), click on the Command tab, choose the Format category, and find the double underline command. Drag the button from this window to your toolbar. Then click Close to close the Customize box.*

How can I format my numbers to show British pounds?

Excel supports a wide variety of currency formats, including the British pound and the new Euro format. Select the cell(s) to which the currency format should apply, then choose Format, Cells, Number. Click on the Currency category. Click the drop-down arrow in the Symbol area and choose from a wide selection of currency formats.

 Note: *If you use a currency format other than the U.S. dollar on a regular basis, you may want to consider changing the currency settings on your computer. From the Start button, choose Settings, Control Panel, Regional Settings, and indicate the language you use, then click the Currency tab to choose a currency format that matches the chosen language. You will need to restart your computer to implement these changes.*

My numbers are right-aligned and the headings above them are left-aligned. How do I get everything lined up properly?

By default, Excel presents numbers right-aligned in their cells, and text appears left-aligned. Change the alignment of any element on your worksheet by selecting the cell(s) to change, then clicking on the appropriate alignment buttons at the top of the worksheet.

 ● **Right Align**. Click this button to make cell contents line up at the right side of the cell. Numbers are automatically right-aligned. Numbers with an accounting format appear right-aligned with a small space separating the number

from the right edge of the cell. This space leaves room for a parentheses which might apear if this is a negative number.

 ● **Center**. Click this button to center the cell contents in the existing cell. If the cell contents exceeds the width of the cell, and the surrounding cells are empty, the contents of the centered cell will spill over to the left and right adjacent cells.

 ● **Left Align.** Click this button to make cell contents line up at the left side of the cell. Text aligns to the left by default.

 Note: *Numbers do not lose their integrity if they are left-aligned or centered within a cell.*

How can I add shading to some cells to make them stand out?

 Click on the cells to which you wish to add shading. Click the Fill Color button on the Formatting toolbar. Click one of the colors to add shading to your cells. If the available shades are not appropriate for your cells, follow these steps to see more choices:

1. Select the cells to which you wish to add shading.

2. Choose Format, Cells. The Format Cells window will appear.

3. Click the Patterns tab. Choose from the available array of colors by clicking on a color that is appropriate, or click the drop-down arrow in the Pattern area, and choose from various patterns of dots and stripes.

4. Click OK when you have made your selection. The background color of the selected cell(s) will display the color you have chosen.

 Note: *Shading does not affect the color of text in your cells, it only changes the background color.*

 Is there a toolbar button for changing text color?

 Change the color of text or numbers in your cells by selecting the cells to which you wish to change text or number color, then clicking the Font Color toolbar button on the Formatting toolbar. Choose from the array of available colors.

To select from additional colors, follow these steps:

1. Select the cells to which you wish to apply color to the text or numbers.

2. Choose Format, Cells. The Format Cells window will appear.

3. Click the Font tab, and click the drop-down arrow in the Color area. Click on the color you wish to use.

4. Click the OK button. The contents of the selected cell(s) will appear in the color you have chosen.

 My titles are too large to fit in one cell without extending the width of the cell more than I want to. Can I wrap the text within the cell so that I can use a long title?

Excel gives you the capability of wrapping text within a cell, so that multiple lines of text will appear within a single cell. If your headings are too wide for your cells, consider wrapping text as an alternative to using a smaller font size or truncating the words in the title.

Follow these steps to wrap text on your worksheet:

1. Select the cell(s) in which you want the text to wrap.

2. Choose Format, Cells, and the Format Cells window will appear.

3. Click the Alignment tab. Click the Wrap text option to place a check in the checkbox.

4. Click OK. The text in the selected cells will be wrapped to fit the designated width of the cells.

USING STYLES

 I use the Comma style frequently, and I always have to decrease the decimal places to zero because my reports don't require decimal places. Is there a way to change this style so that when I click the Comma button I automatically get no decimal places?

Excel has three preset styles that are available on your Formatting toolbar (although there are other styles that are not on the toolbar):

- **Comma**: comma separators, two decimal places, no dollar or percent sign
- **Currency**: comma separators, two decimal places, dollar sign

---

 Note: the Currency tool is not a true currency style: the $ stays on the left of the cell, and does not appear beside the numbers.

- **Percent**: no decimal places, percent sign

If these styles are not useful to you with their normal attributes, you can change the attributes so that the style will fit your needs. To change the attributes of the Comma style, for example, so that it presents numbers with no decimal places, follow these steps:

1. Choose Format | Style. The Style window will appear.
2. In the Style name list box, choose Comma.
3. Click the Modify button. The Format Cells window will appear.
4. Choose the Number tab. Change the number format to meet your requirements. For this example, change the number of decimal places from 2 to 0.
5. Click OK in the Format Cells window, then click OK in the Style window.

From this point forward, your Comma button will return a style containing comma separators with no decimal places. Note that if you wish to add decimal places to a range formatted with the Comma button, you can do so easily by clicking on the Increase Decimal button.

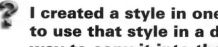 **I created a style in one of my workbooks. If I want to use that style in a different workbook, is there a way to copy it into the new workbook instead of having the recreate the entire style?**

Excel calls this process "Merging a style," and the way you begin is to have both the sending and the receiving workbook open at the same time, then follow these steps:

1. In the workbook that is to receive the style, choose Format | Style, and click on the Merge button. A window will appear listing all open workbooks.

2. Click on the name of the workbook containing the styles(s) you wish to merge. You must merge all styles from the originating workbook—you cannot pick which style(s) you wish to merge.

3. Click the OK button. You will be asked if you wish to merge styles of the same names. Answer Yes to merge the styles. (If you answer No or Cancel, the operation aborts.) The styles from the originating workbook are immediately merged into the current workbook.

4. Click OK to close the Style window.

 I use conditional formatting to change the appearance of sales numbers when they reach a certain level. How can I remove the conditional formatting feature once I no longer need it?

Excel's conditional formatting feature enables you to establish criteria for determining which cells receive certain types of formatting. Up to three levels of criteria may be set with this feature.

Should you choose to remove or change one or more levels of criteria, but you still want to use the conditional formatting option, choose Format | Conditional Formatting, and click the Delete button in the Conditional Formatting window. A check box will appear in which to indicate which criteria you wish to delete. The remaining criteria will remain in place.

Remove conditional formatting altogether by following these steps:

1. Click on a cell that doesn't contain conditional formatting.

2. Click on the Format Painter button. If there is more than one contiguous area from which you wish to remove the conditional formatting, double-click on the Format Painter button so that its effect will remain activated as you paint various areas of your workbook.

3. Click on or drag through any cells that contain conditional formatting that you want to return to normal formatting. If the Format Painter button is still depressed when you have finished removing conditional formatting, click the Format Painter button again, or press the ESC key to turn off its effect.

 I like to dress up my worksheets with fancy titles. What options are available for turning text on an angle?

You can turn text on its side by entering the text in a cell, then following these steps:

1. Choose Format | Cells. The Format Cells window will appear.

2. Click on the Alignment tab. Notice the illustration at the right side of the window that looks like half of a clock.

3. In the clock illustration, there is a text line. Drag this line around the clock face to change the degree of rotation for your text. Alternatively, you can enter a precise degree of rotation in the Degrees box.

4. Click OK when you have finished making your adjustments. The text in your worksheet will be aligned at the angle you selected, as shown in Figure 5-7.

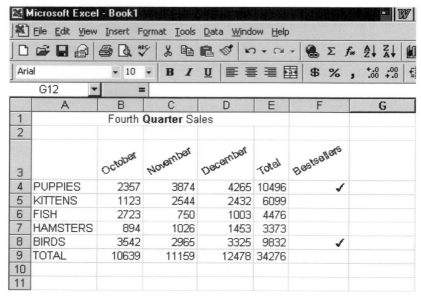

Figure 5-7 Add attention-getting rotated titles to your report

TROUBLESHOOTING

 Somehow my column letters have turned into numbers. How can get my display of column letters to return?

When your column letters are numbers instead of letters, an adjustment must be made in the Options window. Choose Tools | Options, and click on the General tab. In the Settings section of this tab, there is a check box labeled **R1C1 reference style.** Uncheck this box, then click OK. Your column letters should magically reappear!

Chapter 6

Advanced Formula Construction

Answer Topics!

Advanced Formula Construction @ a Glance

Linking to Other Workbooks. You can incorporate information from other workbooks in your formulas by linking to cells in other workbooks, and by copying information from one workbook to another. Be sure to keep track of files containing links—you can change the name or location of a linked file, but you must then update your links to make sure the linked information is still available to you.

Absolute and Relative References. Sometimes you will copy formulas and want only to copy the logic of the formula (multiply the cell to the right by the cell above), and other times you will want to copy the actual formula (multiply cell E5 by cell F4). Excel provides techniques for both types of copying.

Array Formulas. You can use simple formulas to perform calculations on a vast collection of cells by using Excel's array formulas. Use an array formula to find cells that meet particular criteria, or to perform calculations on many items at once.

Other Advanced Formula Considerations. For those Excel users who prefer to work with the keyboard instead of the mouse, there are several shortcuts for entering functions using the function keys on the keyboard.

LINKING TO OTHER WORKBOOKS

 How do I copy information from one workbook to another so that when the information in the original workbook changes, it will also change in the other workbook?

You can create a *link* between workbooks so that when information is copied from one workbook (the originating workbook, or the *source*) to another (the receiving workbook, or the *target*), the information in the target workbook will always reflect the most current information from the source workbook. By linking information, you will be able to use data from one workbook in other workbooks without having to re-enter the information.

To link information between workbooks, follow these steps:

1. Select the information in the originating workbook by dragging over the cells you wish to link. Cells being linked must be adjacent to one another.

2. Click the Copy button on the standard toolbar. The highlighted cells will be surrounded with a moving border.

3. Click on the taskbar button for the workbook that is to receive the linked information, or open the target workbook if it is not already open.

4. Click in the upper-left-most cell of the area in which you want the linked information to appear.

5. Choose Edit | Paste Special (or right-click on the cell mentioned in step 4 and choose Paste Special). The Paste Special window will appear.

6. Click the Paste Link button, as shown in Figure 6-1, to paste the copied information into the target workbook. Click on any of the linked cells, and note that the contents of the linked cells in the formula bar include the name of the worksheet to which they are linked.

7. Press the ESC key to turn off the border surrounding the linked cells in the source workbook. Alternatively, as soon as you make an entry in any cell in either workbook, the copy border will disappear.

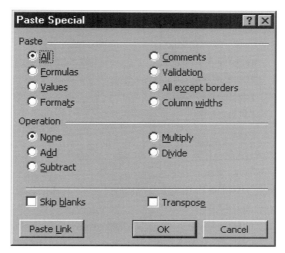

Figure 6-1 Click on Paste Link to link copied information to the currently selected cell(s)

From this point forward, each time you open the target workbook, Excel will look for the source workbook and bring in the latest cell information to the target workbook.

 Tip: *When saving linked files, save the source file first. This way, the target file will know the name of the file providing the linked information.*

Is there a way to copy an entire worksheet to a new workbook other than using the clipboard to copy and paste every cell?

You can easily move or copy worksheets from one workbook to another. If you plan to move or copy a worksheet or group of worksheets to another workbook, the receiving workbook should be open, as well as the workbook containing the original sheets.

With both workbook files open, follow these steps to move or copy worksheets.

 Tip: *To move or copy more than one worksheet, select the worksheet group (click on the first worksheet tab, hold down the SHIFT key, then click on the last tab in the group; or use the CTRL key while you click on non-contiguous sheet tabs) before beginning these steps.*

1. Place your mouse pointer over the sheet tab on the worksheet you wish to copy or move.

2. Right-click. A pop-up menu will appear.

3. Select Move or Copy.

4. Choose the name of the destination workbook. Choose New workbook if you want Excel to open a new workbook.

5. Indicate where in the order of sheets you wish the destination worksheet(s) to be placed.

6. Click the Create a copy box if you wish to copy rather than move the worksheet(s).

7. Click OK. The selected worksheet(s) will appear at the requested location in the destination workbook.

Tip: *If you are moving a worksheet from one workbook (the source) to another (the target), you can display the two workbooks on-screen simultaneously (choose Window | Arrange), then drag the sheet tab of the source worksheet to the target workbook. If both workbooks are displayed, you can copy worksheets from one workbook to another by holding down the* CTRL *key while you drag a sheet.*

When I link cells from one workbook to another, I either use the Copy and Paste Special combination, or I enter the path and name of the source file along with the cell reference. Is there an easier way to create a link?

You can save time when linking cells over workbook boundaries if you have both workbooks open at once. Click in the cell in which you wish to place the link. This cell will be in the target workbook. If you plan to use the linked cell (from the source workbook) in a formula, begin entering the formula in the target cell. If you plan to merely enter the link without any other information in the cell, enter the equal (=) sign.

When you are ready to add the link to the cell, click the Window menu and click on the name of the file containing the cell to which you wish to link. The source workbook will appear. Click once on the cell containing the information you want to

link. If there is nothing else you want to enter in the cell along with the link, press the ENTER key. Otherwise, continue entering the formula you began previously.

The link, including the path and file name of the source file, will appear in the target file. Keep in mind that links are automatically absolute references, which means that the formula can't be copied as can one with a relative reference.

If I change the location of a file to which another file is linked, what happens to the linked information?

Excel can't keep up with you if you move linked files to new locations. Whenever you open an Excel file that contains links to other files, you will see a message like the one shown in Figure 6-2, asking if you want Excel to update this workbook with the latest information from the linked source(s). Answer No to this question, and Excel will leave the information in the workbook as it is, without trying to search for the files containing the source of the links. It won't matter if the file to which this workbook is linked has been moved to a new location. Answer Yes and Excel will examine any files to which this workbook has links and retrieve the current value of all linked cells.

When you ask Excel to update linked information in a workbook, Excel assumes the filename and its location have not changed. If either the filename or the location of the file (or both) has changed since the link was created, you will see the message shown in Figure 6-3, indicating that the file can't be found.

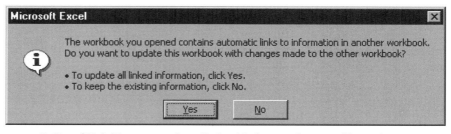

Figure 6-2   Click Yes to update linked information, or No to leave everything in the workbook as is

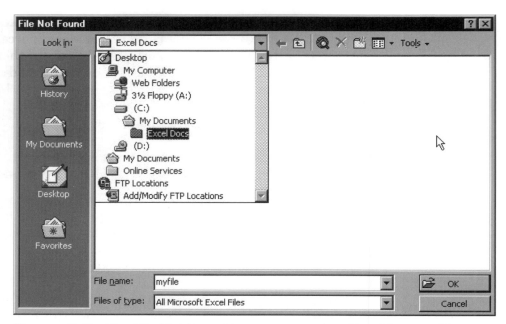

Figure 6-3 The File Not Found box appears when Excel has trouble locating files to which the current file is linked

Use the drop-down list in the Look in field to select the folder that contains the linked file. When you have found the file, click on the file name and click OK. Indicating the new location of the linked file in the File Not Found box enables Excel to update the links in your workbook with the current information from the linked files. Note, however, that if you save your workbook at this point, Excel saves the original linked file name and location, rather than the information you provided in the File Not Found box. The next time you open this file you will once again need to indicate the new location and/or the name of the file containing the linked information.

To revise the links in your workbook so that the next time Excel tries to update links it will know where to go to find the linked files, follow these steps:

1. With the workbook containing the links open, choose Edit │ Links. The Links dialog box will appear showing a list of all existing links in the current worksheet.

2. To indicate a new file name or location for a linked file, click on the link that needs revising in the Source file list. That filename will become highlighted (if there is only one link in this workbook, the link is already highlighted).

3. Click the Change Source button (see Figure 6-4). The Change Links dialog box will appear.

4. Indicate the correct folder and file name for the linked source file, then click OK. The Links window returns, showing the new name or location for the source file.At this point the linked information in the workbook is also updated with the new source file data.

5. Click OK to return to the worksheet. Be sure to save this worksheet before closing it so that the updated link(s) will be saved.

When working in a workbook that contains links, how can I be sure all links are up to date?

Normally you don't have to worry about making sure your linked information is up to date—Excel will do this for you

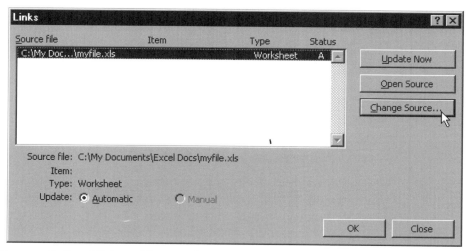

Figure 6-4   Click on Change Source to open a window in which to identify the new name or location for the linked source file

automatically. Each time you open a workbook that contains links, you will see a message asking if you want to update links to your worksheet. Click Yes and Excel examines the file that contains the source of the linked information and displays the most current information for the links.

At any time, you can choose Edit, Links, select the links listed in the window displayed, and click the Update Now button to make sure all links are up to date.

If you are working on two files that are linked and both files are open, linked information in one file is automatically updated when the source information changes.

If your worksheet is not automatically updating linked information, it is likely that the automatic calculation feature has been turned off. You can test this easily—by pressing F9 to recalculate, your worksheet formulas will recalculate and all links will be updated. Turn automatic calculation on by choosing Tools, Options, Calculation, and clicking the Automatic option. Click OK to close the Options window and save this change.

I don't need these links any more. How can I remove links from my worksheet?

Remove links from your worksheet by changing the linked cells to values. Select a cell containing a link (or a group of cells containing links). Choose Edit Copy (or click the Copy button). With the cell(s) still selected, choose Edit, Paste Special. Click the Values button, then click OK. The cell contents will be replaced with the actual value of the cell; the link to another source will be removed.

What's the difference between linking and embedding, and how do I embed an object in Excel?

A link retains its connection to the source file, but becomes a part of the Excel file to which it is linked. The linked information can be changed in the Excel file, using the tools available within Excel.

An embedded object appears in its own boxed frame, and by double-clicking on the object you activate the toolbar and menus of the originating program. In this way you can use

the features of the originating program to edit and enhance the embedded object.

The embedded information is not linked, so changes to the original information will not have an affect on the file containing the embedded information.

To place an embedded object in your Excel worksheet, go to the source document, select the information you wish to embed, and click the Copy button. Return to your Excel worksheet, choose Edit, click on the appropriate description of the object to be embedded, click the Paste option (as opposed to Paste Link), then click OK.

Tip: *This process is referred to as Object Linking and Embedding, and is supported by most Windows programs. You can use Microsoft Word, for example, to create and format text, then copy and embed the text in Excel, preserving the formatting design chosen in Word, without disrupting the formatting in your Excel worksheet.*

ABSOLUTE AND RELATIVE REFERENCES

 When I copy formulas in a worksheet, the cell references in the formula change. Usually this is what I want, but occasionally I want to lock in the cell references before I copy a formula. How can I do this?

Copying cells containing formulas usually results in the logic of a formula getting copied, rather than the exact formula. For example, suppose cell C7 contains the formula =B7/B24. Copy that formula down one cell to cell C8 and it will change to read =B8/B25. Copy the formula to cell D7 and it will change to read =C7/C24. Copy the formula to any other cell in the workbook, and the formula will change to read =☆/♥, where ☆ represents one cell to the left of the cell in which you are copying the formula, and ♥ represents one cell to the left and 17 cells down from the cell in which you are copying the formula.

The fact that Excel copies the logical rather than the actual references in a formula is because Excel copies what is

known as *relative references* when you copy a formula. If you want Excel to copy the exact cell references, you want to request that the *absolute references* be copied.

To use absolute references, you must enter cell references with a dollar ($) sign to the left of the reference(s) that should be absolute. For example, in the previous formula, =B7/B24, if you want to copy it down from cell C7 to cell C8 and keep the denominator of the fraction from changing (i.e., make the "24" absolute), you would write the formula as =B7/B$24. When the formula is copied from C7 to C8, the formula will read =B8/B$24. Continue copying the formula down, and the numerator will continue to change relative to the direction in which you are copying, but the denominator will remain constant in each rendition of the formula.

If you plan to copy the formula across, and at the same time keep the denominator constant, it is the column reference that must be made absolute. Thus, =B7/B24 becomes =B7/$B24. When copied from C7 to D7, the formula will read =C7/$B24.

To enter a formula in which you want to include an absolute reference, you can enter the dollar sign(s) when you type the formula or edit the formula and include the symbols later. Or, while entering the formula, press F4 after entering the cell reference. To edit the formula, click on the cell reference and press F4. This causes dollar signs to appear and disappear in the following order (C is the column reference and R is the row reference):

First F4 CR

Second F4   C$R

Third F4 $CR

Fourth F4   CR

Tip: Assign a range name to a cell that is to be used in a formula. Then, when you copy the formula, the cell reference will always be correct, because named cells are always absolute.

When I refer to a cell in another workbook in my formula and then try to copy the cell containing the formula, the cell reference from the other workbook doesn't change. Is there a way to make the linked cell a relative reference rather than an absolute one?

References to cells from other workbooks are automatically absolute. Thus the formula:

=C5+[myworkbook.xls]Sheet1!$A$1

will always refer to the cell A1 in the linked workbook, even when copied to another cell. You can edit the cell containing the formula and remove the absolute reference symbols by removing the dollar signs. Then, when you copy the formula down one cell, for example, the resulting formula will read:

=C6+[myworkbook.xls]Sheet1!A2

ARRAY FORMULAS

I have a large list of numbers in my worksheet. I would like to be able to find the nearest number in the group to a given amount. Is there a way to do this without sorting the numbers?

Excel's array formulas can operate calculations on large groups of numbers and return a single result, or results for every cell where you want an answer to appear. The advantage of working with an array formula is that an operation that would normally take a large quantity of repeating calculations can be performed as one calculation, thus saving time and space in your worksheet. The following comprehensive example should give you a healthy introduction to working with array formulas.

In this example, you will use an array formula to find a number that matches certain criteria within a group. In the group of numbers shown in Figure 6-5, suppose you want to find the number closest to the average of the group.

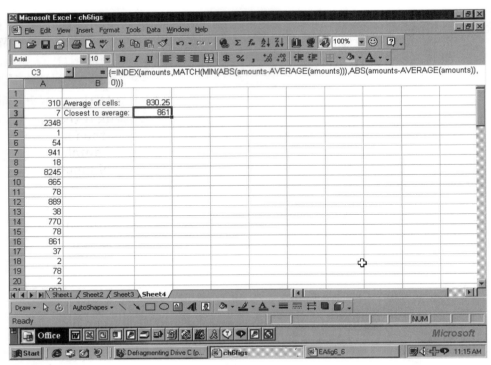

Figure 6-5 Use an array formula to determine the number that comes closest to the average of all the numbers in the range

The range of numbers under consideration spans cells A2 to A21 (in reality you would take advantage of the array formula to perform an operation on a much larger group of numbers). First, to find the member of the range that is closest to the average, you must determine the average (=AVERAGE(A2:A21)) of the group. Next, create a formula that will compare each number in the range to the average, consider the difference between the two, and return the number presenting the smallest difference between itself and the average.

As with all complex formulas, it is important to break the formula down into smaller parts, calculating one piece at a time and eventually combine all elements to make the complete formula. For this formula, perform the following steps:

1. Determine the difference between each member of the group (which we will name *Amounts*) and the average (which resides in cell C2):

   Amounts-AVERAGE(Amounts)

   If *Amounts* represents each number in the group, and if the formula is treated as an array formula (executed by pressing CTRL-SHIFT-ENTER after constructing the formula), this piece of the formula will return an array of numbers. Each number in this array will be one of the original amounts minus the average.

   Tip: *When creating an array formula, you must always press CTRL-SHIFT-ENTER. Even if you edit an array formula, you must press this key combination, or the formula will be written as a normal, nonarray formula.*

2. Once you have collected this group of numbers representing the difference between each of the original amounts and the average, you must determine the smallest member of this group. In addition, since some of the numbers in this group are negative numbers, you must request the absolute value of each number when considering which is the smallest. Thus the formula:

   ABS(MIN(x))

   Where "*x*" is the amount determined in step 1.

3. Using the MATCH formula, request a match between the number representing the smallest difference from the average with the array of all the numbers. The "0" at the end of the formula indicates that you want the MATCH formula to return an exact match:

   MATCH(ABS(MIN(amounts-AVERAGE(amounts))), ABS(amounts-AVERAGE(amounts)),0)

4. Finally, you want Excel to return to you the number whose difference from the average is the smallest, as

determined in step 2 above. The INDEX formula returns the contents of a cell in a selected range or array.

> =INDEX(amounts,MATCH(ABS(MIN(amounts-AVERAGE(amounts))),ABS(amounts-AVERAGE(amounts)),0))

Remember to press CTRL-SHIFT-ENTER to create this as an array formula. Excel places braces around the formula when you press this key combination. The final formula will look like this:

> {=INDEX(amounts,MATCH(ABS(MIN(amounts-AVERAGE(amounts))),ABS(amounts-AVERAGE(amounts)),0))}

I have a range of numbers that includes positive and negative numbers. How can I find the smallest positive number in the range?

You can use an array formula to find the smallest number in your range. The innermost part of the formula, the IF argument, sets out the premise that you only want to consider positive numbers. Use the MIN function to find the smallest number from the results of the IF function, then finish the formula by pressing CTRL-SHIFT-ENTER to make the formula an array formula (pressing CTRL-SHIFT-ENTER will place curly brackets around the formula):

> {=MIN(IF(A1:A10>0,A1:A10))}

Figure 6-6 displays the finished result.

I need to calculate the total cost of various pieces of computer equipment that will be purchased for my office, and each type of equipment has a separate price. Can this calculation be accomplished in one formula?

An array formula can produce the results you need from the cost and quantity information you provide. Say, for example, that you plan to purchase the following items:

Equipment	Quantity	Cost per item
Printer	12	$275
CPU	25	$995
Modem	15	$87
Monitor	25	$175

You can produce four separate multiplication formulas to determine the cost of each item of equipment, then add the four products to arrive at a total cost for all the equipment. Or, you can use an array formula like the one below (see Figure 6-7) to perform the calculation in one easy formula. Remember to press CTRL-SHIFT-ENTER when placing the formula in the cell.

{=SUM(B2:B5*C2:C5)}

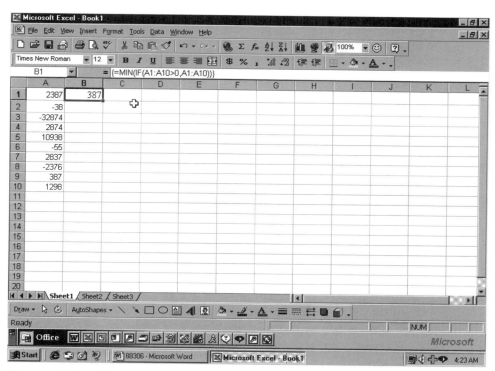

Figure 6-6 You can use an array formula to find the lowest positive number within a range

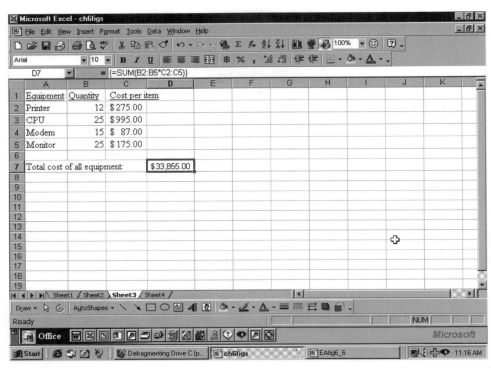

Figure 6-7 An array formula solves the problem of calculating the cost of several differently priced items

OTHER ADVANCED FORMULA CONSIDERATIONS

The more you use formulas in Excel, the more you will appreciate shortcuts and quick methods for performing these tasks. Table 6-1 provides you with some of the most common keyboard shortcuts for working with formulas in Excel.

I'm trying to calculate payments on a loan where the payments are made at the end of the period, but Excel seems to want to calculate with the payments made at the beginning of the period. Can I override this assumption to calculate with end of the period payments?

There is an optional argument when using the loan payment function that lets you assign either the beginning or end of

Keystroke	Results
CTRL-A	Open Paste Function window after you type function name Also: Select Entire Worksheet
CTRL-SHIFT-A	Enter the function arguments names in a formula after you type the function name
F2	Edit the active cell
F3	Choose from a list of defined names to place into a formula
SHIFT-F3	Paste a function into a formula
F9	Calculate all sheets in open Excel workbooks
SHIFT-F9	Calculate the active worksheet only
ALT-=	Enter AutoSum formula into active cell
CTRL-;	Enter current date into active cell
CTRL-SHIFT-:	Enter current time into active cell
CTRL-SHIFT-"	Copy value from cell above into active cell or formula
CTRL-' (quotation mark in upper left corner of keyboard)	Toggle between displaying cell values and formulas in all cells of worksheet
CTRL-' (quotation mark on right side of middle letter row of keyboard)	Copy formula from cell above into active cell or formula
CTRL-"	Copy value from cell above into active cell or formula

Table 6-1   Shortcut Keys for Working in Formulas

period for the timing of the payment. If you don't use this argument, Excel uses the beginning of the period for payment calculations.

The arguments requested by the PMT function for calculating loan payments are:

RATE	The interest rate applied per period
NPER	The number of periods, or number of payments
PV	The present value, or the current amount of the loan
FV	(optional) The value of the loan when all the payments have been made (assumed to be zero)
TYPE	(optional) The timing of the payment: Enter 1 for beginning of the period or 0 for end of the period (assumed to be 0)

For a loan with a principal of $10,000, an interest rate of 8 percent per year, a term of 48 months, and payments to be

made at the beginning of the month, utilizing the formula, =PMT(Rate/12,Nper,PV), the calculation for the payment would be:

=PMT(.08/12,48,10000,1)

? How can I quickly edit a function that has been placed in my worksheet?

Click on a cell containing a function, then click the Paste Function button on the Standard toolbar. The function window will open, displaying all the components of the function, along with a description of the information required of the function. Make any changes that are necessary, clicking the OK button when you have finished.

? Where can I go for detailed information about Excel's function library?

You can check the index in this book, looking up specific Excel functions, to see descriptions and examples of the functions described throughout the pages of this book. For a detailed analysis of all of Excel's functions, go no further than your Excel program itself. Choose Help, and enter the name of the function for which you want information when the Office Assistant appears. If you have turned off the Office Assistant (see Chapter 1 for more information about turning the Office Assistant on and off), choose Help, Microsoft Excel Help, to open the list of Help Topics. Enter the name of the function for which you want information. Excel provides a definition of each function, along with a hyperlink to specific examples and tips relating to the function.

Chapter 7

Excel Workbooks

Answer Topics!

Excel Workbooks @ a Glance

Grouping Multiple Sheets. You can use the multiple pages of workbooks to create spreadsheets that are similar in appearance and/or contents. Also, you can use workbooks as a tool to store supporting information that provides details for the numbers on the main page of your workbook. In this chapter you'll learn to remove sheets you no longer need, and add and rearrange more sheets easily.

Creating Formulas while Using Multiple Sheets. Create formulas that draw from information on different sheets without having to worry about preserving links to other files. Enter references to cells on other sheets, or click on cells in other sheets to use those cells in formulas. Create three-dimensional formulas that "drill down" through the sheets to collect information from many sheets at once.

Formatting Multiple Sheets. With workbooks, you can design one workbook page, with formatting features such as bold titles and decimal number formats, and apply that design to any other pages in the workbook. Or select several workbook pages and apply formatting changes to all the selected pages at once. You can copy sheets from one to another, or copy sheets from other workbooks. Excel provides workbook sheets in numerical order, but you are not limited to that order, or to the generic names of Sheet1, Sheet2, and so on. Name your worksheets with names that make sense to you, and rearrange them in a logical order. You can use range names on your worksheets and refer to those names on other worksheets, or refer directly to the cells on other sheets. References to cells on other worksheets contain the sheet name as well as the cell reference.

Troubleshooting. Control the use and display of your worksheets by hiding sheets. Choose which sheets you want to display, and find sheets that have gone astray. Choose which sheets you want to print, and preview the sheets before printing.

GROUPING MULTIPLE SHEETS

How do I switch from one sheet to another?

When you open a new Excel workbook, Sheet1 is the active sheet. The active sheet is the one that is displayed on top of your screen. You can also tell which sheet is active by looking at the Sheet tabs at the bottom of the screen. The tab that is white is the active sheet.

Move from one sheet to another by clicking on the various sheet tabs. Clicking on the Sheet2 tab places Sheet2 on the top of your screen and turns the Sheet2 tab white.

Switch rapidly between sheets by either clicking on the sheet tabs at the bottom left of your Excel screen or by pressing CTRL-PAGE DOWN to advance to the next sheet and CTRL-PAGE UP to go to the prior sheet. If you have more than a few sheets in your workbook, you can move even more quickly among your sheets by clicking the arrow keys at the left of your sheet tabs as shown in the following illustration. Click the respective button to go:

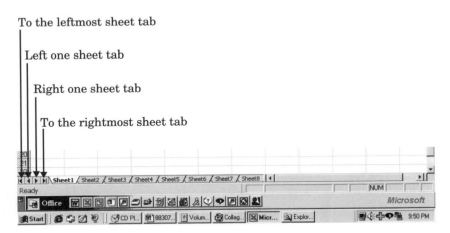

Note that clicking on these scrolling arrows changes the display of sheet tabs at the bottom of the screen, but it doesn't change the active sheet, the one that is displayed on top of your screen. You can right-click on these little scrolling sheet arrows and choose the particular sheet you want to display from the pop-up menu that appears. Choosing a sheet in this manner changes the active sheet to the one you have chosen.

I only see three sheet tabs at the bottom of my Excel screen. How can I increase the number of sheets?

By default, Excel provides you with three sheet tabs on each new workbook. You are entitled to open files containing up to 255 sheets in a workbook by requesting an increase to the original three. You can choose to increase the number of sheets in a particular workbook, or you can choose to increase the default number of sheets in all workbooks.

To add one sheet to your current workbook, choose Insert Worksheet. A new sheet will appear before the current worksheet, numbered chronologically with the next highest number available. For example, if there are three sheets in your workbook, and Sheet 2 is the active sheet, choosing Insert Worksheet will add a Sheet 4, and the new sheet will appear between sheets 1 and 2.

You can add multiple sheets to your workbook (up to the number of sheets already in existence in your workbook) in one step. Simply hold down SHIFT while you click on as many worksheet tabs as you wish to add new worksheets, and choose Insert Worksheet. The same number of sheets on which you clicked will be added. For example, if you wish to add three sheets to your workbook, hold down SHIFT while you click on three sheet tabs (the tabs on which you click will change color). The new sheets will be inserted to the left of the active sheet.

Tip: *It seems there is an unlimited number of sheets that can be added to a workbook file. Although you are limited to having a maximum of 255 sheets available when you open a new file, once the file is open you can add as many additional sheets as you like. Beware! The more sheets you add, the more time Excel will need to execute calculations.*

If you find you are frequently increasing the number of sheets in your workbooks, consider changing the default number from three to something higher. Adjust the number of sheets that will appear in new workbooks by choosing Tools | Options, then clicking on the General tab. Change the Sheets in new workbook option to any number from 1 to 255 (see Figure 7-1), then click OK. From this point forward, each

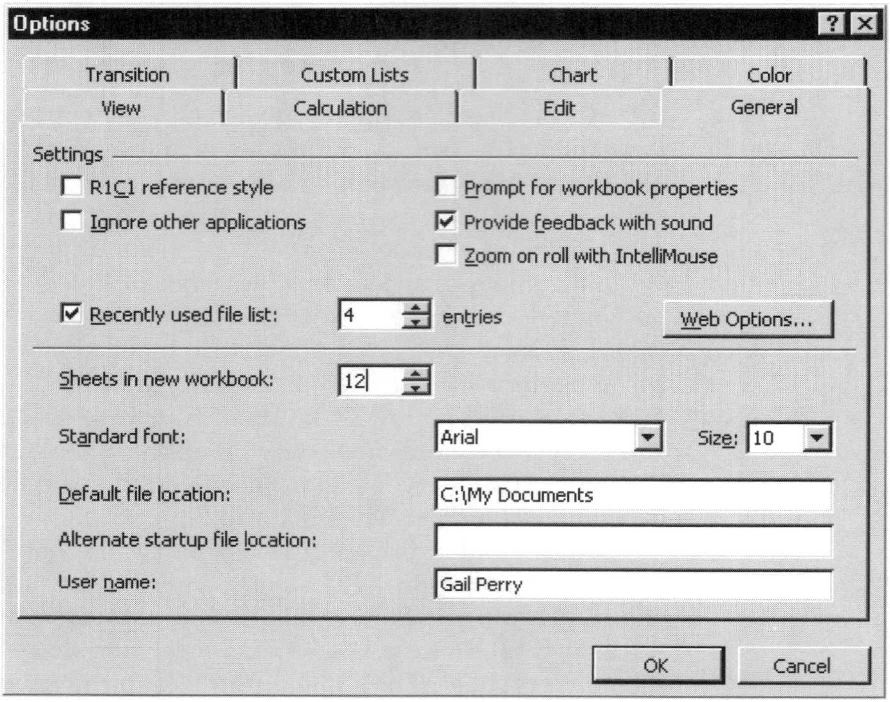

Figure 7-1 Designate the number of sheets you want to have appear in future workbooks

new workbook you open will have the newly designated number of sheets. Existing workbooks will not be affected by this change.

Tip: *You can insert a new sheet in your workbook quickly by pressing SHIFT-F11. Having inserted one new sheet, you can insert additional sheets even more quickly by pressing the F4 key. This key causes Excel to repeat your most recent action.*

Is there a way to change the number of sheet tabs that I see at the bottom of the screen?

When working in multiple worksheets it can be helpful to see more of the sheet tabs at the bottom of the screen, so you don't have to rely on the arrow buttons at the left side of the tabs to change the view of sheet tabs.

Just to the right of the last sheet tab, and to the left of the horizontal scroll bar on the bottom of your Excel screen, there is a small vertical bar. This box is called the tab split bar. You can drag this little bar to the right or left, thus extending or shrinking the view of sheet tabs in your worksheet. When you're finished sliding the bar around, return the bar to its normal position by double-clicking on it.

How do I indicate which sheets I want to include in my group?

Select adjacent sheets for inclusion in your group by clicking on the tab of the leftmost sheet in the group, holding down the SHIFT key, and clicking on the tab of the rightmost sheet in the group. The two sheets on which you clicked, as well as all the sheets in between, are members of the group. The tabs of grouped sheets change color (to white, if you use a standard Windows color scheme) when they are selected.

To include nonadjacent sheets in your group, hold down the CTRL key while clicking the tabs of additional sheets you wish to include. Each sheet on which you click will be included in the group.

My sheet numbers have gotten out of order. Can I change the order of the sheets without having to redo them?

You can easily rearrange your sheets by dragging the sheet tabs to the location where they belong. For example, if your sheets are numbered from the left, Sheet1, Sheet4, Sheet2, Sheet3, and you wish to present them in ascending order, drag the Sheet4 tab to the right of Sheet3. A tiny arrow appears above the tabs, indicating the location where the sheet will appear when you release your mouse button.

The dragging method works well if you don't have a lot of sheets in your workbook. When the quantity of sheets gets large, it is sometimes easier to move a sheet to a new location by using the menu options for relocating. Select the sheet you wish to move by clicking on the sheet tab. Select Edit, Move or copy Sheet. In the window that appears, click on the sheet before which you want to move the original sheet, then click

OK. Your sheet will move to its new location, with all sheet contents intact.

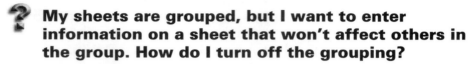

My sheets are grouped, but I want to enter information on a sheet that won't affect others in the group. How do I turn off the grouping?

Holding down the SHIFT key, click on the tab of the active sheet. The grouping feature is no longer in effect, so any changes you make to an individual sheet in your workbook will affect only that sheet. Alternatively, you can right-click on the sheet tab of the sheet you want to be active and select Ungroup Sheets from the pop-up menu.

Tip: *A quick way to ungroup sheets using the keyboard instead of the mouse is to press CTRL-PAGE UP or CTRL-PAGE DOWN until you have activated a sheet that is out of the group.*

If you want to make changes to some but not all sheets in your group, you can create a new subgroup by turning off the grouping on the main group and then choosing particular sheets to form a new group.

It would be helpful if I could see information on more than one sheet at a time. Is there a way to view multiple sheets simultaneously?

To view more than one sheet from the same workbook file at a time, open a new window on your Excel screen for each sheet you wish to view. Choose Window, New Window, to open a new window. Choose Window, Arrange to display a little Arrange Windows box wherein you can decide if you want to see your windows in tiles on your screen, horizontally or vertically displayed, or cascaded (one on top of another with the title of each window showing). Click OK when you've made your choice, and the new window will appear with the original.

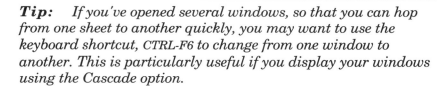

! ***Caution:*** *When using Window, Arrange to display multiple sheets of the same workbook, you may get more than you bargained for. If more than one workbook file is open on your computer, make sure the Windows of Active Workbook checkbox option is checked, otherwise, Excel will display a separate window for each open workbook instead of a new window within the same workbook.*

You can click on any sheet tab in the new window, thus displaying a different sheet from the same workbook file. Click in either of the windows to make that window active.

+ ***Tip:*** *If you've opened several windows, so that you can hop from one sheet to another quickly, you may want to use the keyboard shortcut, CTRL-F6 to change from one window to another. This is particularly useful if you display your windows using the Cascade option.*

To bring a window up to full size, click the Maximize button (the one in the middle of the three buttons at the upper right corner of the active window). Take this window back down to its smaller size by clicking the Restore button (the same button).

To close a window, just click the "x" in the upper right corner of the window, and Excel will close the window without closing your workbook file (if you choose File, Close, instead, the entire file will close).

How do I remove unwanted sheets?

Sometimes you can overdo it and add too many sheets to a workbook. No harm is done of you leave the extra sheets in the file, but if you're pressed for disk space, you may want to remove the empty sheets because they do take up space in your file. You may also want to remove the sheets so that others who may use your workbook won't get confused. To

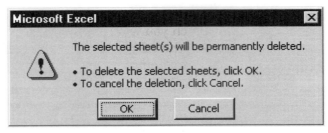

Figure 7-2   Deleting a sheet is permanent!

remove an unwanted sheet, right-click on the tab of the sheet you don't need, and choose Delete. Click OK in the window that appears, and your sheet will be permanently removed from the file (see Figure 7-2).

Caution: *Deleting a sheet from a workbook is not an undoable procedure. You cannot click the Undo button to reinstate the sheet, so be certain you no longer want this sheet before deleting it. The only way to recover a deleted sheet is if the file was saved previously with this sheet intact. If you have not resaved the file since you deleted the sheet, you can close the file without saving, then reopen the file. The previously saved version of the file will appear.*

Remove several sheets at once by selecting the sheets as if to include in a group, then right-clicking on any one of the selected sheets, and choosing Delete. Click OK in the resulting window and all selected sheets will be removed from the workbook.

CREATING FORMULAS WHILE USING MULTIPLE SHEETS

How do I create a formula referring to data from another worksheet?

You can make a reference to a cell in another sheet by typing the cell reference yourself or by clicking on the cell when it's time for that cell to be referenced in your formula. When entering the cell reference, the format is: SheetX!CellCR, where

SheetX is the name that appears on the sheet tab containing the cell to which you wish to make reference, C is the column designation of the cell, and R is the Row designation of the cell. The exclamation point separates the sheet name from the cell reference.

For example, if you want to use the contents of cell B12 on Sheet4 in a formula on Sheet1, refer to that cell as **Sheet4!B12** in your formula.

Can I use the mouse to refer to cells on other sheets in my formulas?

The mouse can help you construct formulas that refer to cells in other worksheets. An easy way to enter the cell reference in your formula rather than typing it yourself is to go to the cell and click on it while you are constructing the formula. For example, if you want to create a formula on Sheet1 that multiplies the cell B12 of Sheet4 by cell A26 on Sheet1, follow these steps to constructing the formula:

1. With Sheet1 active, enter your formula by typing the equal (=) sign (or clicking = on the formula bar).

2. Click the sheet tab for Sheet4, making that the active sheet. With Sheet4 visible, click on cell B12. Notice the construction of the formula as it appears in the formula bar at the top of the screen: at this point the formula bar displays =Sheet4!B12.

3. Continue the formula by entering the * (multiplication) sign. The formula construction proceeds and you are returned to the sheet on which the formula resides.

4. Enter **A26**, or click on cell A26, to complete the information for the formula.

5. Press ENTER (or click the green check mark on the formula bar) to complete the calculation.

Is there a quick way to create a formula that sums the same cell in several sheets?

One of the nicest results of working in groups is the ability to create formulas that drill down through the layers of your sheets, extracting the contents of a single cell or group of cells from all selected sheets. You work with cells in multiple sheets in the same way as you work with cells in a range on a two-dimensional sheet, by referencing the first and last cell of the range and letting Excel include all the cells in-between.

When preparing to add the contents of the same cell on several sheets, think of the cell as a range of cells that spans the collection of sheets. Think of calling for the contents of cells A1 on Sheet1, Sheet2, Sheet3, and Sheet4 as using the contents of cells A1 on Sheet1 *through* Sheet4. The cells still form a range, but the range drills down through four sheets instead of across some cells on a single sheet.

Enter the addition formula that will add cells A1 in Sheet1 through Sheet4 and place the contents in cell A1 of Sheet5, by following these steps:

1. Click on the cell in which you wish the formula to appear. In this case, click on cell A1 in Sheet5.

Σ

2. Begin the formula by entering **=sum** (or by clicking on the AutoSum button).

3. Click on the tab containing the first cell in the range, then click on the cell you wish to include in the formula. In this case, click on the Sheet1 tab and on cell A1.

4. Holding down the SHIFT key, click on the tab of the *last* sheet on which there is a cell you wish to include in the range. In this case, click on the Sheet4 tab.

5. Complete the formula by pressing ENTER or by clicking on the AutoSum button again.

FORMATTING MULTIPLE SHEETS

 I need to apply several different formatting features to the information on my worksheets. How do I accomplish this on several worksheets at once?

Before applying any formatting that will appear on several sheets, select the sheets as a group. When all sheets to receive

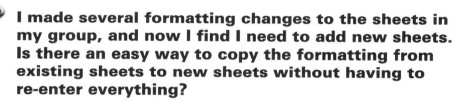

the formatting have been selected, apply your formatting on one of the selected sheets. *Anything* you enter on one sheet will appear on all sheets in the selected group. This includes type styles, such as boldface or italics; font selection; justification, such as centering or right-alignment; number formatting; shading; borders; underlining; and so on. In addition, any text you enter on one sheet will appear on all sheets in the selected group.

When you have made all of your universal entries, turn off the group selection (SHIFT-CLICK on the active sheet tab), and any additional formatting or entries you make will apply to only the active sheet.

 I made several formatting changes to the sheets in my group, and now I find I need to add new sheets. Is there an easy way to copy the formatting from existing sheets to new sheets without having to re-enter everything?

This is quick and easy. To copy the format from an existing sheet to a new sheet, follow these steps:

1. Click the Select All button in the upper left corner of your worksheet, as shown in Figure 7-3. The entire worksheet will be selected.

2. Click on the Format Painter button on the toolbar. The button will appear depressed.

3. Click on the sheet tab of the worksheet that is to receive the formatting.

4. Click on the Select All button of the worksheet that is to receive the formatting. All the formatting (and none of the text) from the original worksheet will be copied to the new worksheet.

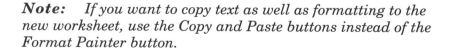 **Note:** *If you want to copy text as well as formatting to the new worksheet, use the Copy and Paste buttons instead of the Format Painter button.*

Click here to select the entire worksheet

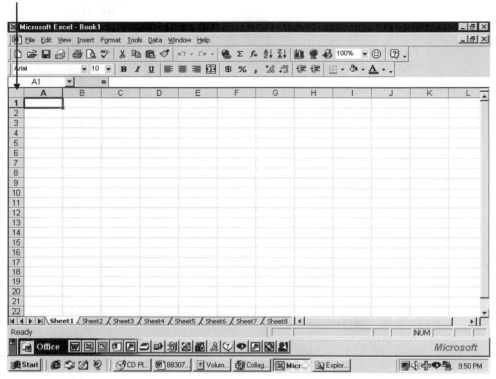

Figure 7-3   The Select All button resides at the upper left corner of each worksheet

Is there a quick way to copy an entire worksheet to a new sheet?

This is quick and easy to do. To copy the contents, formatting, everything from one worksheet to another, press the CTRL key and drag the sheet tab of the sheet you wish to copy. When you drag the tab to the right, a new sheet is created, and the new sheet is a duplicate of the original. The new sheet tab will be named with the same name as the original, followed by a (2). Double-click on the new sheet tab to give it a new name.

If dragging the sheet is difficult, due to the existence of many sheets in your workbook, you can use a menu option to copy the worksheet. Click on the sheet you wish to copy.

Choose Edit, Move or Copy Sheet. Click on the name of the sheet before which you wish to copy the original sheet. Check the Create a Copy checkbox, then click OK. A new sheet will appear in the location indicated, and this new sheet will be an exact copy of the original.

Can I copy a worksheet to a different workbook?

You can copy an entire worksheet to a completely different workbook if you open both workbooks at the same time, display them both on-screen (use Window, Arrange, to display both workbooks), then drag the sheet tab from one workbook to another.

The copied worksheet in the new workbook file will bear the same information, formatting, and name as the original worksheet.

These sheet names (Sheet1, Sheet2, and so on) are so uninspired—can I change the names to something more fitting to my spreadsheet material?

Sheet tab names are easy to change. Just right-click on a sheet tab and choose Rename, or double-click on the sheet tab. In either case, the name of the sheet will be selected and you can type a new name to replace the old one. Your new name is limited to 31 characters, including spaces.

If you like, you can create a formula that will refer to the name of your file and the name of the sheet in your worksheet. If you rename the sheet, the reference in the worksheet will change as well. The formula is =CELL("filename",A1). Entering this formula anywhere in your worksheet will return the name of the file and the name of the sheet. Note that you must save the file before generating this formula, or else it will return a blank cell.

Is it possible to apply the same range name to the same range in different worksheets?

Technically, you must use a unique range name for each area you name in your workbook. You can, however, sidestep this rule by using the sheet name with the range. For example, if you name the area A5 to A45 *Computer_equipment* in Sheet2 and wish to name the same range *Computer_equipment* in

Sheet3, assign the names *Sheet2!Computer_equipment* and *Sheet3!Computer_equipment*.

You can assign like range names to several sheets at once if the same titles appear in cells on each of the sheets. Figure 7-4 shows a spreadsheet with column titles in columns A, B, and C, and data through row 10. Assuming those titles appear on other sheets, assign the titles as range names on all sheets at once by following these steps:

1. Select all the sheets for which you want to assign the range names.

2. On the active sheet, select the range of cells, including the titles, which will be included in the named range.

3. Choose Insert | Name | Create from the Excel menu. The Create Names window will appear.

4. Select Top Row to indicate the location of your range names, then click OK. The title of each column is now assigned as a range name to the nine rows beneath it on each sheet in the selected group.

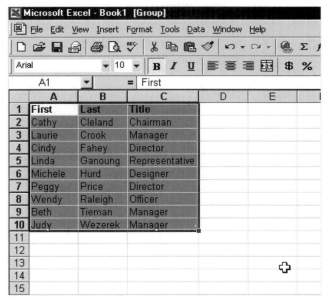

Figure 7-4 Select the entire area, including column titles, and select multiple sheets to apply range names to all selected sheets simultaneously

From this point forward, any reference you make to the named range must be preceded by the sheet name and an exclamation point (for example, Sheet1!Computer_Equipment), so that Excel can distinguish one range from another with the same name. If you are referring to the range on the active sheet, you don't need a sheet reference.

How do I use the Sheet Background feature that comes with Excel?

Excel offers an opportunity to display a background design on your worksheet. Note that this background applies to the screen view of the worksheet only and does not print.

Choose a background by selecting Format, Sheet, Background. The Sheet Background window will appear. In this window you can select a background display from graphic images you have saved on your computer. Built-in background options are available from Microsoft and are found in the Program files/Office2000/Clipart/Backgrounds folder. Select a background, then click Open to apply the background to your worksheet.

For a better display of the background, you may want to turn off the display of gridlines. Choose Tools, Options, click the View tab, and uncheck the Gridlines checkbox, then click OK to remove the gridlines display. Cells that contain data may benefit from a solid color background instead of the background design you chose for the rest of the sheet. Select any cell or group of cells, then click the Fill Color button on your Formatting toolbar to choose a background color.

Remove the background graphic by choosing Format, Sheet, Delete Background.

TROUBLESHOOTING

There are no sheet tabs in my workbook. I know there are multiple sheets, because I can use CTRL-PAGE UP and CTRL-PAGE DOWN to display them. But what happened to my tabs?

The visibility of sheet tabs is dependent on the viewing options assigned to your workbooks. Choose Tools | Options

and click on the View tab. There is a checkbox for Sheet tabs. When this box is unchecked, sheet tabs do not display. Checking the box causes Excel to show your sheet tabs.

 Note: *Another possible explanation for sheet tabs not displaying properly is that a macro virus has infected your machine. It's wise to check for viruses on a regular basis. Microsoft posts free fixes for macro viruses on its Web site.*

Multiple sheets are still saved with your workbook, but the tabs are only visible when this checkbox option is activated.

 ### I want to print some, but not all, of the sheets in my workbook. How do I indicate this print request?

Your print options, with regard to printing sheets, are:

- **Print entire workbook** This option prints all sheets in the workbook that contain data. Blank sheets are not included. If a print range has been designated on a sheet, only that range will print. (See "Printing Worksheets" in Chapter 10 for more information on print ranges.)

- **Print active sheets** This option prints only the sheets you select. While holding down the CTRL key, click on the tabs of sheets you wish to print, or click on one tab, hold down the SHIFT key, and click on another tab to select the two sheets and all sheets between them.

Select the sheets you want to print, then choose File | Print, from the Excel menu. When the Print window appears, choose your print option, then click OK.

 ### I've lost one of my sheets! I know I created a sheet, but the sheet tab is now missing. How can I find a lost worksheet?

It's easy to hide a worksheet and then forget the sheet has been hidden. Unlike hiding a column, where the column letters

suddenly appear out of sequence, you can hide a sheet and not necessarily realize a sheet is missing, particularly if your sheets have been renamed so that they are not numbered sequentially.

You can hide a worksheet by making the sheet you want to hide active, then choosing Format | Sheet | Hide.

To check for hidden worksheets, select Format | Sheet | Unhide. The Unhide window will appear and all hidden sheets will be listed (see Figure 7-5). Click on a sheet name, then click OK to unhide the sheet. Sheets must be unhidden one at a time.

When I select Print Preview, only one sheet is visible. How can I preview all my worksheets at once?

Choosing File | Print Preview enables you to preview the active sheet before printing. You can preview multiple worksheets by selecting all the worksheets you wish to view first. If you select multiple sheets, then choose File | Print Preview, and all sheets will be available to preview at once. Click the Next and Previous buttons or use your PAGE UP and PAGE DOWN keys to move from one sheet to the next in Preview mode.

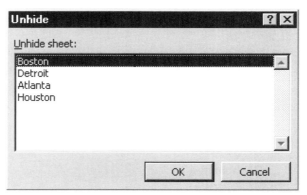

Figure 7-5   Choose Format | Sheet | Unhide to display a list of hidden sheets

 When renaming a sheet, some of the characters I enter don't appear. Are there unacceptable characters for sheet names?

There are a few characters that don't work when giving names to sheets. The following characters will be rejected by Excel:

[ ]	Square brackets
:	Colon
/	Forward Slash
\	Backward Slash
?	Question Mark
*	Asterisk

Chapter 8

Working with Ranges

Answer Topics!

Working with Ranges @ a Glance

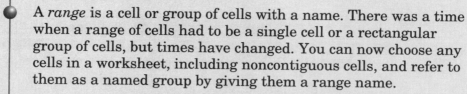

- A *range* is a cell or group of cells with a name. There was a time when a range of cells had to be a single cell or a rectangular group of cells, but times have changed. You can now choose any cells in a worksheet, including noncontiguous cells, and refer to them as a named group by giving them a range name.

- You can get to a range quickly and without having to remember the cell references by pressing F5 and asking for the range by name.

- You can refer to a range name in a formula, saving you from having to look up the cell addresses—this is especially useful in situations where you need to refer to the same range of cells frequently.

- A range is absolute. Copy a cell that contains a reference to a range, and the range reference copies too.

- It's easier to recall a range name than a group of cell references.

- You can use range names as a method of printing particular sections of your workbook.

NAMING RANGES

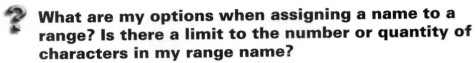

What are my options when assigning a name to a range? Is there a limit to the number or quantity of characters in my range name?

There is quite a bit of flexibility available in your choice of a name, but it is subject to certain limitations. The range name must follow these guidelines:

- The first character of the range name must be either a letter (upper- or lowercase) or an underscore.

- After the first letter, characters in your range name may include letters, numbers, periods, and underscores. Both upper- and lowercase letters are allowed.

- Range names cannot duplicate cell coordinates. For example, you cannot name a range GG25 because there is already a cell with that name.

- There are no spaces allowed in range names.

- You are limited to a maximum of 255 characters.

! Caution: *Don't get too carried away with the length of your range name. Even though you are entitled to use up to 255 characters for your name, a lengthy name may be truncated when it appears in lists of range names, and a name that is long may take up valuable space in your formulas, which are limited in how many characters they can contain.*

Range names are not case sensitive. Therefore, if you name a range *Computer_Expenses* and later refer to the range in a formula as *computer_expenses* your reference will refer to the range you originally named. This can be convenient, but be aware that if you decide to name another range *COMPUTER_EXPENSES* in the same worksheet, the latter name will replace the original name, and your original range, *Computer_Expenses,* will be replaced with the new range.

Is there a limit to the quantity of range names allowed in one workbook file?

Nope. You can have as many named ranges as you desire in a single file.

Can the same cell exist in more than one range?

It's okay for range names to overlap. One cell can show up in several different ranges. In fact, you can give several different names to the exact same range on your worksheet. Excel doesn't care.

Is it possible to apply the same name to ranges on different sheets in the same workbook?

Technically, you must use unique names throughout the workbook. If you name a range on Sheet1 *Sales*, you cannot use *Sales* to name a range on Sheet2 without replacing the range name from Sheet1.

There is an option, however, of using the sheet name with the range name, which will enable you to duplicate the range name throughout the sheets. In this situation, a range called *Sheet1!Sales* will refer to the designated range on Sheet1, while *Sheet2!Sales* will refer to a range on Sheet2.

***

Note: *For a description of shortcuts for naming ranges on multiple sheets, see "Is it possible to apply the same range name to the same range in different worksheets?" in Chapter 7.*

How do I assign range names in my workbook? Are there some shortcuts I should know?

The formal method for naming a range in your workbook is accomplished by following these steps:

1. Select the cell(s) that will be included in the range.
2. Choose Insert | Name. A side menu will appear.
3. Choose Define. The Define Name dialog box will appear (see Figure 8-1).

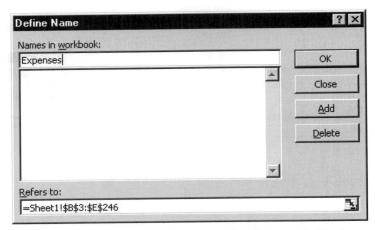

Figure 8-1 The name you enter in the Define Name dialog box will be assigned to the range shown in the *Refers to* field

4. Enter the range name in the Names in workbook field. Notice that the Refers to field displays the cell references of the selected cells.

5. Click OK. The name you entered will be assigned to the range you highlighted.

A shortcut to performing the steps above is to select the cells to be included in the range, click in the Name box (see Figure 8-2), enter the range name, then press the ENTER key.

Another quick way to assign range names is to use the titles already in place on your worksheet. For example, the titles in Column A of the worksheet shown in Figure 8-3 refer to the amounts in Columns B through E. You can assign the Column A titles to their associated amounts by following these steps:

1. Select the entire area, including the titles and the cells to which they refer. In this example, you would select cells A4 through E9.

Click here, then type a range name.

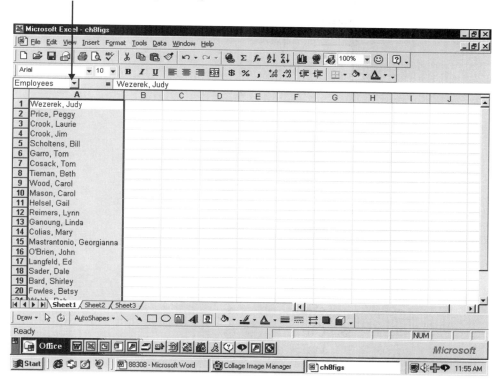

Figure 8-2 Range names can be assigned without opening the Define Name dialog box

2. Choose Insert | Name | Create from the main menu. The Create Names dialog box will appear (see Figure 8-4).

3. Select Left column to assign the titles in the leftmost column to the selected area.

4. Click OK and the assignment will be completed.

5. If you want to assign both row titles and column titles as range names, you can select both the left and top check boxes, as shown in Figure 8-4. All names will be created.

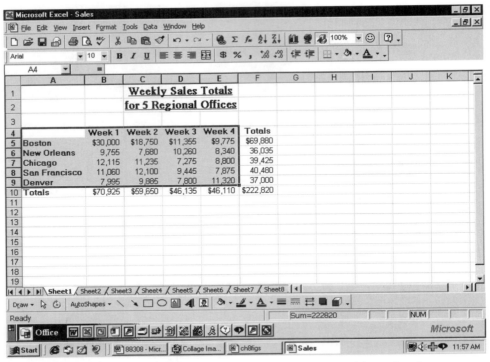

Figure 8-3 Assign existing labels as range names without having to re-enter the names by choosing Insert | Name | Create

What's the difference between Insert ½Define, and Insert ½Create?

Although both of these commands apply a range name to selected cells, these two commands behave in different ways.

Use the Define command to open the Define Name dialog box. In this dialog box, you can type the name you want to assign to the selected cells.

Use the Create command to use existing labels from your worksheet as range names. Select the entire range, including titles, then choose Insert | Name | Create. The Create Names dialog box appears and you can use the checkboxes to indicate in which location(s) your range names appear. When you are ready, click the OK button to apply all selected titles as range names.

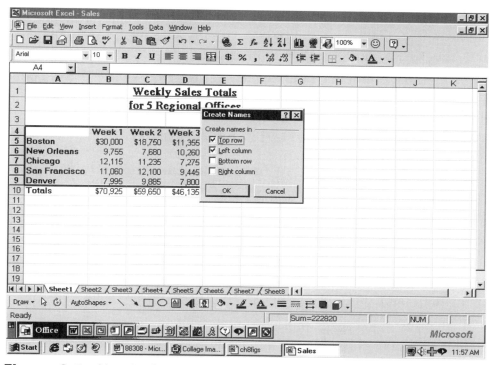

Figure 8-4   Use the Create Names dialog box to indicate the location of titles that will be used as range names

 I've assigned a range name, but now I want to change the name to something else. How can I do this?

Changing a range name is a two-step process. You must first assign a new name to the range by following the steps shown above.

Assigning a new name to a previously named range will give you two names assigned to the same range. You can leave the two names intact (in which case you are finished), or you can remove the original name.

To remove a range name, follow these steps:

1. Choose Insert | Name | Define. The Define Name dialog box will appear. Note that you do not have to first select the range when making this menu choice.

2. Click on the range name you wish to remove.

3. Click the Delete button. You will receive no warning that you are about to remove a name. The range name will be removed immediately.

4. Click the Close button to close the Define Name dialog box.

USING NAMED RANGES

 Now that I've named some ranges in my workbook, how can I quickly move from one range to another?

The quickest way to move from one range to another using the mouse is to click the down-arrow in the Name Box, then click on a range name from the list that appears. The entire range will be selected, and the cell in the upper-left corner of the range will be active.

Range names from all sheets in your workbook are listed in the Name Box, so you can use a range name as a quick method to move to a designated range on a different sheet. There is an exception to this rule, however. If a range name is duplicated on more than one sheet (for example, *Sheet1!Sales, Sheet2!Sales*), the name from the current sheet is the only one that will appear in the Name Box.

Another way to move to a named range is by pressing the F5 key (or choosing Edit | Go To). The Go To dialog box will appear (see Figure 8-5) with all named ranges in the workbook listed (including names that are duplicated from one sheet to another). Click on the name of the range to which you want to move. Click OK, and the entire range will be highlighted, with the upper left cell in the range as the active cell.

 I've named several ranges in my worksheet. Is it possible to select more than one range at a time using the range names?

You can select multiple ranges, including ranges in different sheets of the same workbook, by following these steps:

1. Select one range by dragging the mouse through the cells and using either the Name Box or the Go To (F5) feature.

Figure 8-5 Choose from this list of named ranges, then click OK to be transported to the chosen range

2. Select additional ranges in the same worksheet by holding down the CTRL key and either dragging through the other ranges or clicking on various names in the Name Box.

3. If you want to select ranges in more than one worksheet, select the first range, then hold down the CTRL key and use the Name Box to select additional ranges. You may select as many range names as are listed in the name box. All chosen names are selected.

An alternative to step 3 is to use the F5 key and the CTRL key. Select one range, press F5, then press the CTRL key. Make sure to do it in that order; if you press the CTRL key before opening the F5 Go To window, the CTRL key will reduce your worksheet to a window size.

Can I copy a whole range at once?

You can copy a range just as you would copy a cell. Select the entire range, click the Copy button (or choose Edit, Copy), click in the place where you want to make a copy of the range, and click the Paste button (or choose Edit, Paste).

 Note: *When you copy spreadsheet cells, Excel places a moving border around the copied information. After you paste the information, the border remains. To turn off this moving border, press the ESC key.*

The place to which you copy the range can be on the same worksheet, a different sheet in the same workbook, a sheet in a different workbook, or a location in a different program (for example, you can copy a range to a Word document).

When you click in the place where you want the copy to appear, you need only click in the top left corner of the destination. For example, if you are copying a range to a new worksheet, and the range covers an area of 24 cells, you don't need to select the 24 cells where you want the copied range to appear. You only need to click in the single cell in the top left corner of the new location. Excel will figure out that the rest of the cells should fall into the proper places, starting with the cell you clicked.

 Tip: *You can use a drag-and-drop technique for copying a range if you are copying to a location on the same worksheet (or another worksheet that is visible). Select the cells you want to copy, then press the CTRL key. Place your mouse pointer on an outside edge of the selected range. You will see the mouse pointer turn into a white arrow and a small plus sign appear next to the arrow. The plus sign indicates that you can copy the range by dragging.*

 ## How do I move a range to a new location?

Moving is a lot like copying, only you don't leave the original information behind. To move a range of cells to a new location (whether it is a new location in the same worksheet, a different sheet, or a different file altogether), select the original range of cells, click the Cut button (or choose Edit | Cut), click in the new location where you want the range to appear, and click the Paste button (or choose Edit | Paste).

You can use a drag-and-drop technique for moving a range if you are moving the range to a new location on the same worksheet (or another worksheet that is visible). Select the cells you want to move. Place your mouse pointer on an outside edge of the selected range. The mouse pointer will turn into a white arrow. When you see this arrow, drag the range to its new location.

If I move or copy a named range, does the name relocate with the range?

You can move a range by selecting the range and dragging the border of the range to another location on the same worksheet, and the name of the range relocates along with the contents of the cells in the range.

You can also move a range by cutting and pasting the range to a new location (as described in the previous answer), be it on the same sheet or a different sheet within the same workbook, and the range name gets pasted with the cell contents. Use either the Cut and Paste toolbar buttons or the Cut and Paste commands on the Edit menu. The results will be the same.

You can't, however, cut and paste a range from one workbook to another and preserve the range name associated with the range. The cell contents will move, but the range name will be lost from both the originating and the destination workbook.

Copying a range does not relocate the range name in any situation.

When I attempt to move a range of cells, I get a message about replacing the contents of destination cells. What is this message all about?

If you attempt to move a range of cells to a location that includes at least one non-blank cell, you will receive the following message:

DO YOU WANT TO REPLACE THE CONTENTS OF THE DESTINATION CELLS?

Your choices are OK and Cancel. Choose OK to execute the Move command, replacing all non-blank cells in the new range with the contents of cells from the range you are moving. The cells being replaced will lose their original contents. Choose Cancel to cancel the Move command.

Avoid this message by examining the contents of the cells in the range to which you want to move and making sure all cells are empty before you attempt to execute the Move command.

⁇ Is it possible to drag-and-drop a range into a new location of the worksheet without replacing the existing cell contents?

Looking back to the previous answer, you can see that if you attempt to move a range into a range where the cells are occupied, you have a choice of either replacing the existing cell contents at the destination, or aborting the move.

A nice alternative is to perform a little surgery, inserting your moving range right in between the existing cell contents.

When you drag a range to a new location, press the SHIFT key before you begin to drag. Instead of dropping the range right over the existing cells, you will see the shape of an I-beam, which moves with your mouse pointer. This I-beam shows you where the cells will be inserted, and all the surrounding cells in the new location will slide aside to make room for the cells you are moving (see Figure 8-6).

⁇ Now that I've created some range names, how do I utilize the names in formulas?

Named ranges appear by name in formulas in lieu of the cell references contained in the range. For example, a simple formula that adds a column of numbers might read:

=SUM(A1:A275)

If the cells A1 to A275 are given the name *Expenses*, the formula can read:

=SUM(Expenses)

By using the range name in the formula, the formula may be easier to understand at a glance.

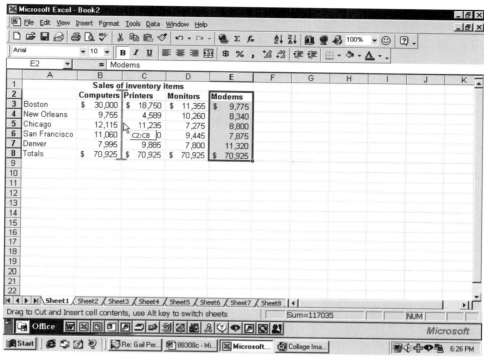

Figure 8-6   The I-beam shows that cells will be inserted between the existing cell entries in columns B and C

   Tip: *If you are examining a worksheet created by someone else with range names in formulas and you wish to discover which ranges make up the names you see, click the arrow in the Name Box and choose the name of a range about which you are curious. The range will be highlighted.*

When using range names in your formulas, you can type the name of the range to which you wish to refer. Alternatively, you can begin the formula and, at the location where you want to use a range name, press F3. The Paste Name dialog box will appear (see Figure 8-7). Click on the range name you wish to use, then click OK. The range name will be inserted into the formula you are creating.

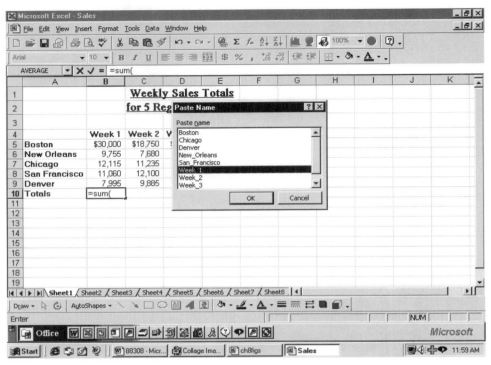

Figure 8-7 Choose a range name from the Paste Name dialog box, and that name will be placed in your formula

I use ranges to designate print areas on my worksheet. What's the easiest way to print a specific range?

Give names to ranges you wish to be able to print, and you'll save yourself the time of having to select specific cells each time you want to print an area. To print a named range, follow these steps:

1. Click in the Name Box, and select the range you wish to print. The range will be highlighted on your worksheet.

2. Choose File | Print. The Print dialog box will appear.

3. In the Print what area of the window, click the Selection option (see Figure 8-8), then click OK. Only the selected range will print.

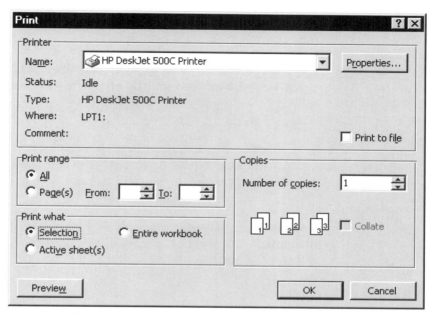

Figure 8-8   Choose Selection, and only the range you indicated on your worksheet will print

 Note: *If you plan to use a print area more than once during the same Excel session, you can save time by highlighting the print area and then choosing File | Print Area | Set Print Area. As long as the worksheet is open, you can click the Print button and only the defined print area will print. As soon as you close the worksheet, the print area is cleared.*

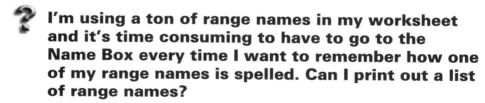 **I'm using a ton of range names in my worksheet and it's time consuming to have to go to the Name Box every time I want to remember how one of my range names is spelled. Can I print out a list of range names?**

> You can easily keep track of the range names in your workbook by producing a list of all the range names you've

created and their corresponding cells. To produce a list of range names, follow these steps:

1. Click in the cell where you want the list to begin. This cell can be located on any sheet in your workbook.

2. Choose Insert | Name | Paste. The Paste Name dialog box will appear (see Figure 8-9).

3. Click the Paste List button. A complete list of all ranges in your workbook, along with the cell references that make up those ranges, will appear across two columns at the location you selected.

To print a copy of this range name list, select the range of cells containing the list, choose File | Print | Selection, then click the OK button.

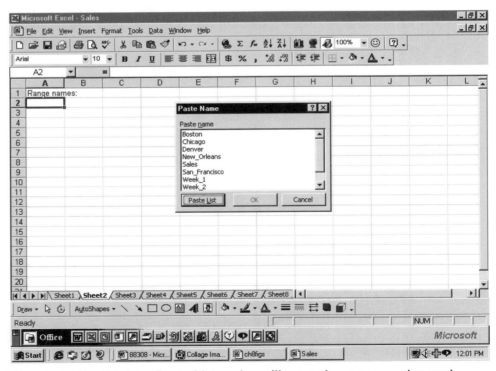

Figure 8-9 Click on Paste List and you'll never have to wonder again what names you've given to ranges

 I don't want others to be able to change some of the information on my worksheet. How can I protect a range on my worksheet?

You can protect a particular range or group of cells on a worksheet by following these steps:

1. Select the cells you *don't want to protect*. In other words, select the cells that it's all right for someone to change. Do not select the range of cells you wish to protect.

2. Choose Format | Cells, and click the Protection tab. Uncheck the Locked checkbox. With this step you are disabling protection on the selected cells of the worksheet. Click OK.

3. Choose Tools | Protection | Protect Sheet. Enter an optional password if you want to prevent users from being able to turn off the protection. (If you enter a password, you will be asked to enter the password a second time.) Click OK.

At this point, the entire worksheet, except the cells you did not select earlier, will be protected. Anyone who attempts to enter information in a protected cell will be prevented from doing so until the protection is turned off.

You can disable the protection by choosing Tools, Protection, Unprotect Sheet. If a password was assigned when protection was initiated, the password will need to be entered before protection can be disabled.

TROUBLESHOOTING

 I need to combine several noncontiguous cells into one range. The problem is that if I try to combine these cells to make one large range, there isn't room to list all the cell references in the Refers to area of the Define Name window. Is there a way to work around this problem?

You can break a large group of noncontiguous cells into two or more smaller groups, give each group a range name, and

then assign a master range name to the combination of groups.

For example, suppose your worksheet contains two ranges of noncontiguous cells named *CellGroup1* and *CellGroup2*. Combine these two groups into one range by defining a new range name and entering the names of the two groups in the Refers to box as follows:

=CellGroup1,CellGroup2

An example of this type of range combination is shown in Figure 8-10.

I'm getting a #NAME? error in my worksheet which I assume is somehow related to range names. Why am I getting this, and what should I do about it?

The #NAME? error message relates to Excel's inability to decipher a range name to which you have referred in your

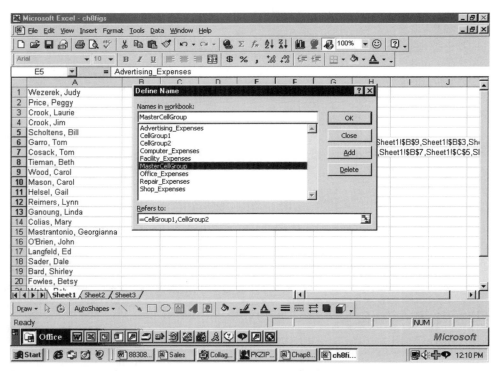

Figure 8-10 Combine range names in the *Refers to* area by separating them with a comma

worksheet. This message usually results from one of two circumstances.

First, there may be a spelling error. You may have named your range *Expenses*, but in your formula you refer to the range as *Expense*. Although case sensitivity is not a problem (*Expenses* and *expenses* will be treated as the same name), you must be very careful to spell your range names consistently. When you see the #NAME? error message, the first thing you should do is click on the cell containing the formula and look at the way the range name is spelled. Then click on the Name Box and compare spellings. If there is a difference in spellings, edit the formula to change the spelling, and the error message should go away.

The other problem may be that you are referring to a nonexistent range in your formula. You may have meant to assign a range name and then created a formula using the range name without having first defined the range name. In this case, make the correction by creating your range name, and the error message will correct itself.

Chapter 9

Charting Techniques

Answer Topics!

Charting Techniques @ a Glance

Overview. Numbers on spreadsheets have a tendency to look like, well, a lot of numbers. The reaction of someone looking at a lot of numbers can range from overwhelmed and intimidated to bored and not caring, with a dose of incomprehension somewhere in the middle. The person who created the spreadsheet may have a solid grasp of what the numbers mean, but for anyone else looking at the mass of numbers, it can be difficult to pick out trends, spot troublesome areas, notice subtle upswings, or even to figure out which numbers are the important ones. By turning your numbers into a visual display in the form of a chart, you can make the numbers easier on the eye. You can also choose the type and design of the chart, so that the important information is obvious to even the most uninitiated spreadsheet viewer.

Creating Charts. Use the Chart Wizard to easily create charts ranging from the simple to the incredibly elaborate. Control the location of your chart, adjust the scale to show an appropriate chart range, and print hard copies of your charts, both in color and black and white.

Enhancing Charts. Control the appearance of your charts with various formatting techniques, drawing tools, and color display. Add titles, and dress up your charts with custom images right inside the chart columns.

Troubleshooting. Fix draw objects on the top layer of your chart so they don't disappear when you click on the chart. Save your favorite chart styling features in a default chart style, so it will be available every time you create a new chart.

CREATING CHARTS

 ### Is the Chart Wizard the only way to create a chart? What's the best way to use the wizard?

Technically, you must use the Chart Wizard to create a chart in Excel. How much of the wizard you use, however, is your choice. You can choose to accept all of the wizard's defaults (be sure to see the question about saving the default chart style at the end of this chapter), which will create a chart in two simple clicks of the mouse, or you can move from screen to screen in the wizard, making careful selections and choosing the options appropriate for you.

No matter which method you use for creating a chart, the beginning steps are identical: Select the worksheet information you wish to include in the chart by dragging your mouse through the numbers and, if you like, titles, then click the Chart Wizard button (or choose Insert | Chart). The Chart Wizard window appears.

To accept all default chart features, click the Finish button. A chart appears onscreen, probably right on top of your data. You can move the chart to a new location in your worksheet by placing your mouse pointer over the white area of the chart and dragging the chart. If the chart is too big or too small, click once on the chart to activate it. You will see small black "handles" appear in the corners and on the sides; place your mouse over any of the handles and drag the chart to the size you want it to be.

 Tip: *Here's a quick trick for creating a chart using all the default options: Highlight the data in your worksheet that you want to place in a chart, then press the F11 key. A chart will appear on its own sheet (called Chart1).*

Instead of accepting the default features, you can work through the Chart Wizard's four steps and make the following choices and specifications:

● **Step 1:** Choose from several 2- and 3-dimensional chart types. Refer to Table 9-1 for pointers on selecting the chart type that fits your data.

Type of Chart	When to Use It
Column	To compare categories and show changes over a period of time, where each period is important to note separately.
Bar	To compare categories (although bar charts are not appropriate for comparisons where time is important, as most people tend to think of time as moving from left to right, instead of from bottom to top).
Line	To chart data trends over a period of time, where the continuous flow of data illustrates a gradual trend.
Pie	To show the pieces of a whole and the proportion of each piece to the whole. Only one series of data can be displayed in a pie chart.
XY (Scatter)	To show the relationship between two sets of values, one on the X axis and one on the Y axis.
Area	To chart subtle trends without having to follow lines that cross over one another, placing emphasis on the whole and the percentage that each piece occupies.
Doughnut	To show each data series as a part of the whole. Like a multiple-tier pie chart, the doughnut chart allows you to have a separate doughnut, one inside another, for each data series.
Radar	To demonstrate how each piece of data extends from a central location and compares to the other data. Similar to a line chart, but more circular in appearance.
Surface	To show how three axes and three independent sets of data interact.
Bubble	To emphasize the relative importance of types of charted data. This is an extension of the XY Scatter chart with a third piece of data. In addition to an X and Y axes, there is a factor for the size of the bubbles.
Stock	To chart stock activity, with options for charting Volume, Open, High, Low, and Close information.
Cylinder, Cone, Pyramid	To compare categories. Can be shown from left to right or from bottom to top. One interesting feature is that you can display the bar or column object as a percent of a complete object based on the data being charted (for example, a cone without the point at the top—this option is available by right-clicking on the cones of a chart, then choosing Format I Shape and selecting the partial cone option).

Table 9-1   Choosing a Chart Type

● **Step 2:** Verify the data range being charted; indicate if data in rows or columns is being charted.

● **Step 3:** Change and add to the appearance of your chart with titles, legend, gridlines, data labels.

● **Step 4:** Determine the location for your chart, either on an existing sheet or a new sheet of its own.

The numbers I want to use in my chart are not situated in adjacent cells in my worksheet. How do I choose the correct numbers for my chart?

There are two ways to choose nonadjacent numbers for your chart. You can use the CTRL key to select cells that are nonadjacent, or you can make the choice in the Chart Wizard. For example, suppose you want to chart the Week 1 through Week 4 figures for Boston, Chicago, and San Francisco in the worksheet shown in Figure 9-1. Drag through cells A4 through E5 to select the Week titles and the Boston numbers.

To continue your selection, press the CTRL key, then drag through cells A7 through E8. The numbers and related city names for Chicago and San Francisco will be selected. Note that the ranges you select using the CTRL key must be parallel to any other ranges selected. For example, if you

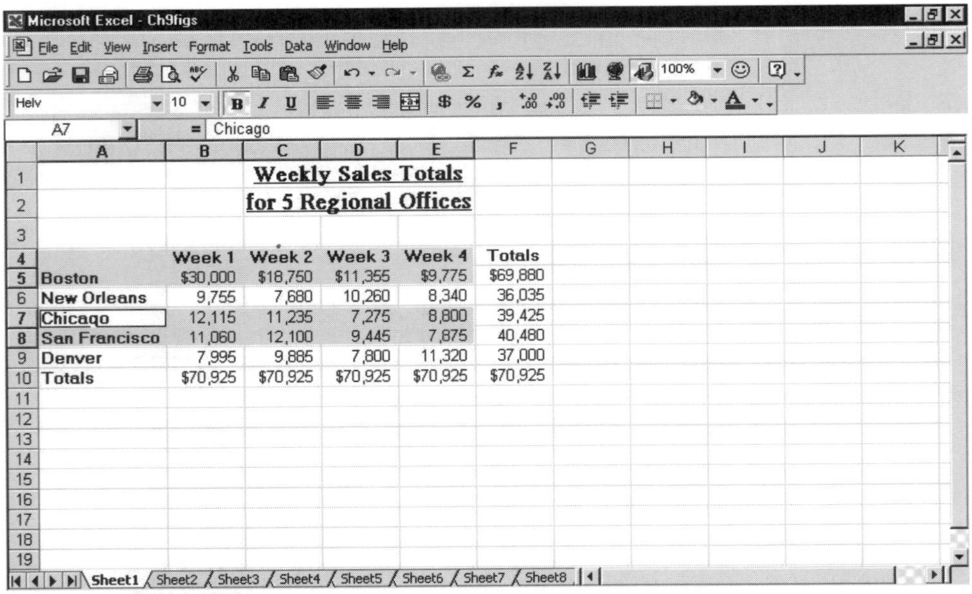

Figure 9-1 Use the CTRL key to select nonadjacent cells for your chart

select columns A through E in one row, you must select columns A through E in any other row you include in the chart data. The intervening amounts for New Orleans will not be selected. After making your selection, continue creating your chart by opening the Chart Wizard.

If you prefer, you can use the Chart Wizard to weed out the cells you don't want to include with your chart. Select an area of your worksheet that includes all the numbers you want to chart (for example, cells A4 through E8 in Figure 9-1). Begin the Chart Wizard. At Step 2, Click the Series tab, and click on any information you wish to exclude from the chart, clicking the Remove button to bump the information off the list (see Figure 9-2).

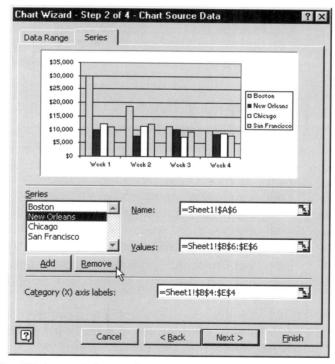

Figure 9-2 Click any information you want to exclude from your chart, then click Remove

Once I've placed a chart on a worksheet, is there a way to move the chart to a different sheet?

You'll find that trying to drag the chart down onto a sheet tab will prove an unsuccessful way to move the chart. Instead, click once on the chart to select it (black handles will appear in the corners and on the sides) and click the Cut button (or choose Edit | Cut). The chart will disappear from the current sheet. Click on the sheet tab for the destination sheet, then click in the approximate location where you want the chart to appear. Click the Paste button (or choose Edit | Paste), and the chart will appear in its new location.

What options do I have for customizing the chart legend?

When you select titles with your data, Excel turns those titles into a little legend that appears in a box next to the data in your chart. You can change the following features in your legend:

● Location of legend
● Size of legend box
● Size, style, and color of legend type
● Background color of legend
● Thickness, color, and style of legend border
● Shadow effect of border

Right-click on the legend, then choose Format Legend from the pop-up menu (or double-click on the legend). The Format Legend window will appear, with three tabs from which you may choose.

Choose the Patterns tab to make changes to the style and color of the border and the background color of the legend box. There is a Shadow option on this tab as well.

Choose the Font tab to change the typeface, style, or color of the text in your legend (alternatively, you can use buttons on the formatting toolbar to apply these changes). All text is

affected—you cannot change the text on one legend title without changing all text in the legend.

Choose the Placement tab to control the location of the legend in your chart window. Alternatively, you can drag the legend to a new location when the Format Legend window is closed. You get a better placement if you use the placement options in the Format Legend window because Excel will move the chart to make room for your legend if you choose one of these options. Moving the legend is a lot more work if you try to drag it around by yourself.

Excel decides how high my Y axis should go and where my X axis begins and ends. Is there a way to override these settings?

Excel determines the size and the intervals of numbers on your axes based on the numbers selected for charting. This information is called the scale of the axes. You can change the beginning and ending number on either axis, and you can set the intervals to give you the appearance that is most useful for you.

To change the scale on a chart, right click on the Y axis, choose Format Axis, and click the Scale tab. Change the settings for maximum and minimum amounts, major and minor unit intervals, and the point at which the X and Y axes cross. Click OK to implement your changes.

For example, suppose you want to create a chart to display the New Orleans sales results, as shown in Figure 9-3. The default chart, which shows a Y axis that goes up to 12,000 with intervals of 2,000, doesn't really emphasize the changes from one week to the next.

Now, try changing the scale so that the Y axis begins at 5,000 (there aren't any amounts under 7,000, so the spaces under 5,000 are unnecessary to this graph). Change the major unit to 500 so the intervals will be smaller and the columns will appear more distinct from one another. You may need to adjust the size of the chart so that the display will be more easily read. See Figure 9-4 for the result of these changes.

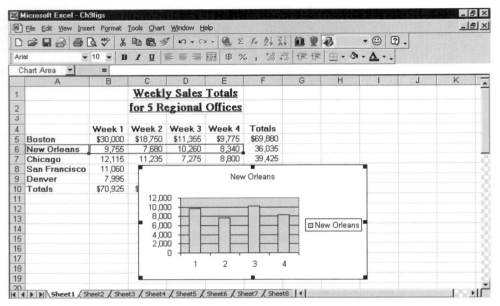

Figure 9-3 The default chart for New Orleans' sales performance

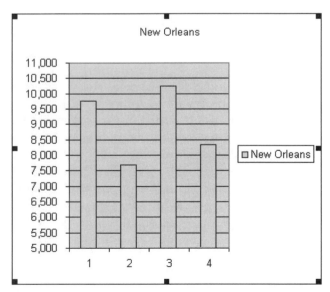

Figure 9-4 Some simple changes in scale make a more meaningful statement for the New Orleans sales figures

My chart is on the same sheet as the data. How do I print the chart but not the data?

Click once on the chart to select it. Choose File | Print. The Print window will appear with Selected Chart chosen. Because you selected the chart, Excel assumes you want to print only the chart (in fact, that is your only option). If you prefer to print the data and the chart together, click off of the chart on a cell in the worksheet before opening the Print window.

You can choose to print more than one chart, exclusive of the data from which they were created, by placing the charts together on a separate sheet (see the question "Is there a way to move a chart to a different sheet?" above), making that sheet the active sheet, then printing the sheet (as opposed to the individually selected charts).

ENHANCING CHARTS

 I chose the default chart for my data, but everything looks out of proportion. How can I alter the chart size so that it doesn't look so strange?

Sometimes the chart you get is not very attractive when it first appears. You may be able to correct the proportion problems by simply changing the size of the chart. Click on the chart once, then drag the black handles that appear in the corners.

A problem I run into frequently is that the size of the font used for the axis titles is much larger than I need. Reducing the font size on the axes may make your chart appear more proportional. Right-click on either axis and choose the Format Axis option at the top of the pop-up menu that appears. Click the Font tab and choose a typeface and size that is more appropriate to the size of the chart you are using (see Figure 9-5).

My chart title is too long to fit on one line. Is it possible to enter more than one line for a title?

The Chart Title field will accept up to 255 characters and no more. You can enter all these characters in step 3 of the Chart Wizard in the Chart title field. Excel will wrap the text

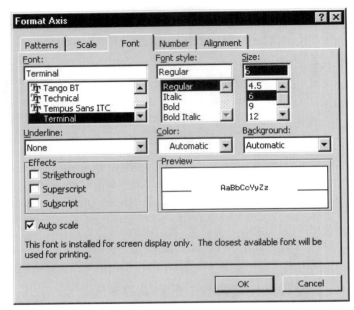

Figure 9-5 The Format Axis Font tab provides a preview of the font and size that you choose

onto additional lines if the entire title won't fit on one line. You can control how the text wraps after you have finished using the Chart Wizard by clicking once in the chart title to select it, then clicking at the place where you want the text to wrap. Press the ENTER key, and the text will wrap at that point.

If you finished the Chart Wizard without entering a title, you can enter a title at any time on your chart by clicking once on the chart, then choosing Chart | Chart Options from the menu (the Chart menu is only available when you have selected a chart by clicking on it). Enter title information on the Titles tab in the Chart Options window that appears (see Figure 9-6).

How do I change the format of the numbers and text on my chart?

Right-click on any object in your chart (such as an axis, the legend, the title) of which you want to change the format, and choose Format at the top of the resulting pop-up menu. You

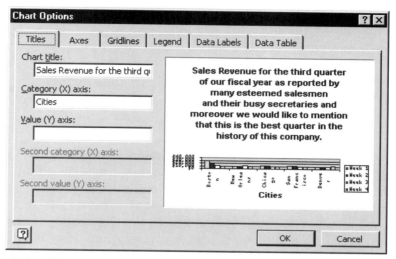

Figure 9-6   Enter up to 255 characters for your chart title

will see an array of formatting choices applicable to the object you clicked. Choose Font if you wish to change typeface; number if you wish to change number format. You will also see options for changing the color, pattern, alignment, and special effects such as underlining.

Change the appearance of all the text on a chart at once by double-clicking in the white area surrounding the chart. When the Format Chart Area window appears, the font characteristics you choose will apply to all titles and text boxes.

 Is there a way to include text from my worksheet in a chart?

This is a bit tricky, but it can be done. You can link worksheet text to a text box in your chart, so that whenever the text in the worksheet changes the text in the chart will change also. Follow these steps to link text:

1. Enter the text you wish to link in a blank cell in your worksheet.

2. Click once on your chart to select it.

3. Enter the = sign.

4. Click once on the cell containing the text you wish to link.

5. Press ENTER. The text will appear in a selected text box somewhere on your chart.

As long as the text box is selected, you can use your mouse to drag the text box to a new location on your chart. You can also resize the text box by dragging its handles. You can right-click the text box and choose the Format option to make a font style selection. *But be careful!* Once you click off the text box and deselect it, it's very difficult to reselect the box and make further changes. If you can find the border of the text box and click on it, you can reselect the text box. If you think you will need to select the text box, consider formatting it with a thin border. If you want to change the font or appearance, make changes to the appearance of all text in the chart (including text boxes) by double-clicking on the chart as described above.

To change the content of the text box, change the text in the linked cell from your worksheet.

 Tip: *If you link text from your worksheet to a text box in your chart and decide you no longer want that text to appear in your chart, you can delete the text in the worksheet. This will have the effect of removing the text from the chart. Alternatively, select it and press DELETE.*

The best way to add text to a chart and keep it easy to manipulate is to click once on the chart to select it, then enter some text. When you press the ENTER key, the text will appear in a text box on your chart. You can move the text box, change the font, format the box, change the alignment, and so on. More importantly, you can easily access the text again by simply clicking on it at any time.

 ### Are there any features on the Drawing toolbar that are helpful with chart construction?

The more artistic you are, the better advantage you can take of the Drawing toolbar that comes with your Excel program.

To display your toolbar, choose View | Toolbars and click on Drawing on the side menu that appears (or click the Drawing button on your Standard toolbar). Some of the features on this toolbar are particularly useful when it comes to enhancing your charts. Here's a sampling of some of the common drawing elements that are used in charting:

- **Arrows** Use an arrow to call attention to areas of interest in your chart (see Figure 9-7). Click the Arrow button (shown in the left margin, top) and drag your mouse to draw an arrow. The arrowhead will appear at the point where you release your mouse button. While the arrow is selected, you can click on the Arrow Style button (shown in the left margin, bottom) to choose from various types of line weights and arrowhead styles.

- **Geographic Shapes** Use the Rectangle and Oval shapes to drag shapes on your chart. Hold down the SHIFT key while drawing to force the Rectangle to a square shape or the Oval to a circle shape. When a shape is selected, you can enter text inside of the shape.

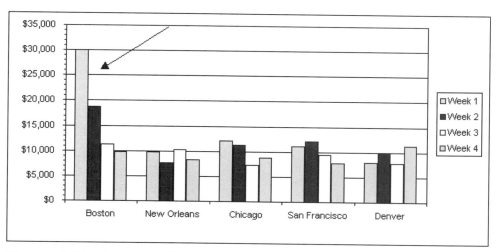

Figure 9-7   An arrow directs the eye to an important aspect of your chart

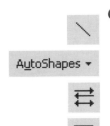

● **Lines**   Use graphic lines to draw on your graph. Click the Line button (shown in the left margin, top) and then drag your mouse to draw. Or click AutoShapes (shown in the left margin, second) to draw a free-form line. Select a line on your graph by clicking on it, and then click the Arrow Style button (shown in the left margin, third) to assign an arrowhead to the end of the line. Or, use the Line Style (shown in the left margin, fourth) or Dash Style (shown in the left margin, bottom) button to change the consistency of the line itself (see Figure 9-8).

● **Rotate**   Select a drawing object on your chart (such as an arrow or a line), then click the Rotate button (shown left). Place your mouse pointer on any selection point on the object and drag to change the angle at which the object appears. Lines and arrows can also be rotated if you point to a selection point on the object and hold down the CTRL key while rotating. Objects like rectangles and ovals require the use of the Rotate button if you want them to turn.

● **Snap**   If you have trouble moving objects around your chart—if the objects seem to jump from one location to another instead of sliding smoothly when you drag them—click the Draw button on the Drawing toolbar,

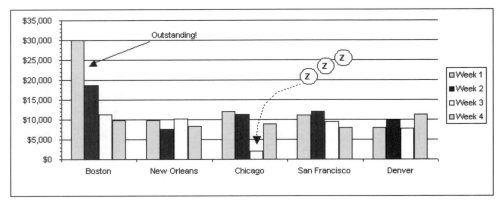

Figure 9-8   Use the different features on the Drawing toolbar to add a personal touch to your charts

choose Snap from the pull-down menu, and turn off any Snap to features that are in use by clicking on the To Grid or To Shape option if the button is depressed.

What color options are available to me when I'm working with charts?

Use colors to brighten your chart, take advantage of a company color scheme, or make a point by emphasizing or downplaying certain areas of your chart. Here are some examples of situations in which color can be used to change the appearance of your chart:

- **Text and Numbers** Change the color of your chart text. To change the color of all chart titles, numbers, and text boxes at once, right-click on the background area of your chart window (within the chart window, but outside the confines of the actual chart), choose Format Chart Area, then select the Font tab and make your choices. To change individual titles or text, right-click on the specific object, choose Format, then make your changes on the Font tab.

- **Chart window background and border** Right-click on the background area of the chart window, choose Format Chart Area, and select Patterns. Choose colors and styles for your chart border (note also the Shadow and Round Corners options in addition to size, style and color of the border).

- **Chart background** Right-click on the chart area itself, choose Format Plot Area, and make selections for border and background area.

- **Chart bars, columns, lines, pie pieces** Change the color or pattern of the data columns, lines, and so on by right-clicking on the item you wish to change, choosing Format Data Series, and then making choices on the Patterns tab of the window that appears.

Is there a way to incorporate my company logo into the background of my chart?

You can put any pictorial image you want on your chart background. Some pictures may get stretched, depending on

the height or width of your chart, so you may need to experiment a little or refine your graphic image in a graphics program before bringing it to your chart.

To place a graphic image in the background of your chart, follow these steps:

1. Right-click the chart area. A pop-up menu will appear.

2. Choose Format Plot Area. The Format Plot Area dialog box will appear.

3. Click the Fill Effects button. The Fill Effects dialog box will appear.

4. Click the Picture tab, then click Select Picture. You will be expected to indicate a file that contains the picture you want to use as your chart background. Click Insert when you have selected the file. Click OK and OK again and the picture will appear as the background on your chart.

Is there a way to place images or labels inside the columns on my chart?

In much the same way you incorporated a company logo into your chart background (see previous question), you can right-click on a chart image—column, bar, tube, pyramid, and so on—and choose the Format Data Series option, then choose Fill Effects and work with colors and pictures to enhance the images on your chart.

To place labels in your chart columns (see Figure 9-9), you can right-click on the column (or any type of data depiction), choose Format Data Series, then click the Data Labels tab. Click the Show label option, then click OK. The data labels will appear on your chart outside the columns or bars. To place a label inside a column, drag it where you want it. If you need to change the alignment of the labels (for example, I changed the alignment to vertical in Figure 9.9), right-click on a data label (they're all selected when you click on one), choose Alignment, and indicate the alignment you desire.

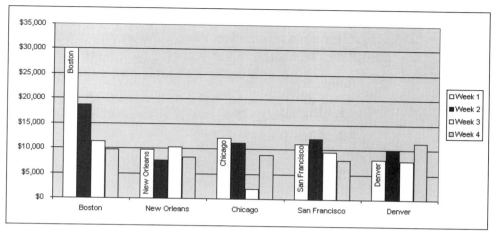

Figure 9-9   You can place labels in the bars on your chart

TROUBLESHOOTING

 My draw objects disappear when I click on the chart. How can I keep them on top of the chart?

When adding draw effects to your chart, the key is to click on the chart first to select it, then click on the appropriate button on your drawing toolbar and add your effects. If you don't select the chart first, you can add your draw effects, but the effects actually belong to the worksheet instead of the chart. Select the chart after adding an effect in this manner, and the effect (such as an arrow or a text box) disappears behind the chart. Move the chart, and the effects stay put on your worksheet instead of moving with the chart.

By selecting the chart before adding the draw effects, the effects become part of the chart, staying on top of the chart even when the chart is selected and moving with the chart when it is relocated.

 Every time I make a chart, I go through the same steps to enhance the chart with my particular style choices. Is there a way I can save these choices so I don't have to redo them with every chart?

If you use the same features over and again, you can alter the default chart style to use your own style choices. Right-click the background of the chart window and choose Chart Type (or choose Chart | Chart Type), make sure the default style of chart is the one selected, then click Set as default chart. You will be asked if you are sure you want to set the current chart as your default. Click Yes.

From this point forward, when you are ready to create a chart, select the information you want to chart from your worksheet and click the Chart Wizard button. You can click Finish at any time, and your chart will be created in the style to which you have become accustomed. Feel free to indicate any titles or legend information you want to change while in the Chart Wizard, or make such changes later.

Chapter 10

Printing and Viewing Results

Answer Topics!

Printing and Viewing Results @ a Glance

Overview. Creating a worksheet that provides all the information you need in an eye-pleasing presentation can be a time consuming but very rewarding process. It can be very disappointing when the printed output doesn't look like the worksheet you created onscreen. This chapter presents you with basic information about the printing techniques used in Excel so that you can produce hard copies of your information just the way you want them to appear.

Printing Worksheets. There are different printing methods you can use in Excel, including setting specific areas to print and page breaks and making your worksheet fit on a specific number of pages. You can have Excel print your file name in your worksheet, as well as printing borders, gridlines, and row and column headings. Excel provides a quick way to repeat row and/or column titles on every printed page of your worksheet.

Printing Charts. You can print your charts on your worksheet with your numbers or on a separate page. You can control how many charts print. There are special considerations for black and white printers.

Other Printing Considerations. You can choose the sheets you want to print and set up your own custom views for printing. If you use the Comments feature in Excel, you can print a hard copy of your comments.

PRINTING WORKSHEETS

 ### What's the quickest way to print a worksheet?

The quickest and easiest way to print is to click the Print button on the Standard toolbar. There are several other ways to print as well, and you can choose the one with which you're most comfortable.

- Press CTRL-P to print the active sheet(s) in the current workbook

- Open the File menu and choose Print to open the Print dialog box, where you can specify several print criteria.

- Press ALT-F (for File), then P (for Print) to open the Print dialog box.

 ### How do I indicate which areas of a worksheet I want to print when I don't want to print the entire worksheet?

If you normally print the entire worksheet but just this once want to indicate a specific area of a worksheet that you want to print, highlight the area you want to print, then choose File | Print, and click the Selection button. Only the area you highlighted will print. If you want to print this same area again, you will need to highlight it again before printing.

If the area you selected to print contains cells that are not adjacent to one another, each block of adjacent cells will print on a separate page.

If you would like to designate a print area that will be available for future use, rather than just for a single print session, select the area you wish to print, then choose File | Print Area | Set Print Area. You will see dashed lines surrounding the area you have designated.

Note: When you designate a print area using the Set Print Area command, dashed lines appear around the selected print area. If you save the file and then open the file at a later time, you won't see these dashed lines. The print area still exists, however, and only the designated print area will print when you choose File | Print.

Choose File | Print at any time to print the assigned print area. Save the file if you wish to save the print area for future use.

Tip: You can use range names as quick printing shortcuts if there is more than one area of your worksheet you wish to print. Highlight an area and choose Insert | Name | Define, to open the Define Name window. Enter a name and click OK. Name several ranges in this manner and you can quickly print a named range by clicking on the name in the Name Box, then choosing File | Print | Selection.

How do I clear a print area?

If you don't need a print area anymore, or if you wish to print a different area of your worksheet, choose File | Print Area | Clear Print Area.

Excel determines where a new page should start, but sometimes I need the break to be at a different location. How do I override the page breaks?

You can create your own page breaks in your worksheet, forcing Excel to begin printing on a new page at the best location for you. To create a horizontal page break, place your cellpointer in column A, in the row *below* the row in which you wish to insert a page break. Choose Insert | Page Break. A horizontal dashed line will appear across your worksheet,

indicating the location where the page will break (see Figure 10-1).

Create a vertical page break by placing your cellpointer in row 1 in the column to the *right* of the column in which you wish to force a page break. Choose Insert | Page Break. A vertical dashed line will appear across your worksheet, indicating the location of the page break (see Figure 10-2).

 Note: *The page breaks are ignored when the Scaling/Fit To options in Page Setup are set (see the question about scaling, below).*

	A	B	C	D	E	F	G	H
24	21	Cotton Candy	621	438	600			
25	22	Sno Shak		355	350			
26	23	Bingo	284	205	300			
27	24	Where in USA is Carmen Sandiego	205	125	175			
28	25	Madame X	n/a	44	200			
29	26	Golf	374	302	350			
30	27	Makeover Shop	n/a					
31	28	Basketball	399	350	375			
32	29	Bounce House	377	400	400			
33	30	Brain Quest	433	276	300			
34	31	Bucket Game	271		300			
35	32	Bake Sale						
36	33	Popcorn	270	154	200			
37	34	Speed Pitch	n/a	300	350			
38	35	Goldfish	373	382	385			
39	36	Pick a Pencil	770	936	950			
40	37	Gone Fishing	458	281	450			
41	38	Snakes Alive	596	513	550			
42	39	Stroll for Sweets	451	468	475			
43	40	Toss for Pop	336	308	350			
44	41	Pan for Gold	378	509	500			
45	42	Cup Toss	281	379	375			
46	43	Pocket Lady	375	358	375			
47	44	Face Painting	200		200			

Figure 10-1 Clicking in cell A45 and choosing Insert | Page Break will make row 45 the first row at the top of the next page

	A	B	C	D	E	F	G	H
1		Booths 1998	prior years	1997	1998			
2			avg # of people	# of people	expected			
3								
4	1	Basketball	399	350	375			
5	2	Bounce House	377	400	400			
6	3	Brain Quest	433	276	300			
7	4	Bucket Game	271		300			
8	5	Bake Sale						
9	6	Popcorn	270	154	200			
10	7	Speed Pitch	n/a	300	350			
11	8	Goldfish	373	382	385			
12	9	Pick a Pencil	770	936	950			
13	10	Gone Fishing	458	281	450			
14	11	Snakes Alive	596	513	550			
15	12	Stroll for Sweets	451	468	475			
16	13	Toss for Pop	336	308	350			
17	14	Pan for Gold	378	509	500			
18	15	Cup Toss	281	379	375			
19	16	Pocket Lady	375	358	375			
20	17	Face Painting	200		200			
21	18	Cane Toss	396	335	350			
22	19	Tic Tac Toe	344	323	325			
23	20	Staff Sensation	385	532	550			
24	21	Cotton Candy	621	438	600			

Sheet1 / Sheet2 / Sheet3 /

Figure 10-2 Clicking in cell G1 and choosing Insert | Page Break will cause column G to be the first column on the second page of your worksheet

You can create a horizontal and vertical page break simultaneously by placing your cellpointer in your worksheet in any cell other than one in the first column or first row. Choose Insert | Page Break, and a break will occur horizontally across the row above your cellpointer and vertically down the column to the right of your cellpointer (see Figure 10-3).

How do I remove a page break?

Remove a page break by placing your cellpointer in the row beneath a horizontal page break or in the column to the right of a vertical page break and choosing Insert | Remove Page Break.

		C	D	E	F	G	H
	A	B					
46	43	Pocket Lady	375	358	375			
47	44	Face Painting	200		200			
48	45	Cane Toss	396	335	350			
49	46	Tic Tac Toe	344	323	325			
50	47	Staff Sensation	385	532	550			
51	48	Cotton Candy	621	438	600			
52	49	Sno Shak		355	350			
53	50	Bingo	284	205	300			
54	51	Where in USA is Carmen Sandiego	205	125	175			
55	52	Madame X	n/a	44	200			
56	53	Golf	374	302	350			

Figure 10-3 Clicking in cell F56 and choosing Insert | Page Break causes a horizontal page break to occur after row 55 and a vertical page break to occur after column E

How do I move a page break?

You can move a page break by dragging it to a new location if you are looking at your worksheet in Page Break Preview mode. Choose View | Page Break Preview. Your page breaks will appear as heavy blue lines on your worksheet (see Figure 10-4), and can be moved to a new location by placing your mouse pointer over the lines and dragging. While in this view, you can also drag a page break line right off the page to remove it. Choose View | Normal to leave the Page Break Preview mode.

Note: Page breaks run the distance of your worksheet. A horizontal page breaks goes from column A to column IV, a vertical page break goes from row 1 to row 65,536.

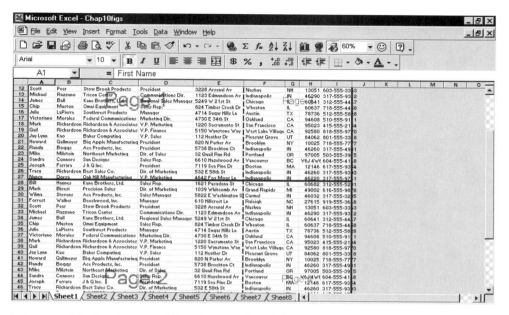

Figure 10-4 Choose View | Page Break Preview to drag your page break lines to a new location

 My worksheet is just a little too big to fit on one sheet of paper. How can I change the margins so that the worksheet will fit?

There are two primary ways of making your worksheet fit on a page: adjusting the margins and using the scaling feature (covered in the next question). You can decrease the margins of your worksheet page so that there is less white space around the edges of the worksheet. Any margin adjustments you make will be limited by your printer, which has the right to override any changes you make to the margins.

To change the margin settings, choose File | Page Setup. In the window that appears, click the Margins tab (see Figure 10-5), and make the adjustments you feel are necessary to the right, left, top, and bottom margins. If you like, you can even set these margins to zero; your printer will then change your settings to the minimum allowable space.

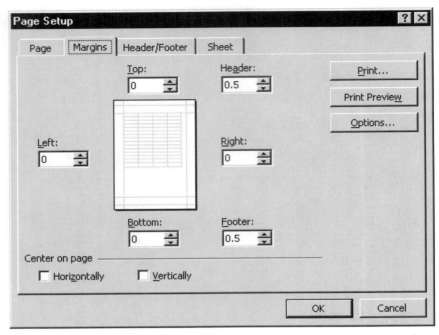

Figure 10-5   File | Page Setup lets you adjust your margins to make your worksheet fit on a page

There is an alternate method for setting margins that you can try, although some people find this method difficult because you must be very precise with your mouse. Open the Print Preview screen (File | Print Preview), click the Margins button, and see the actual margins appear as gray lines on your previewed document. These lines can be dragged to a new location with your mouse. This may be a better way to attempt to make a worksheet fit on a page because you can actually see the page and determine how much of an adjustment you need to make.

How does scaling work?

Another option for squeezing a large worksheet onto a required number of pages is the scaling feature. Use scaling to either indicate a specific percentage by which you want

Excel to reduce your entire worksheet, or request that the worksheet be squished to fit onto a particular quantity of pages. Choose File | Page Setup again to open the Page Setup window, and then click the Page tab.

Under Scaling there are two options: Adjust to and Fit to (see Figure 10-6). The Adjust to option enables you to indicate a specific percentage reduction (or increase) for the entire worksheet. For example, if you indicate an adjustment of 90% original size, every item in the worksheet, including graphic elements such as charts, will be reduced to 90 percent of its original size.

Alternatively, you can choose that the worksheet fit to a specific number of pages. Excel will reduce the worksheet uniformly by whatever percentage is necessary to make everything fit into the number of pages you require.

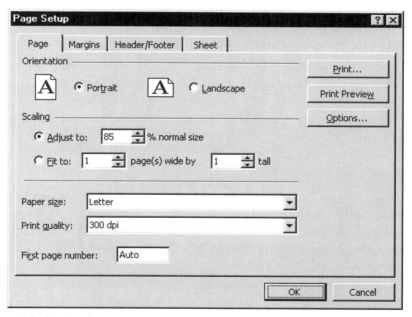

Figure 10-6 Indicate a percent or a page count for uniform reduction of your worksheet

 I decreased the size of my font in hopes of making my worksheet fit on one page, but the page count is unchanged. Why doesn't a smaller font force the worksheet to take up less space?

Changing the size of your font doesn't alter the width of your columns. Lowering the point size of the font is a good start, but you must then change the column width to take advantage of the extra space.

If your worksheet spans several columns, you can adjust all columns at once to the best fit (the smallest width that will accommodate the largest entry in a column). By selecting all cells in the worksheet (click the Select All button in the upper left corner of the worksheet, or press CTRL-A), then double-clicking on the bar separating any two column letters, all columns will be adjusted to achieve the best fit to their contents.

 Is there a way to print the path and file name of my document in the worksheet itself?

You can insert the name and location of your file anywhere in your worksheet by following these steps:

1. Click on the cell where you want the path and file name to appear.

2. Enter the function (or use the Paste Function button to access this function) =CELL("filename"). This function will place the name and complete path of the file in the current cell (see Figure 10-7). Note, however, that the cell will remain blank if you have not yet named the file.

Once placed in a worksheet, the CELL formula can be moved to any other cell without disrupting the integrity of the function.

 Is there a way to enter the path and file name in a header or footer?

Excel would have you believe that this can't be done, since there is no easy command to perform this task. But, never fear! Here's a little macro that will do the job nicely. Choose

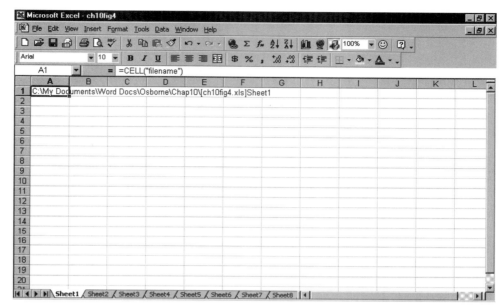

Figure 10-7   Use the CELL function to place the path and file name in a cell

Tools | Macro | Macros, then enter a name (such as **Path**) for your macro. Choose PERSONAL.XLS as the location for your macro so that the macro will be available to any workbook. Click the Create button, and enter the following information in the Module area, between the Sub and End Sub lines.

> **ActiveSheet.PageSetup.RightFooter =**
> **ActiveWorkbook.Path & "\" &**
> **ActiveWorkbook.Name**

Each time you want to run this macro, choose Tools | Macro | Macros, then click on the name of the macro and click the Run button.

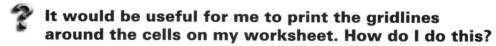

It would be useful for me to print the gridlines around the cells on my worksheet. How do I do this?

The border technique works, especially if you want to have some control over the size and style of the gridlines. A border can be easily placed around your cells by clicking on the cells in question, then choosing Format | Cells, clicking the

Border tab, then choosing the type, style, and color of border you want. A border of this sort is extraordinarily easy to remove later by simply selecting the area again, clicking the border button on the toolbar and choosing the No Border option.

Is there a way to print Excel's gridlines without having to place a border around each cell?

The alternative to using Excel's Border feature to place printing gridlines on your worksheet is to choose File | Page Setup, then click on the Sheet tab, and check the Gridlines box. (Note, in some earlier versions of Excel, this box was checked by default.)

How can I print a column heading (A, B, C, and so on) at the top of my worksheet?

Besides the Gridlines feature, there are a couple of other options on the Sheet tab of the Page Setup window that might be of interest. The Row and Column Headings check box provides you with the option of printing the A, B, C column headings and the 1, 2, 3 row numbers. This is a great tool if you plan to print a worksheet that will be discussed in a group because the row and column headings allow group members to say, "Look at the information in row 14," or "Take a look at cell D23," and have everyone in the group be immediately able to get to that location.

What does it mean to print in Draft quality?

Another interesting option on the Sheet tab of the Page Setup window is the ability to print in Draft quality. Worksheets that contain a lot of graphics may print very slowly. Printing in Draft quality prints at a lower resolution, so graphic images may not appear as sharp as you would like them, but you make up in speed what you lose in quality. If you want to examine your worksheet on the printed page and are willing to sacrifice the clarity of graphic elements on your rough draft, choose this option.

My worksheet extends beyond one page. How can I reuse the column and row headings from the first page on subsequent pages?

You can lock in column and row headings so that they repeat page after page and you won't have to reenter them at the top of each page. To do this, choose File | Page Setup, and click on the Sheet tab. To assign rows that will repeat at the top of each page, in the Print titles area, click in the field that reads Rows to repeat at top, and then click on the row number of the row from your worksheet that contains the column titles that should repeat on each printed page (see Figure 10-8). You don't have to close this Page Setup window, just move your mouse right over to your worksheet and click on the row number (or drag through multiple row numbers) of the row(s) you want to have repeated at the top of each printed page. Click OK.

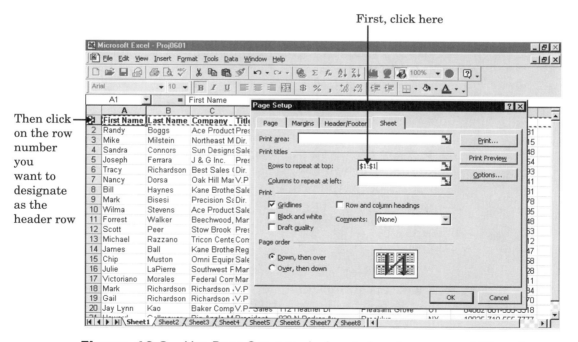

Figure 10-8 Use Page Setup to designate header rows and title columns. These rows or columns will repeat on each printed page

To repeat columns at the left, click in the Columns to repeat at left field in the Page Setup box, and then click on the column letters for the columns that have the titles in them that you want to have repeat on your worksheet. Then click the OK button.

How do I clear column and/or row titles?

To clear these rows or columns that repeat on each page, return to the Page Setup window and empty the fields where you entered row and/or column information. Note that although you have access to the Page Setup window from the Setup button at the top of the Print Preview screen, the repeat fields in Page Setup are dim and you can't access them. You must open the Page Setup window from your regular worksheet in order to use these options.

Which printer settings can be controlled from within Excel?

There are several printer settings, including a choice of printer, which can be controlled from the Print and Page Setup windows in Excel. For computers that have access to more than one printer, choose a particular printer by choosing File | Print. When the Print window appears (see Figure 10-9), click the drop-down arrow in the Name area, and a list of available printers (including a fax machine if that is an option on your computer) will appear. Click on the name of the printer (or fax) you wish to use. Click Properties in the Print window, and you can choose from options applicable to the printer you have chosen, such as print quality, type of paper, size of paper, and portrait or landscape orientation. These options will vary depending on the type of printer you use.

Choose File | Page Setup and more options are at your disposal. Here you also have a choice between portrait and landscape orientation, and you can access the printer properties by clicking the Options button.

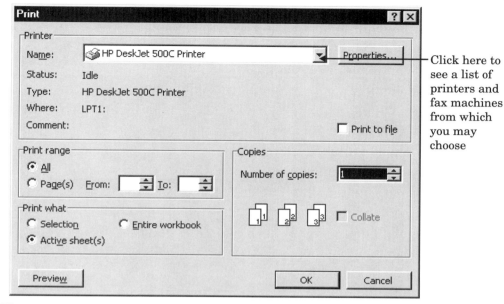

Click here to see a list of printers and fax machines from which you may choose

Figure 10-9   Use the printer of your choice

PRINTING CHARTS

How can I control the number of charts that appear on a printed page?

When you create charts, you have the option of placing them on the same page that your numbers from the worksheet occur, or placing them on separate pages. The Chart Wizard gives you this option (see Figure 10-10) when it asks if you wish to place the chart as a new sheet or an object in the current sheet. You can place as many charts as you want on a page, but obviously, the more charts you choose to appear on one page, the smaller they will have to be.

To move a chart to a different page, you can either insert a page break in your current worksheet and drag the charts to the other side of the page break, or you can place your charts on separate sheets in your workbook. Each sheet containing a chart will print as a separate page.

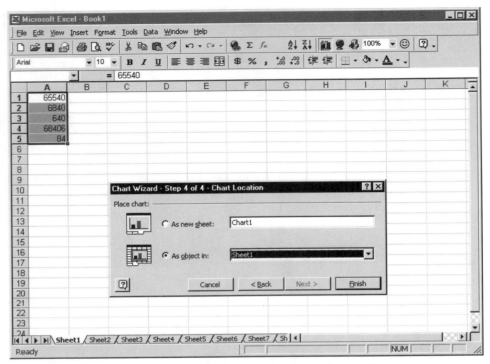

Figure 10-10 Click the Chart Wizard button on the toolbar to open a chart. The last step asks if you want your chart to appear as part of the current worksheet, or on its own page

Tip: *You can move a chart to another sheet within a workbook by selecting the chart (click on it once to select it), then click on the Chart Menu, which only appears when a chart is selected. Choose Location | As New Sheet, then click OK. The chart will move to a new sheet.*

**My chart's colors end up looking black when I print the chart. Is there a good method for printing charts on a black and white printer?**

If you have a black and white printer, or if you're going to photocopy your chart in black and white after you print it, you may want to change the settings so that the chart will be printed in black and white. Excel will substitute gray tones

for the colors in your chart, and you'll get a crisper image than if you were to print the chart as a color chart.

Create the chart on a sheet of its own, then choose File | Page Setup. In the window that appears, click the Chart tab (this tab only appears for charts on separate sheets; although you can request to print only a chart that's embedded in a worksheet, you won't see this Chart tab). Select Print in black and white. Figures 10-11 and 10-12 show the difference between a color chart printed on a black and white printer, and as a black and white chart.

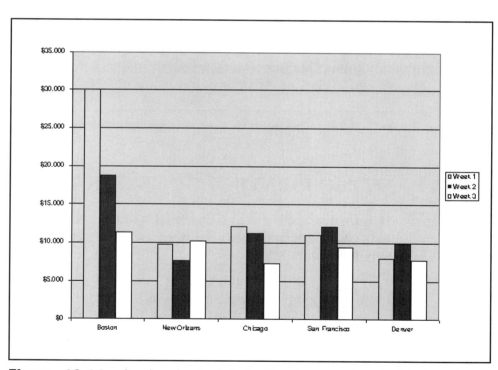

Figure 10-11   A color chart printed without requesting the black and white option

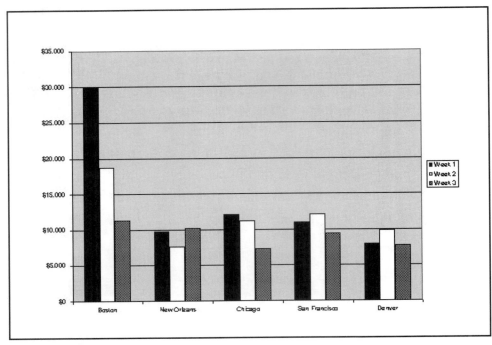

Figure 10-12 The same chart printed with the black and white option

OTHER PRINTING CONSIDERATIONS

 How can I print particular sheets of my workbook as opposed to the top sheet or all the sheets of the workbook?

You need to select the sheets that you want to print by holding down the CTRL key while you click on the sheet tabs of the sheets you want to print. Choose File | Print, and the

Print window will appear (see Figure 10-13). Choose Active sheets, and only the sheets that you selected will print.

 ## What is a custom view and how can I get one?

Excel allows you to store certain settings, including print settings, as a custom view. You can use this feature to return to these settings each time you use a particular worksheet. You can store as many custom views as you need with your worksheet. A custom view is saved with the worksheet in which it is created.

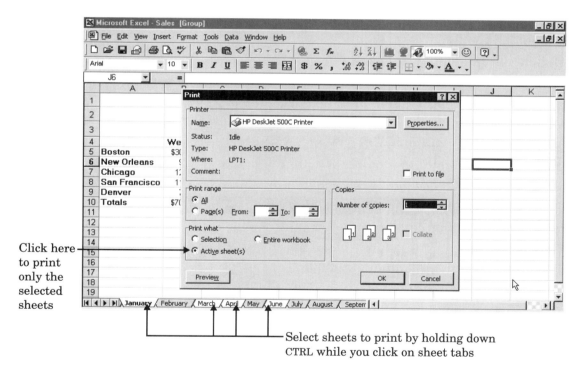

Click here to print only the selected sheets

Select sheets to print by holding down CTRL while you click on sheet tabs

Figure 10-13   Choose Active sheets to print all selected sheets

The types of settings you can save with a custom view include:

- Window size and position on the screen
- Window splits
- Frozen panes
- Which sheet is active
- The cells that are selected
- The location of the cellpointer
- Hidden sheets, columns, and rows
- Filter settings
- Print settings including print area, titles, gridlines, headers and footers

To create a custom view, follow these steps:

1. Apply all the settings you wish to save in a particular view to the current worksheet.
2. Choose View | Custom View. The Custom View window will appear (see Figure 10-14).

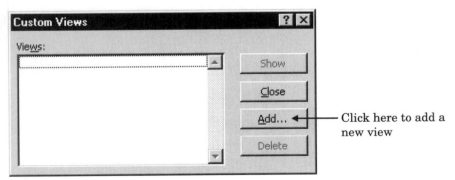

Figure 10-14 The Custom View window

3. Click the Add button.

4. Enter the name for this view.

5. Indicate if you want to include print settings and hidden areas.

6. Click OK to save your view (you must resave the worksheet to save this view with the worksheet).

If you have entered multiple views in your worksheet, switch among them by choosing View | Custom View, clicking on the view you want, and choosing Show.

Tip: *I save a view called Normal before I begin creating other custom views. This way I can always get back to an unadorned view in my worksheet.*

I've created comments in my worksheet. Are these for onscreen viewing only, or is there a way to print the comments?

You can print your comments, and you have two choices for printing them. To print comments all together at the end of your worksheet, listing a row and column reference with each comment, choose File | Page Setup. When the Page Setup window appears, click on the Sheet tab. In the Print area of this screen, click on the down arrow in the Comments field and choose At end of sheet. Comments will be printed on a separate page at the end of your worksheet. Even if your worksheet only consists of one entry, the comment(s) will print on a separate page.

You can also choose to print your comments right in the worksheet, adjacent to the cells to which the comments appear. You must display your comments on your worksheet in order to print them alongside the worksheet entries. Choose View | Comments. If comment boxes overlap with cells containing data, or if the boxes are too big, you can move

and resize the boxes as necessary. Once you are satisfied with the position of the comment boxes, choose File | Page Setup. On the Sheet tab, click the Comments option and choose As displayed on sheet. When you print the sheet, you will see both the worksheet information and the comments (see Figure 10-15).

Weekly Sales Totals
for 5 Regional Offices

	Week 1	Week 2	Week 3	Week 4	Totals
Boston	$30,000	$18,750			69,880
New Orleans	9,755	4,589			32,944
Chicago	12,115	11,235			39,425
San Francisco	11,060	12,100	9,445	7,875	40,480
Denver	7,995	9,865	7,800	11,320	37,000
Totals	$70,925	$70,925	$70,925	$70,925	$70,925

Gail Perry:
The bad weather really hurt us here.

Gail Perry:
Sales were unusually high due to favorable weather conditions.

Figure 10-15 You can print your comments right on the worksheet by indicating the setting on the Page Setup screen

Chapter 11

Data Manipulation

Answer Topics!

Data Manipulation @ a Glance

Overview. The basic column and row design of a spreadsheet is the perfect setting for repetitive lists of information, such as lists of customers, lists of inventory items, employee lists, and more. You may refer to such lists as databases; Excel calls them lists. The concept is essentially the same: a database is another word for an organized list. There are advantages and disadvantages to using Excel for your data needs, but if you do choose Excel over its more sophisticated database counterparts (such as Microsoft Access), this chapter will provide you with some insights about creating and using data lists.

Creating a Data List. Before you begin entering data, you must plan the design of your data list and determine the potential uses of the list. Enter data directly on the list or use Excel's forms. After sorting and rearranging data, you can return to the original order of your entries.

Searching for Data. Once you've created a data list, you can poke around and find all sorts of things. You can have Excel point to data that meets your search criteria, or you can extract the data to a new location. You can also use Excel's data features in conjunction with an external database.

Sorting and Subtotaling Data. Sort your data by up to three criteria, in either ascending or descending order. You can create subtotals within your database to help group your data logically. There are built-in functions that specifically work with data lists.

CREATING A DATA LIST

 I'm going to use Excel to store my customer list. Where do I start when creating a data list?

Contrary to popular belief, your starting point for creating a list in Excel is not entering titles across the columns in a worksheet and then entering your data in rows beneath those titles. The place to start is at a desk or a table with a pencil (and a good eraser!), some paper, and lots of ideas.

Before you begin listing all the pieces of data you want to enter (such as customer name, address, city, state, and so on), perform this *very important step:* Make a list of all the information you want to be able to *retrieve* from your database. What will you use this data to accomplish? Do you plan to create form letters? Will you produce mailing labels? Will you make comparative studies of the type of services you perform for your customers? Are you interested in regional data about your customers? Do you want to know how long it has been since each of your customers did business with you?

These are the questions that will determine the direction of your data creation, and if you don't ask all the questions first, the odds are strongly in opposition to your being able to create a useful database. A database is a tool for obtaining information first, and a list of information second. Look at your data in that way, and you'll be able to create a database that serves your needs. Look at your data as a list of information from which you can derive interesting results, and you'll be very lucky if you are able to obtain the information you need.

Once you've determined the information thar you need to retrieve from your data list, make a list of the information you need to input into the list so you can achieve the desired results. When planning the arrangement of your data, consider who will be using your database, who will be entering data, and the skills of those users. Think about the entry of data in your list—in what order would the information be most easily accessed for data entry, as opposed to what order you want to see the data appear on your screen. You can always reorder the information on your

screen, but the data entry forms are more difficult to change. (For more information on data entry and forms, see Chapter 14, "Using Forms in Excel.")

Once you've made the above-mentioned determinations, plan the appearance of your actual database, considering the kind of information you need to input in order to achieve the desired results. Your database will include a single row of column headings (called *fields*), with each heading being unique. Plan the order in which you will enter your data (each row of data representing one *record*). See Table 11-1 for more information about database terms such as fields and records.

With all of these tasks accomplished, the actual setup of the database in Excel will be much more efficient and meaningful.

 ## I've created the framework for a data list in Excel, determining the data needed. How do I actually create the database?

The first step in creating a database is to determine the field names for each type of data you plan to enter. You will set up the structure of your database in Excel by entering a field name in each column. Each column name must be unique, even if you plan to collect similar data in multiple columns.

Term	Definition
Field	A category of data, displayed in an Excel list as a column heading.
Record	A database item including a maximum of one entry per field. In Excel each record occupies one row.
Data Form	A fill-in-the-blank input device used for entering data into an Excel list. Display the form by choosing Data Form from the menu.
Criteria	A test used for searching for data within a list.
Criteria Range	A cell or group of cells containing the descriptive information (criteria) from which a selection will be made.
Extract	To copy data records from a list to another location on the worksheet.

Table 11-1   Common Terms Associated with Lists

Make field names short, yet make them descriptive enough so that any user of the database will understand what is meant by the name.

Tip: *Enter field names in a bold or otherwise outstanding typeface so that they will be easily distinguishable from the data in your list.*

Each field must inhabit a separate column, and all columns of the database must be adjacent to one another.

Adjust columns widths to appropriate sizes and enter any formatting—such as currency or number formatting, typeface, or alignment that is applicable for the fields you have created.

Caution: *Don't separate records with blank rows. When you sort your data or search for records meeting certain requirements, the blank rows will distort the results of these actions.*

There are two methods for entering actual data in your database. You can use a database form (see Chapter 14 for a complete analysis of database forms), or you can enter information directly into your data list. To enter information directly into the list, begin with the first record (each row of information will represent one record, and each record will inhabit only one row), and enter information from left to right, one piece of information in each field. Complete one record, then advance to the next row and enter another complete record.

Tip: *As your data list expands, the titles may scroll out of sight. To keep column titles in view at all times, freeze them by placing your cellpointer in the leftmost column of your list, in the row immediately under your titles. Choose Window | Freeze Panes. From this point forward, as your data list scrolls down the screen, the titles for your data fields will remain visible.*

I sorted my list into alphabetical order, but now I want to restore it to the original entry order. Is there a way to go back to the original order?

As with any Excel operation, if you catch it early enough, you can choose Undo and go back to the previous step (and sometimes go back several previous steps). If, however, you changed the order of your data list, and then saved and closed the file, the new order reigns, and the former order is no longer retrievable.

Here's a tip that has been useful to many people I know who work with data lists. Once you begin sorting lists (see the "Sorting and Subtotaling Data" section later in this chapter) and changing the order of information, the integrity of the original list can be lost. To enable yourself to always return to the original list in the order in which entries were made, incorporate a separate field into your database that is a numerical field (you can call this field *Number*, *Order*, or some other appropriate term).

Allow this field to increment by one each time you make a new entry in the list, so that the first record you enter will be record number 1, the second number 2, the third number 3, and so on. Later, when you have manipulated your data and reorganized the order of the records, you can return to the original order by simply sorting the entire list based on this Number field (sorting techniques are covered later in this chapter).

SEARCHING FOR DATA

 All the information has been entered in my data list. Now how do find the information I'm looking for?

There are several techniques for finding data, ranging from a basic find command that locates one piece of information at a time, to a more sophisticated find command that locates all records that match in a particular field, to advanced search techniques that find records meeting multiple criteria.

For a very basic search, forget about the data commands and choose Edit | Find. In the box that appears (see Figure 11-1), enter the word(s) or number(s) for which you want to search, and click the Find button. You will be taken to the first occurrence of the information you typed. Continue to click Find Next in this box and the search will continue throughout the list, identifying each member of the list that matches the information you typed, one by one.

Use Excel's AutoFilter feature for a more extensive search. Click anywhere in your list (you don't have to select the list first). Choose Data | Filter | AutoFilter. An arrow will appear at the top of each column in your database across from the field title. Click the arrow for the field within which you want to search. A list will appear showing each unique entry in that field. Click on the entry you wish to find.

For example, if you want to locate all of your customers with a 46464 zip code, turn on AutoFilter, click the arrow in the zip code column, and click on 46464. Your data list will now include only those members with the matching zip code.

Get your full date list back onscreen by clicking the zip code AutoFilter arrow again and choosing All. Alternatively, choose Data | Filter | AutoFilter to turn off the feature and return your entire list to the screen. See Table 11-2 for an explanation of all of your AutoFilter choices.

Find	? X
Find what:	
snakes	Find Next
	Close
Search: By Rows ▼ □ Match case	Replace...
Look in: Formulas ▼ □ Find entire cells only	

Figure 11-1 Choose Edit | Find to perform a basic search

AutoFilter Feature	What It Does
(All)	Displays the entire list of unfiltered data.
(Top 10…)	Displays the top *x* items or percent (by default, the top ten, but you can change this number to any amount) in terms of frequency with which they appear in your list.
(Custom…)	Enables you to customize the filtering choices (for example, find entries amounts greater than, less than, or equal to a certain amount).
Exact values	Choose from each of the unique values of records in this field.
(Blanks…)	Show only records containing a blank in this field.
(NonBlanks…)	Show only records containing an entry other than a blank in this field.

Table 11-2   AutoFilter Options

Just because data is not visible doesn't mean the missing records have left the building. If you look closely at a filtered list (see Figure 11-2), you will notice that the row numbers for items not included in the filtering have been hidden. The rows containing the missing records are still there, they are just not visible at this time. If you save and close the file in this filtered state, the filtering will still be in place the next time you open the file. You will always have the option to bring the hidden records back into view.

Tip: *Should you want to preserve a more permanent record of your data as it appears when certain filtering has been applied, you can print the worksheet, or you can copy the filtered data and paste it onto a new worksheet. Only the filtered portion of the data will copy, not the entire list.*

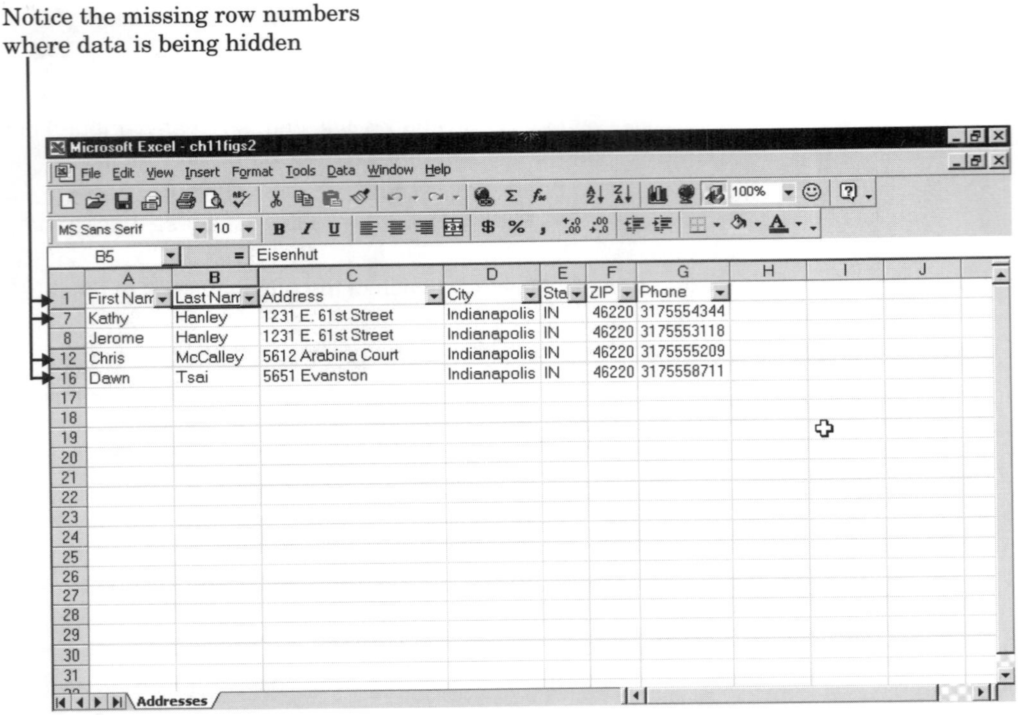

Notice the missing row numbers
where data is being hidden

Figure 11-2 The results of filtering a list to show only zip codes of 46220

AutoFilter doesn't perform advanced, complex tasks. For example, how can I show customers who live in one of four cities, whose last names begin with A–G, and who earn over $50,000?

The more complicated your search requirements, the more likely it is that you will need to go beyond the capabilities of the AutoFilter. You can use the Advanced Filter option to perform an advanced criteria search in which you create an area on your worksheet (called the *criteria range*) where you can enter any and all ingredients for your perfect matches.

Follow these steps to perform an advanced search:

1. Turn off the AutoFilter so that your entire database is displayed.

2. Create a blank area at the top of your database for entering criteria by inserting blank rows. This area will be called the criteria range. The number of blank rows you need will vary, depending on the quantity of criteria for which you wish to search. Inserting four blank rows is a good place to start—you can always add more rows later if you need to. (In the case of the example described in this question, you would want to have six blank rows, one for a header row, four for the criteria for which you will search, and one to separate the criteria range from the database.)

3. Use Copy and Paste to copy the header row from your database to the first row of your criteria range. Be sure to use Copy and Paste rather than retyping the header rows—this will ensure that every character in both sets of header rows matches. If the headings in your criteria range don't match those in your data list *exactly*, the Advanced Filter feature won't work.

4. In the first row under the headings of your criteria range, enter the information that you want to match. For example, if you want to find customers who live in a particular city, enter that city in the first blank row of the *City* column of your criteria range. To enter additional locations, enter each additional location in the next row of the criteria range. To search for other information, such as last names that begin with A–G, enter this information in the name column for each row that contains a city in the criteria range. In addition, enter the salary requirement in each of the criteria rows (greater than $50,000 should be entered as >*50000*).

5. Click somewhere in your main database, and choose Data | Filter | Advanced Filter.

6. In the Advanced Filter dialog box (see Figure 11-3), choose Filter the list, in-place, or choose Copy to another location. Click in the Criteria range text box, and then select the actual criteria range (include the header row, but do not include any blank rows). Click OK to perform the search.

 Tip: *Here's an option that might work for you: Give your criteria range a range name. That way you can refer to that name in the Criteria range text box in the Advance filter window. Be sure that there are no blank rows in your criteria range before assigning a range name.*

 Caution: *If the results of your advanced filter include the entire database, check the dimensions of your criteria range. Probably what happened is that you included a blank row with your criteria range.*

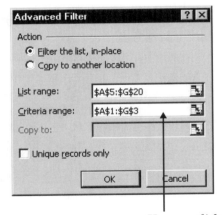

You can click here to temporarily collapse this window while you drag over the data range

Figure 11-3   Perform more sophisticated filters using the Advanced Filters dialog box

To return your entire database to the screen after you have performed an advanced filter, choose Data | Filter | Show All.

 Rather than reducing my onscreen database to show the results of my search, can I leave the database intact and place a copy of the search results in a new location?

When performing an advanced filter, choose Copy to another location in the Advanced Filter window. The Copy to area of this window will become available, and you can enter the range where you want the results of your filtering to appear.

You need only indicate one cell for your Copy to area; this cell will become the upper-left corner of your filtered data. You do not need to prepare this area of your worksheet with titles, because Excel will copy the title row from your database to this location.

Notice that your database and copy to range must occupy space on the same worksheet (see Figure 11-4). You cannot use other sheets for this information. The criteria range may appear on a separate sheet (sometimes this can be useful if the process is going to be automated for other users to keep the absolute integrity of the data worksheet intact). Once you have performed the filtering operation, you can copy the filtered data to another sheet.

Figure 11-4   This message appears if you attempt to refer to a location on another sheet in your filtering operation

 I have data stored in a relational database in Microsoft Access. How can I pull some of that information into Excel so that I can work with the data in a spreadsheet format?

Microsoft Query is a little program that provides a communication link between Excel and other database programs. With MS Query, you establish the criteria for the type of data you want to cull from the database, and then you command the program to search the database for qualifying data and enter that data into your Excel worksheet.

Start by opening an empty worksheet. Choose Data | Get External Data | New Database Query (see the Note below if this procedure results in an error message).

 Note: *Should you see a message indicating that MS Query has not been installed on your computer, choose Tools | Add-Ins. Check the MS Query Add-in option, then click OK. Follow the on-screen prompts to install MS Query.*

In the Choose Data Source window that appears, indicate the source of your data (an MS Access Database, for example), and then click OK. In the window that appears, indicate the name of the file containing your data and click OK. The Query Wizard will appear, listing all the tables in the chosen database (see Figure 11-5).

Indicate a table by clicking on the table name, then clicking the > button. All fields in that table will appear. You can add fields from additional tables by clicking on each table and clicking the > button. When all fields you want to use are displayed in the Columns in your query list, click Next.

Choose a column from which you want to filter data. For example, choose a date column and indicate a range of dates that is acceptable for this query, such as:

is greater than or equal to	1/1/98
is less than	1/1/99

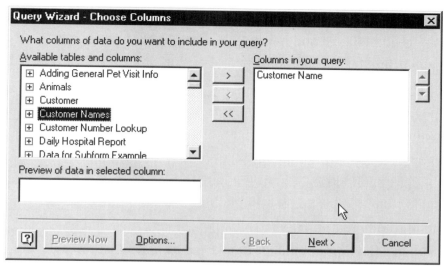

Figure 11-5 Step 1 of the Query Wizard

Click on any additional columns you want to filter and enter the filtering information. When you have entered all filtering information, click Next. Choose the fields (up to three) by which you want to sort the data, then click Next. Indicate that you want to Return the data to Microsoft Excel, and click Finish.

You will be asked for the location where you want to place the data (see Figure 11-6). You need only indicate one cell, which will become the upper-left corner cell of the incoming data. When the data appears in your worksheet, you may make changes to the data without affecting the information in your database.

 I have a large database of items that need to be tested randomly. How can I perform a random selection of items in my database?

You can request Excel's random number generator to produce the desired results by combining the RAND function (which returns a random number between 0 and 1) with the INT

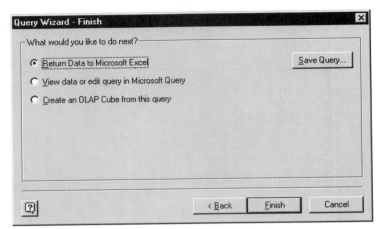

Figure 11-6 Choose Return Data to Microsoft Excel so you can manipulate this data in your worksheet

function (which will request an integer instead of a decimal), and the INDIRECT function (which returns a string of text). The result will be the random selection of a cell reference.

Here's a function you can use to randomly choose a cell in column A from row 3 to row 128:

=INDIRECT("a"&INT(RAND()*(128-3)+3))

RAND()*(128-3)+3 produces a random number from 3 to 128.

INT forces the random number to be an integer

INDIRECT requests a cell reference in column A ("a")

Tip: *Whenever a RAND function exists in your worksheet, you can force the function to recalculate by pressing the F9 key. Each time you press F9, you get a new random selection.*

SORTING AND SUBTOTALING DATA

I can sort my database one column at a time by using the A–Z and Z-A sort buttons on my standard toolbar. But how do I perform more sophisticated sorts?

Don't be deterred by the simplicity of the sort buttons on the toolbar. The sort buttons will work for multilevel sorts, they

just work backward. For a two-layer sort, the secondary sort is done first and the primary is done last. This reverse sort technique is especially useful if you need to sort by more than three criteria because the Data Sort command (discussed next) only provides a sort by three criteria.

Sort your data by up to three different criteria at once using the Data Sort command. Choose Data | Sort, and the Sort window will appear (see Figure 11-7). Click Header row or No header row to indicate whether the first row of the list contains data or titles. Choose the primary sort column in the Sort by area and indicate whether this sort is to be in ascending or descending order. Choose one or two more sort criteria if desired. Click OK to perform the sort on your list.

Excel assumes you want to sort the entire list. If you only need to sort a portion of the list—the first 100 rows, for example—select that portion of the list before requesting the sort.

How are subtotals entered into an Excel list?

You can choose to enter subtotals at appropriate stopping points in your list by first sorting your list so that the information you want to subtotal is grouped together. Then

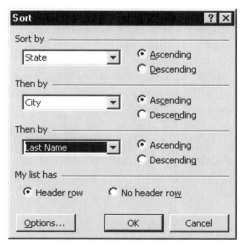

Figure 11-7 Choose up to three sort criteria for sorting a data list

choose Data | Subtotals. Indicate in which field of the database you want subtotal breaks to occur. There are eleven options for calculating the subtotal:

- **Sum** provides the sum of numbers in the group.
- **Count** provides the quantity of items in the group.
- **Average** provides the average of the numbers in the group.
- **Max** provides the highest number from the group.
- **Min** provides the lowest number from the group.
- **Product** returns the product of all numbers in the group multiplied together.
- **Count Nums** returns the quantity of all items in the group that are numeric.
- **StdDev** returns a measure of how widely the numbers in the group vary from the average.
- **StdDevp** returns the measure of how widely numbers in a group vary from the average of the entire population.
- **Var** returns a measure of the variance of numbers in the group.
- **Varp** returns a measure of the variance of the numbers in the group compared to the entire population.

Indicate in which column you want the subtotal to appear. If earlier subtotals exist in the list, check Replace current subtotals if you want to remove the earlier subtotals before inserting the new subtotals. You don't have to remove earlier subtotals—you may want to leave the original subtotals intact and include additional, nested subtotals within subtotaled groups. Indicate if you want each subtotaled group to appear on a separate page, and check Summary below data if you want the subtotal to appear beneath the data being totaled, instead of above the data. Click OK to execute the subtotal command.

Tip: *You can collapse a database that contains subtotals so that only the lines containing subtotals appear. Click the minus signs that appear to the left of the worksheet (see Figure 11-8) to collapse the data; click the resulting plus signs to expand the data to its original form.*

What is the purpose of the database functions that are available in Excel?

Excel's database functions (called *d-functions*, because they all begin with the letter *d*), work with the information in your criteria range, enabling you to perform familiar functions on only the portion of the data that meets certain criteria. For example, in the Prize Inventory list shown in Figure 11-9, you can sum all the prizes that will be used as consolation

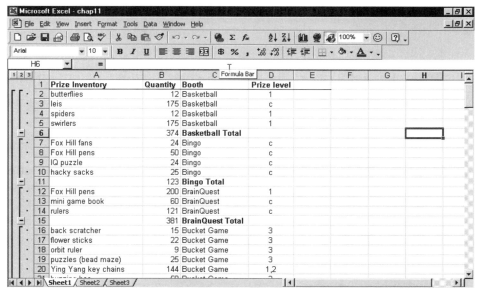

Figure 11-8 Minus signs at the side of your data list indicate collapsible sections

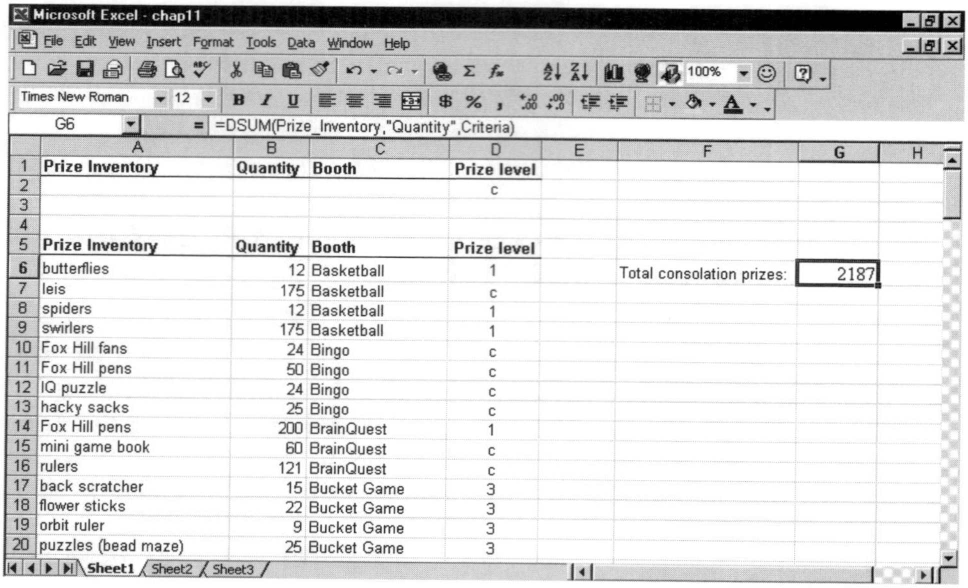

	A	B	C	D	E	F	G	H
1	**Prize Inventory**	**Quantity**	**Booth**	**Prize level**				
2				c				
3								
4								
5	**Prize Inventory**	**Quantity**	**Booth**	**Prize level**				
6	butterflies	12	Basketball	1		Total consolation prizes:	2187	
7	leis	175	Basketball	c				
8	spiders	12	Basketball	1				
9	swirlers	175	Basketball	1				
10	Fox Hill fans	24	Bingo	c				
11	Fox Hill pens	50	Bingo	c				
12	IQ puzzle	24	Bingo	c				
13	hacky sacks	25	Bingo	c				
14	Fox Hill pens	200	BrainQuest	1				
15	mini game book	60	BrainQuest	c				
16	rulers	121	BrainQuest	c				
17	back scratcher	15	Bucket Game	3				
18	flower sticks	22	Bucket Game	3				
19	orbit ruler	9	Bucket Game	3				
20	puzzles (bead maze)	25	Bucket Game	3				

Figure 11-9 Use database functions to apply the function to only the designated portion of the data

prizes in the carnival games (designated by the letter *c*) by entering **c** in the designation area of the criteria range, then using the DSUM function to total the prizes as follows:

=DSUM(Prize_Inventory,"Quantity",Criteria)

Use other database functions in the same manner, referring to the criteria range to designate to which members of the database the function applies.

Available database functions include:

- **DCOUNT** Returns a count of the quantity of items that meet the criteria in the designated field.
- **DCOUNTA** Returns a count of the quantity of items with numerical value that meet the criteria in the designated field.
- **DMAX** Returns the highest number of items that meet the criteria in the designated field.

- **DMIN** Returns the lowest number of items that meet the criteria in the designated field.

- **DSUM** Returns the sum of all items that meet the criteria in the designated field criteria.

- **DPRODUCT** Returns the product of all items that meet the criteria in the designated field.

- **DAVERAGE** Returns the average value of all items that meet the criteria in the designated field.

- **DSTDEV** Returns the estimated standard deviation for items that meet the criteria in the designated field, if the data is a sample of the total database.

- **DSTDEVP** Returns the standard deviation for items that meet the criteria in the designated field, if the data includes the entire database.

- **DVAR** Returns the variance for items that meet the criteria in the designated field, if the data is a sample of the total database.

- **DVARP** Returns the variance for items that meet the criteria in the designated field, if the data includes the entire database.

- **DGET** Returns a single item that meets the criteria. If more than one item meets the criteria, an error message is encountered.

Chapter 12

Customizing Excel

Answer Topics!

Customizing Excel @ a Glance

Evolution of Spreadsheets. I can still remember the first time I ever used a computer spreadsheet program. The year was 1980 and the program was VisiCalc. Rows and columns, numbers and formulas. Each formula changed automatically when I entered a new number. That's all. No fancy selection of typeface (no way, not with a nine-pin dot matrix printer). No centering, no borders, no underlining. No bold type, no changing the height of rows. Just rows and columns, numbers and formulas. We spreadsheet pioneers took what we got, and gladly. After all, we were fresh from the ledger books and art gum erasers. So what if the typeface was boring—at least we didn't have to write it by hand! So what if the column width was limited? We just limited the number of decimal places. Now, 20 years later, spreadsheet programmers give us a program that not only has interesting typefaces and stretchable columns, but capabilities beyond our wildest circa 1980 imagination. We're no longer stuck with the dimensions and styles chosen by the programmers. We can create our own spreadsheet world by customizing our program to suit ourselves. This chapter presents information about a numbers of customizing techniques. Experiment with the topics discussed here, and you'll no doubt be ready to head off in your own direction, finding new frontiers to customize.

Changing Excel's Default Features. Create your own default settings that will be available to you every time you open a new worksheet in Excel. Some defaults can be easily set right from within the Excel program.

Changing and Creating Menus. Tired of the same old menu bar? You can remove menu choices that you never use, add your own custom menu, and place frequently used commands on the menus. Remove a menu choice by mistake? It's no problem to reinstate the default Excel menus.

Creating Custom Toolbars. Don't stop with the menus. You can add and remove buttons from Excel's toolbars, or even create your own personal toolbar filled with only the commands you use most often.

 Other Customizing Options. Do you find that nutty little Office Assistant a bit too annoying? You can make him behave with a few clicks of the mouse. You can also create your own functions and make them available in the same way that the other functions in Excel are.

CHANGING EXCEL'S DEFAULT FEATURES

 Every time I create a worksheet, I have to change several of the settings. How can I change the overall default layout of my worksheet so that it will always include the features I need?

Excel comes to us already packaged with default features such as a typeface (Arial, size 10), a column width (8.43), alignments (right for numbers, left for text), a number format (no commas, no decimal places unless you add them), margins (1 inch, top and bottom, .75 inch right and left), and so on.

These features may be acceptable to you, or you may find yourself frequently changing the basic setup of your workbook to incorporate other features. You can save the features you want to use over and over again in such a way that Excel will always apply your choices when a new workbook is opened.

To create your own default workbook, incorporating any formatting settings you want to use, follow these steps:

1. Open a blank workbook.

2. Without entering information in the cells, make all the formatting adjustments that you want to view on new workbooks from this point forward.

3. Choose File | Save. The Save As window will appear.

4. Enter Book as the name of this file.

5. Change the Save in location to the XLStart folder, which is located as a subfolder under the Excel folder (this folder is not always easy to find—I found mine under Windows\ Application Data\Microsoft).

6. In the Save as type area of the Save As window, enter Template (see Figure 12-1).

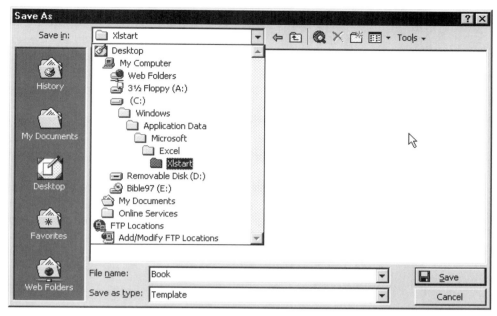

Figure 12-1 Save the Book file containing your default settings in the XLStart folder

Click the Save button. From this point forward, each time you open a new workbook, Excel will look to see if there is a book file in the XLStart folder. If it finds one, the formatting options you used in this file will be applied in the every new workbook you open.

 Caution: Make sure you save your default template in the correct folder. There are two XLStart folders on my computer. One is found in the Microsoft Office folder, and the other is located at Windows\Application Data\Microsoft\ Excel\XLStart. You may have to experiment to learn which one you are supposed to use. I use the XLStart that exists as a subfolder under the Excel folder (where you should save the default template), because Excel has problems finding the file in the other folder. My problem may be a result of having multiple installations of Excel on my machine at one time. In any case, if you place a file in one XLStart folder and nothing seems to change when you open a new workbook, try searching for another XLStart folder and placing the file there.

> ! **Caution:**   *If you are using Excel on a network and the XLStart folder is in a shared location, problems may arise whenever any files are placed in this folder. A wiser solution is to have users rely on the XLStart folder on their own hard drives for saving a default Excel template.*

A similar process applies to individual sheets in your workbook. When you choose the Insert Worksheet command, Excel applies certain default features to the new worksheet. You can choose which features will apply by creating a template called Sheet and saving this template in the XLStart folder, as you did with the Book file. Each time you insert a new worksheet, Excel will look to this file for formatting instructions.

 ## How can I change the default font on my workbooks?

There are several default commands that you can set from within any Excel worksheet, and you don't have to create a book template (as described in the previous answer) to apply these changes. The default settings are available to you in the Options window, which is found on the Tools menu.

Choose Tools | Options. The Options window will appear (see Figure 12-2). Most of the changes you make in this window become default changes and will be applicable in all future workbooks.

To change the default font, click the General tab. In the Standard font area, enter the font and font size you wish to apply to all future workbooks. This change will not affect workbooks created previously in Excel.

Notice that in this window you can also set the default file location. Enter the name of the drive and folder (and subfolder, if you wish) where Excel should look when you choose the File | Open command. This will also be the folder Excel will use to save new workbooks, unless you specify otherwise at the time of the save operation.

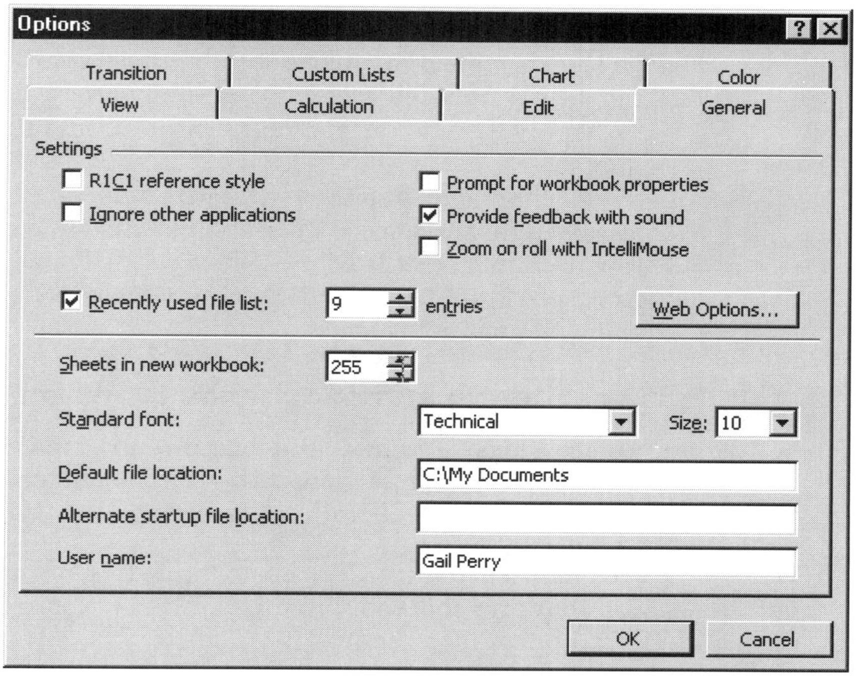

Figure 12-2 Selections made in the Options Window remain in place until you go back and change them

CHANGING AND CREATING MENUS

The menus in Excel keep sliding up and down, sometimes displaying many choices, sometimes only showing a few. What is happening and how can I control this?

Excel has gotten intelligent (if you can call it that) about menus in its 2000 version. Instead of bothering you with commands you never use, the newer, gentler Excel displays short menus that don't include all the commands. To see all the commands from a short menu, click the double arrow at the bottom of a menu. The menu will expand to show the entire array of choices for that menu topic.

How does Excel know which menu choices to include on the shortened menus? Actually, these short menus are constantly updated and customized by Excel, they're designed to display the choices you make most frequently from those menus.

To change this so that the entire selection of menu choices always appears, choose Tools | Customize. Click the Options tab, and uncheck the Menus show recently used commands first box. From this point forward, your Excel menus will show all available choices.

 ## Is it possible to add commands to my menus?

You can choose from a large list of commands to add to your menus. For example, to add the Double Underline command to the Format menu, follow these steps:

1. Choose Tools | Customize (or right-click on the menu bar and choose Customize). The Customize window will appear (see Figure 12-3).

2. Click the Commands tab. A Categories list will appear on the left, showing major groupings of Excel commands. Clicking on a category choice causes Excel to display a list in the Commands area of commands available in that category.

3. Click the Format category, and find the Double Underline command in the Commands area.

4. Use your mouse to drag the command from the Commands area up to the Format menu. The Format menu will drop down, displaying the commands currently listed there. Continue to drag, moving your mouse pointer down the length of the Format menu, until a horizontal bar appears at the location where you want the Double Underline command to appear.

5. Release your mouse button, then click the Close button in the Options window. From this point forward, the Double Underline command will appear on your Format menu.

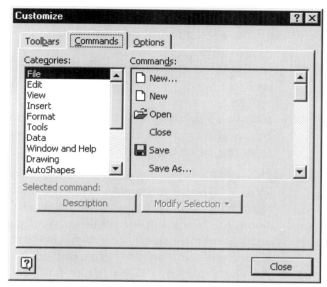

Figure 12-3 You can add to your menus by dragging commands from this window

Okay, I've added a command to my menu. How about going the other way. Can I delete a menu command?

Deleting commands from menus is even easier than adding commands. Choose Tools | Customize. With the Customize window open onscreen (it doesn't matter which tab is active), click on the menu that contains the unwanted command. Place your mouse right over the command you want to remove, and drag the command off the menu and down into the white area of your worksheet.

Click the Close button in the Customize window and the command will be officially removed from your menu.

Now I've done it. I went too far and removed a menu command that I really need. How do I return the menu to its original state?

If you removed a menu command by accident, you have two choices for reinstating the command. You can put the command back on the menu by dragging the command from

the Customize window (as described earlier in the question about adding menu commands).

Alternatively, you can open the Customize window (Tools | Customize), and click the Toolbars tab. Scroll down the list of toolbars until you come to Worksheet Menu Bar. Click on Worksheet Menu Bar to select it. Click the Reset button. Excel will ask you if you're sure you want to reset the menu bar. Click Yes, and then Close, and your menu bar will be restored to its original, default status.

Tip: *When you reset your menus to the default, any customizations that appeared on your menu bar will be removed. If you want to save some of your menu settings but need to restore the default to find some original settings that have been lost, consider creating a new menu that you can save and use later. After all, a menu is nothing more than a toolbar with text instead of buttons. Create a custom toolbar with the commands you want, right-click on each button, and choose Text Only (Always).*

Caution: *When you restore original menu choices by clicking the Reset button, you may find that your menu has disappeared altogether. Don't panic! Return to Tools | Customize, and look closely at that list of toolbars. It's possible you unchecked the Worksheet Menu Bar checkbox when you were resetting the menu. Check the box, then click Close, and presto! Your menu will reappear.*

 Rather than adding commands to an existing menu, is there a way to create my own complete menu and fill it with my own favorite commands?

It's easy to create your own menu. In fact, it's really more efficient to create your own menu than it is to add to the existing menus. When everything you want is on your own menu, your commands are much easier to find than if you have to look through all the existing menus. Be sure to read the following Caution about customizing menus.

> ! **Caution:** *Here's a good argument for creating your own menus and toolbars and leaving the existing ones intact. Every modification to existing menus and toolbars can make it more difficult for someone else who is using the PC, reading and following documentation, or getting support via telephone. If there are instructions that say click x, and x has been removed, it adds a new layer of problems in learning the new task.*

Choose Tools | Customize. The Customize window will appear. Click on the Commands tab. From the Categories list at the left, choose New Menu (see Figure 12-4). Drag the New Menu from the Commands part of the window up to the menu bar, placing it where you would like it to reside. Click the Modify Selection button in the Customize window to change the name of the menu, place an ampersand before the letter you wish to have underlined, and then press Enter (see Figure 12-5).

Select the commands you wish to add to your menu by clicking on categories, then choosing commands from the

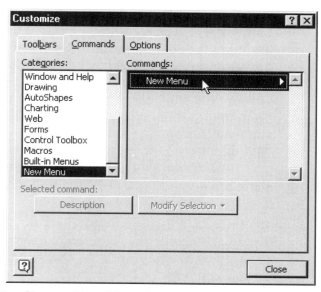

Figure 12-4 Choose New Menu from the Category list, then drag the New Menu command to your menu bar

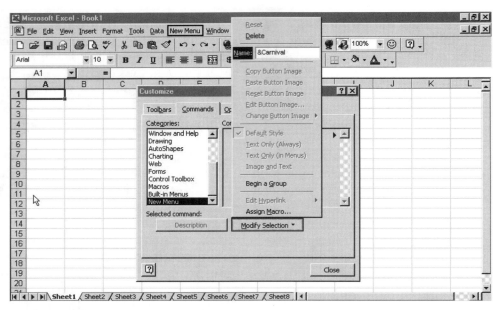

Figure 12-5 Enter a name for your menu, using the ampersand to indicate which letter should be underlined

Commands list. Drag each command to the new menu by dragging the command right onto the menu title, then dragging it down to the box beneath the title. Place each command in the order in which you wish the command to appear (you can change the order of commands by dragging them up or down on the menu). Right-click on menu items if you want to change names (in particular, be sure that you don't have overlapping underlined letters).

You can also establish groups on your new menu. Right-click on a menu choice and then choose Begin a Group to place a horizontal bar above that choice on the menu.

Tip: *You can create a menu to hold your macros. Choose the Macros category from the Customize window, and then drag Custom Menu Item to your new menu. Right-click on the menu item, and choose Assign Macro. Choose the macro you want to assign from the macro list that appears. Right-click again on the menu choice, and change the name to one that describes your macro. (For more information on working with macros, see Chapter 15, "Excel Macros.")*

CREATING CUSTOM TOOLBARS

 There are certain commands I use all the time that I would like add to my toolbar. How can I do this?

Your toolbars are yours to alter, if you like (but see the Caution in previous answer). If there are buttons you don't need, you can either ignore them or get them out of the way. If you are cramped for toolbar space and want to add buttons of your own, consider removing the buttons for commands you rarely if ever use (see the next answer).

Right-click on any toolbar and choose Customize. When the Customize window appears, your onscreen toolbars are completely vulnerable to change.

To add a button to a toolbar, you must have the toolbar you want to edit visible. Generally, the Formatting and Standard toolbars are visible at the top of the Excel screen. If you want to add to a toolbar that is not currently showing onscreen, click the Toolbars tab of the Customize window, then check the box for the toolbar you wish to view.

Click the Commands tab in the Customize window, choose the category that contains the command you want to add to the toolbar, find the command in the command list, and drag the command to the toolbar, placing it where you want it to reside.

 How can I add those little gray bars to the toolbar so that my toolbar buttons are separated into groups?

You may have noticed that some toolbars contain small gray separators, which break the buttons into smaller groups. You can add a separator when the Customize window is open by right-clicking on a toolbar button and choosing Begin a Group. A vertical separator will appear to the left of the button on which you clicked. Change your mind? Right-click again on the same button and choose Begin a Group again. The feature will be deactivated and the vertical bar will disappear.

 There are some toolbar buttons I never use. How can I remove unnecessary toolbar buttons?

Remove unwanted toolbar buttons when the Customize window is open by dragging the buttons off the toolbar and dropping them off on your worksheet. The button will

completely disappear, and the toolbar will shrink and close in around the space vacated by the lost button. Note that there is no undo feature when you are editing your toolbars. If you drag a button off a toolbar by mistake, you can only replace it by finding the button on the Commands list in the Customize window and dragging it back to its original location.

I added a toolbar button and got text instead of a picture. How can I replace the text with a picture like those on the rest of the toolbar buttons?

You may have noticed that sometimes there are no little pictures associated with the command choices, and that if you drag one of these commands on to your toolbar, you get text instead of an icon. You can add your own icon, replacing the text, by following these steps:

1. Right-click on the text button that you want to change. A pop-up menu will appear (see Figure 12-6).

2. Choose Default Style. The text in the button will disappear and you will be left with a blank box (see Figure 12-7).

3. Right-click again, and choose Change Button Image. An array of button image choices will appear (see Figure 12-8).

4. Click on any image to use that image for your toolbar button.

None of the pictures available for toolbar buttons provides a logical illustration of what the button does. Can I create my own toolbar button?

If the selection of available toolbar button images is not to your liking (and if you have a smidgeon of artistic talent), you can create your own image from scratch. With the Customize window open, right-click on the button for which you want to create an image. Choose Edit button image. The Button

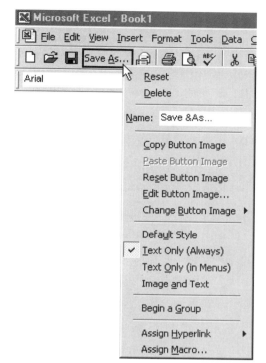

Figure 12-6   You can change the appearance of toolbar buttons with options on this pop-up menu

Editor will appear (see Figure 12-9). Click on a color, then click the little squares in the Picture box to create your own design. You'll see a button-sized preview of your work while you are experimenting. When you are satisfied, click OK. Your image will replace the blank box on the toolbar.

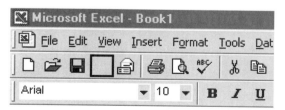

Figure 12-7   The blank button is ready to receive an image

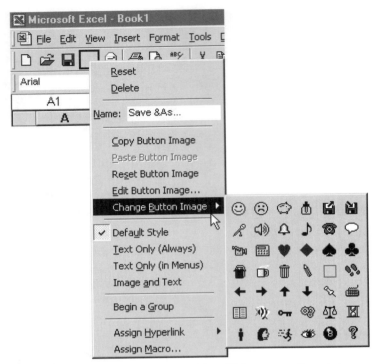

Figure 12-8 Click on any image and it will become the picture on your toolbar button

Tip: Is there a button you see in another Microsoft program that you like and would like to copy onto your Excel toolbar button? Open the other program (Word, for example). Right-click on a toolbar in that program and choose Customize. Either find an example of the button you want to use on a visible toolbar, or find the command in the Commands list and drag the button to a toolbar (you can remove the button from the toolbar as soon as you make a copy of it). Right-click on the button, and choose Copy. (Don't forget to now remove the button if you don't want it on this toolbar.) Close the Customize window and close the program. Return to Excel, right-click on the button that will receive the copied image, and choose Paste. Voilá!

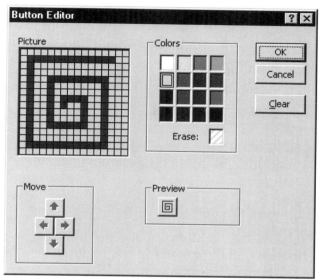

Figure 12-9 Create your own toolbar buttons in the Button Editor

I've created a toolbar nightmare. Is it possible to get my toolbars back to their original state?

If you change your mind after adding buttons to a toolbar and want to return the toolbar to its original state, right-click on the toolbar, choose Customize, click to put an "x" in the checkbox next to the toolbar name in the list on the Toolbars tab, then click Reset. Choose Yes, and Excel will change your toolbar back to the way it looked before you started playing with it.

I can add a button here and there to a toolbar, but I need to add lots of buttons. Can I make a completely new toolbar?

Sometimes it's easier to create your own toolbar, instead of changing one that already exists. There may not be room to add all the buttons you need to an existing toolbar, or you may not need access to the tools all the time. Consider creating your own toolbar that you can display when you need it and hide when you don't.

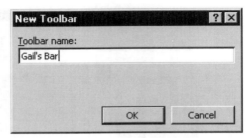

Figure 12-10 Enter a name that will distinguish your new toolbar from others in the program

Choose Tools | Customize (or right-click on any toolbar and choose Customize). On the Toolbars tab, click the New button. In the window that appears, enter a name for your new toolbar (see Figure 12-10). Click OK. The toolbar will appear on your screen, floating on your desktop. Add buttons to this toolbar just as you would to any toolbar, finding each command and dragging the button to your new toolbar.

If you want to add macros to your toolbar, choose Macros from the Categories list on the Commands tab, then drag Custom Button to your toolbar. Edit or replace the button picture as described in the previous question.

OTHER CUSTOMIZING OPTIONS

 The animated paper clip drives me crazy! How can I make this little guy leave me alone, or at least change its appearance?

Excel's Office Assistant (and he doesn't only belong to Excel—you'll see him in other Microsoft Office products as well), is a fairly new form of interactive help. While you're working, and sometimes when you least expect it, the Office Assistant pokes his head into your projects and offers advice, tips, and the opportunity for you to ask questions. You can also call on him yourself by pressing F1, or by choosing Help | Microsoft Excel Help. There is an Office Assistant button on the standard toolbar (see Figure 12-11) that will page the little guy as well.

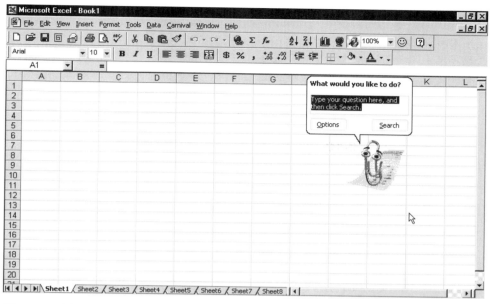

Figure 12-11   If you don't see a place to enter a question, click once on the Office Assistant and his Q&A balloon will appear

The Office Assistant provides you with an area for writing questions. You can enter questions written in plain English or enter key words and forget about sentence structure, then click the Search button or press Enter. The Office Assistant will scurry around through the Help archives searching for the answer to your question. He will provide you with various topics from which you may choose to see more information on (see Figure 12-12).

Choose a topic from the list provided by the Office Assistant and double-click or press ENTER. A detailed Help screen will appear, providing you with a description and examples of the topic you requested.

Change the look of your Office Assistant by right-clicking on the character and choosing Choose Assistant. Click Next (or Prev) to flip through the gallery of animated characters. If the characters have not yet been installed, Excel will give you a message to that effect. The message will provide instructions for installation.

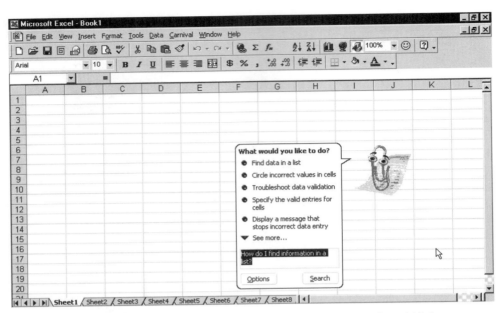

Figure 12-12   Click on one of these topics to see the related Help screens

Click the Options tab to select which features you want to apply to your personal Office Assistant (see Figure 12-13).

If you are not a big fan of the Office Assistant, click the Use the Office Assistant option to uncheck the box and remove him from sight. When the Office Assistant is turned off in this way, you will go right to the Help Index when you press F1 or choose Help | Microsoft Excel Help. Miss the little guy? Bring back the Office Assistant by choosing Help | Show the Office Assistant.

Excel comes with all sorts of built-in functions. Is it possible to make my own complex formulas into functions and add them to the list in the Function Wizard?

You can create your own functions in Excel and add them to the Function Wizard list so that you can easily call up your function just as you would the AVERAGE or the COUNT function. This is a great time-saver if you need to execute complicated calculations. Not only can you condense your calculations into one simple function, this function can be

Uncheck this box if you want the
Office Assistant to leave you alone

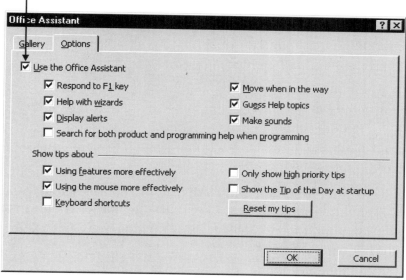

Figure 12-13 Modify your Office Assistant's behavior with this window
of options

made available to all of your other Excel worksheets. Create
the function once, and never worry about having to create
it again.

For example, suppose you need to be able to calculate
corporate income tax on your worksheets. The corporate
income tax is calculated in modules, with the rates changing
depending on the income of the taxpaying entity. The
corporate rate structure (rates effective for 1999) is shown in
Table 12-1.

You could create a nested IF statement to accommodate
this tax structure and calculate the tax. However, this is a
complicated calculation, and having to recreate this formula
every time you want to calculate corporate income tax would
be time-consuming and cumbersome. And what if you want
someone else in your organization to be able to use this
formula, but that person is not adept at creating formulas
and will not be able to figure out how to write an efficient
IF statement?

Create a function called CorpTax using the Visual Basic
Editor. The function will automatically appear in your

Taxable income over...	But not over...	The tax is	Of the amount over...
0	50,000	15%	0
50,000	75,000	7,500+25%	50,000
75,000	100,000	13,750+34%	75,000
100,000	335,000	22,250+39%	100,000
335,000	10,000,000	113,900+34%	335,000
10,000,000	15,000,000	3,400,000+35%	10,000,000
15,000,000	18,333,333	5,150,000+38%	15,000,000
18,333,333		35%	0

Table 12-1 Corporate Tax Rates

function list, so that it will be accessible from the Function Wizard. Just take a look at how easy this process is:

Open the Visual Basic editor by choosing Tools | Macros | Visual Basic Editor. In the Project list at the left of the screen, click VBAProject (PERSONAL.XLS), then create a new module by choosing Insert Module. You will use this module for storing your functions. On the Personal.xls module screen that appears (see Figure 12-14), begin entering your function by entering the following on the first line:

```
Function CorpTax(Income)
```

The word Function tells Excel that this is a function. CorpTax is the name given to the function. This is the name that will appear on the Function Wizard list. Income is the name of the variable. When you execute this function, it will ask you to identify the cell containing Income.

The entire function for calculating corporate income tax looks like this:

```
Function CorpTax(Income)
Select Case Income
Case Is > 18333333: CorpTax = Income * 0.35
Case Is > 15000000: CorpTax = 5150000 + (Income - 15000000) * 0.38
Case Is > 10000000: CorpTax = 3400000 + (Income - 10000000) * 0.35
Case Is > 335000: CorpTax = 113900 + (Income - 335000) * 0.34
Case Is > 100000: CorpTax = 22250 + (Income - 100000) * 0.39
Case Is > 75000: CorpTax = 13750 + (Income - 75000) * 0.34
Case Is > 50000: CorpTax = 7500 + (Income - 50000) * 0.25
Case Is > 0: CorpTax = Income * 0.15
End Select
End Function
```

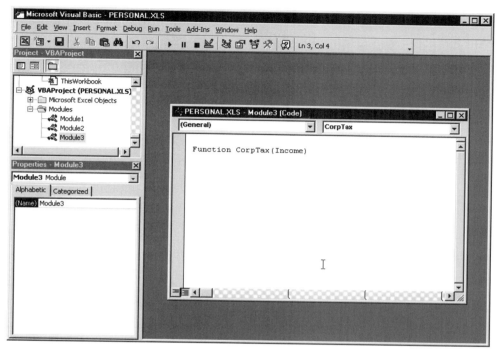

Figure 12-14 Entering your function in a module of the PERSONAL.XLS project will make the function available to all worksheets

Close the Visual Basic Editor, and you will be returned to your worksheet. To try out this function, enter a sample corporate income amount in a cell, then click on the cell where you want the tax to be calculated. Click the Paste Function button and choose CorpTax from the All list. Click OK and you will be asked to identify the cell containing the Income. Click on the appropriate cell, then click OK. The tax will be calculated (see Figure 12-15). Experiment some more by changing the income amount on your worksheet and watch the tax recalculate.

 Note: *You must use the Paste function tool or enter =Personal.xls!corptax(...) for your new function to work. Just typing =Corptax(...) does not work.*

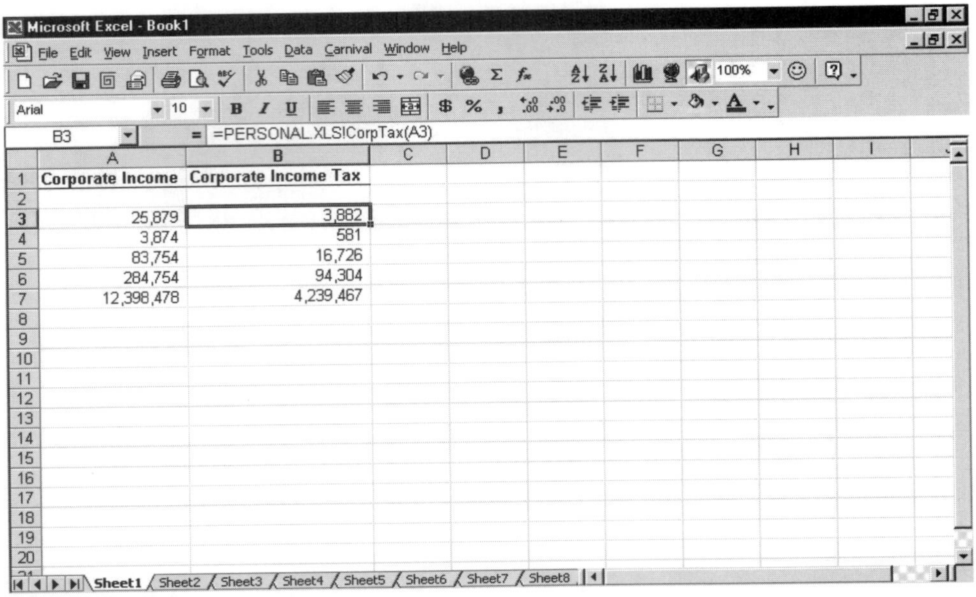

Figure 12-15 Use your new function and you'll save lots of time

Chapter 13

PivotTables in Excel

Answer Topics!

PivotTables @ a Glance

Overview. Excel excels at data analysis—looking at masses of data to summarize and discern trends and patterns that help in decision-making. The PivotTable feature takes an internal list or external database and instantly creates either a crosstab report (results are generated at the intersection of columns and rows) or control break report (results appear in subtotaled groups) that condenses the data into whatever categories you need. You have many options for viewing and formatting the spreadsheet report generated by a PivotTable to make it the most useful to you and to your organization.

Creating PivotTables. Use Excel to generate PivotTables to aid in data analysis. Create PivotTables quickly and manipulate your data easily right on the screen. Place fields where you want them, perform calculations on fields, and control the display of pages in PivotTables.

Controlling the Display of PivotTables. Don't feel you're locked in to the original display of the PivotTable you have created. Change the order and placement of fields, and view hidden details of your report. Delete a PivotTable when you're finished working with it, change the column headings that appear on your PivotTable, change the size of the table, or can even change the contents of cells within the PivotTable.

Working with PivotTables. Once created, a PivotTable can be updated. You can introduce subtotals into your PivotTable, sort by various types of information within your PivotTable, and produce a PivotChart based on the data in your PivotTable. The chart will update with your data.

CREATING PIVOTTABLES

 People keep telling me to make PivotTables from my data. What is a PivotTable, and why should I use one?

A PivotTable is an Excel summary report that can be easily and interactively manipulated so that you can change the type of summary totals that are produced. A PivotTable produces either *crosstab* reports or *control break* reports (these terms are both common in database management systems).

What is a crosstab report?

An example of a crosstab report is a mileage chart in an atlas on which, if you locate a city from the list on the side and a city from the list on the top, the intersection of the two cities tells you how many miles divide each city. Taking that a step further, a PivotTable can also sum, average, or perform other calculations at the intersection

More technically speaking, a crosstab report is a matrix that plots an attribute across the X axis and another across the Y axis. The intersecting matrix cells show the values of x at y. For example, you can create a matrix that shows the average attendance percentage of students at each school in a school district plotted by months. The school names would appear in the first column, and the 12 months of the year would be represented by 12 columns across the top. At the intersection of each school and month you would find the average attendance of students at that school in a particular month. It might come as no surprise that attendance is lighter in July than in months when school is regularly in session. However, this type of chart might also show that some schools in the district seem better able to keep their students in class during certain months in a regular school year. This kind of information would enable the school administration to see if the schools with the better attendance had some technique that could be shared with the other schools.

If you were to create this matrix by hand and enter in the formulas to calculate each cell, building the worksheet would be a lengthy and tedious process. Working from a list that contains the name of the school, the date, and the percent of students in attendance on that day, the PivotTable command builds this matrix for you in less than a minute.

What is a control break report?

You can also use a PivotTable to create control break reports. A control break report is a report that produces multiple levels of subtotals, called *breaks*. A classic example of a control break report is a report of product sales by customer type by region. In such a report, you might wish to see a listing that shows the region as its main break field, then lists all of the customer types in the region. You would see the total sales for each customer type broken down by product. Subtotals would be the sales for each customer type and the sales for each region. The PivotTable could also produce subtotals by product. You can see both row and column totals and subtotals. Figure 13-1 shows an extract from a PivotTable report in the control break style.

One of the main advantages of using the control break PivotTable feature is that it allows you to see totals of sales by region broken down by product, and, with a few clicks, you can change that to a report of products broken down by region, as shown in Figure 13-2.

PivotTables are also very useful as the basis of a chart. When you link a chart to the PivotTable (an option when you initially set up the PivotTable), the chart automatically updates if the PivotTable changes. You can also build very fast summaries of data by linking one PivotTable to another.

Book1

	Qtr (YYYY) Product	Customer Type	CT	MA	MW	NE	NW	SC	SW	TX	Grand Total
Sum of Extension			Region								
199901	Gadget	Large				50					50
		Medium		575							575
	Gadget Total			575		50					625
	Twiddle	Medium								2250	2250
	Twiddle Total									2250	2250
	Waddle	Large						500			500
		Medium	400								400
		Small		3400							3400
	Waddle Total		400	3400				500			4300
	Widget	Large				56					56
		Medium							140		140
	Widget Total					56			140		196
199901 Total			400	3975		106		500	140	2250	7371
199902	Gadget	Medium		575		300					875
	Gadget Total			575		300					875
	Twaddle	Medium					76				76
		Small			135						135
	Twaddle Total				135		76				211
	Waddle	Small				1500					1500
	Waddle Total					1500					1500
	Widget	Large		168							168
		Small								84	84
	Widget Total			168						84	252
199902 Total				743	135	1800	76			84	2838
199903	Gadget	Large	950								950
		Small						75	100		175
	Gadget Total		950					75	100		1125
	Widget	Medium								322	322
	Widget Total									322	322

Sheet4 / Sheet6 / Sheet7 / Sheet9 / Sheet8 \ **Sheet10** / Sheet1 / Sheet2 / Sheet3 /

Figure 13-1 You can get multiple levels of subtotals on a control break PivotTable report

Book1

Qtr (YYYYMM)	(All) ▼					
Sum of Extension	Product					
Region	Gadget	Twaddle	Twiddle	Waddle	Widget	Grand Total
CT	950			400		1350
MA	1150			3400	168	4718
MW		135				135
NE	350			1500	56	1906
NW		76				76
SC	75			500		575
SW	100				140	240
TX			2250		406	2656
Grand Total	2625	211	2250	5800	770	11656

Figure 13-2 You can change the PivotTable report to show sales of products by region

 ## How do I create a PivotTable?

Create a PivotTable using the PivotTable Wizard in Excel. This feature is installed when you install Excel.

1. You first need to have a list or a data region that you plan to use. The list can be on an Excel worksheet, or it can be located in an external database. See also the options noted in Step 3 below.

2. If the list is in an Excel worksheet, select any cell within the list. Note that the entire list must be located in contiguous cells for all of its information to be included in the PivotTable.

3. Choose Data | PivotTable | PivotChart Report. You are presented with the Step 1 dialog box, shown in Figure 13-3, which will ask you to specify the type of data that you will use as your source. Your source can be an Excel list or database, an external database, multiple consolidation ranges, or another PivotTable. Make your selection and then click the Next button.

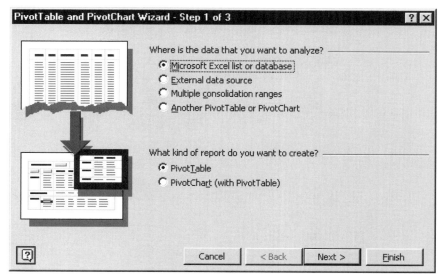

Figure 13-3   Select the source type for your PivotTable report

4. Choose whether you plan to create only a PivotTable or a PivotChart along with the PivotTable.

5. The Step 2 dialog box asks you to locate the source data. If you have already selected a cell in the source range, then the entire data list should be surrounded by a marquee. The full range is also shown in the Source field. Confirm that the range is correct and click on the Next button. If you plan to use an external database as the source data, click the Browse button and indicate the name of the file containing the data. Click OK when you have selected the file name, then click Next to continue the PivotTable Wizard.

6. Click the Layout button to design the PivotTable report, as shown in Figure 13-4. (If you choose not to click Layout at this time, you will design the report directly on the worksheet after the Wizard window closes.) All of the fields are shown as buttons at the right of the dialog box. There are four areas labeled Page, Row, Column,

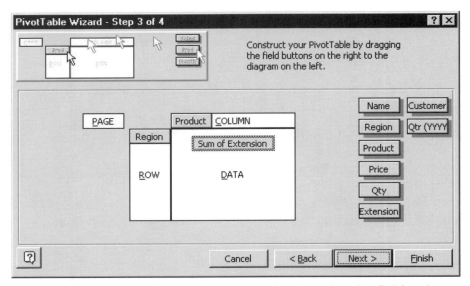

Figure 13-4 You can lay out your report by dragging the fields where you want them

and Data on the report form. You can drag any of the field buttons into any of these areas. Click OK when you have finished.

7. The final dialog box of the PivotTable Wizard asks where you want to place the PivotTable. You may select a new range on an existing worksheet or create a new worksheet. Your safest choice is to place the PivotTable on a new worksheet. Click on the Finish button to construct the PivotTable.

Where on the PivotTable Wizard can I place fields?

You can drag fields from your list onto four areas of the report layout screen. If you drag a field onto the Page area, your PivotTable will be based on the data in that area. For example, if you drag the Quarter field onto the Page area, then you will see one report page per quarter. The table won't break out multiple quarters at once. It will either allow you to view totals for one quarter at a time, or for all of the quarters together.

Note: *Choosing Page fields on your PivotTable layout causes Excel to print portions of the PivotTable on separate pages; it does not create separate workbook pages for each portion of the PivotTable.*

When you drag fields into the Row area, you specify the data that is to be summarized in each row of the report. For example, if you drag the Region field onto the Row area, each row of the report shows a different region. If there are seven regions, then your final report shows seven major rows.

The Column area, as you would expect, sets up the column headings across the top of the report. If you drop the Product field into the Column area, then each product's total is shown across the width of the table. If you have already defined the Rows area to contain the region, then you can see the performance for each product broken down into columns across the report, thus showing the performance for each region.

If you need to cause a field to be mathematically manipulated (or counted), drag that field into the Data area. If you drag a numeric field into the Data area, you will see the SUM OF that field by default. If you drag a non-numeric field into that area, the function defaults to COUNT OF. For example, if you drag the Extended Price field into the Data area, then you will see sales totals for each product and each region. The cell that intersects the Northeast region and the widget product shows the total sales of widgets in the Northeast.

You could also get a total of number of orders for each product by placing the salesperson's name in the data area. Since the name field occurs once per record and is not numeric, the function defaults to COUNT OF, thus giving you a count of orders.

 I don't want my data to show SUM OF or COUNT OF. Can I use any other calculations within a PivotTable?

When you drag a field into the data area of the PivotTable layout dialog box, numeric fields default to the SUM OF calculation, and non-numeric fields default to COUNT OF. You can select a different calculation by double-clicking on the specific field button after you've dropped it into position. The PivotTable Field dialog box opens and gives a choice of many other functions including Average, Min, Max, StdDev, etc.

You can drag a field into the data area multiple times, so that you can see both the sales totals and the average of sales, for example. Because the calculation differs, the PivotTable treats them as two different fields.

When you drag an existing field into the data area, you are limited to using the functions in the PivotTable Field dialog box. A new, advanced feature that first became available in Excel 97, that allows you to define both calculated fields and calculated items. This feature lets you define either a new field in the PivotTable for which you specify the formula, or a new category (such as a new item in the Product list for which no data yet exists). This way, you can forecast the results based on the performance of an existing set of data.

I dropped a field into the Page area on the PivotTable Wizard. Now I see a consolidated report with totals for my entire list. It looks like the PivotTable only added one page to my workbook. How do I find the other pages?

The term *page* in the PivotTable Wizard is probably a misnomer, because selecting this option doesn't add more pages to your workbook. If you look at the Page area at the top of your PivotTable on the worksheet, you'll notice that there is a drop-down box that most likely holds the current value of All. If you click on that box, a list of all values for the Page field pops up. If you select a specific value, all of the totals on the PivotTable will immediately recalculate so that you are filtering your list to only show values for the current page. This feature is similar to the AutoFilter tool that's used to filter information on a data list. Only the data that meets the filtering criteria appears on the list, even though all the underlying data remains intact and can be instantly retrieved by choosing Data | Filter | Show All.

But I really want to see a separate worksheet page for each page of my PivotTable report. How do I force the PivotTable pages onto separate worksheet pages?

You might actually want to see one page in your worksheet for each virtual page in the PivotTable report. If you need to print the PivotTable, for example, you might not want to select each page manually and print it. To add a worksheet for each page to your workbook, double-click on the Page field at the top of the worksheet. Use caution, however, if the PivotTable contains many values for the Page field. Because Excel keeps the entire PivotTable in memory, you could have a problem if you don't have enough RAM.

My database package gives me a control break report that lists the regions and for each region lists the salesperson. For each salesperson, I can get subtotals by product. Can I create a PivotTable that lets me view the data in this manner?

You can drop multiple fields into any of the four areas on the PivotTable Wizard Layout dialog box. To get a traditional-looking control break report, you might want to drop multiple fields into the Rows area. For example, using the Sales list again, if you drop Region, Salesperson, and Product into the Rows area and Extended Price into the Data area, you get a PivotTable that looks like the one in Figure 13-5. This shows a hierarchy of Region, Salesperson, and Product.

	A	B	C	D
1	Sum of Extension			
2	Region	Product	Name	Total
3	CT	Gadget	Coffee, Marlene	950
4		Gadget Total		950
5		Waddle	Coffee, Marlene	400
6		Waddle Total		400
7	CT Total			1350
8	MA	Gadget	Elias, Jack	1150
9		Gadget Total		1150
10		Waddle	Elias, Jack	3400
11		Waddle Total		3400
12		Widget	Elias, Jack	168
13		Widget Total		168
14	MA Total			4718
15	MW	Twaddle	Hunt, Frank	135
16		Twaddle Total		135
17	MW Total			135
18	NE	Gadget	Martin, John	350
19		Gadget Total		350
20		Waddle	Martin, John	1500
21		Waddle Total		1500
22		Widget	Martin, John	56
23		Widget Total		56
24	NE Total			1906
25	NW	Twaddle	Kummings, Anita	76
26		Twaddle Total		76
27	NW Total			76
28	SC	Gadget	Marley, Jeanne	75
29		Gadget Total		75
30		Waddle	Marley, Jeanne	500
31		Waddle Total		500

Sheet4 / Sheet6 / **Sheet7** / Sheet9 / Sheet8 / Sheet1 / Sh

Figure 13-5 A control break PivotTable hierarchy

CONTROLLING THE DISPLAY OF PIVOTTABLES

 What if I change my mind and want to see the PivotTable in a different order?

One of the best features of the PivotTable is that it is very easy to rearrange by either reopening the PivotTable Wizard or dragging the fields onto the PivotTable itself.

The PivotTable cells are not like "normal" cells. Since they are linked to underlying data, the individual cells cannot be typed into or replaced. However, the header fields that control the arrangement of the data can be easily changed.

If you reopen the PivotTable Wizard, you can simply drag the fields where you want them to be. Reopen the wizard by right-clicking on the PivotTable and choosing Wizard from the shortcut menu.

If you prefer to work right on the worksheet that contains the PivotTable, just point to the desired field and drag it around. If you decide that, instead of viewing sales by region, salesperson and product, you want to see the region and then the product sales by salesperson, simply place your cursor on the Name header and drag it to the left between the Region and the Product. Immediately, the PivotTable rearranges itself.

 How can I change the presentation of the data in my PivotTable so that the data fields are side-by-side instead of above and below one another?

The default arrangement of the PivotTable is to show data fields underneath each other if there is more than one field in one area. For example, if you dragged both the Quantity and the Extended Price fields into the Data area, the default report would show the total sales quantity on top of the total dollar value of the sales. However, this is not the way most users like to see the data.

If you want to see the two amounts next to one another instead of above and below one another, drag the Data field (see Figure 13-6) to the right. The report will reformat itself

Book1.xls

	A	B	C	D	E	F	G	H
1			Product					
2	Region	Data	Gadget	Twaddle	Twiddle	Waddle	Widget	Grand Total
3	CT	Sum of Extension	950			400		1350
4		Sum of Qty	38			4		42
5	MA	Sum of Extension	1150			3400	168	4718
6		Sum of Qty	46			34	12	92
7	MW	Sum of Extension		135				135
8		Sum of Qty		3				3
9	NE	Sum of Extension	350			1500	56	1906
10		Sum of Qty	14			15	4	33
11	NW	Sum of Extension		76				76
12		Sum of Qty		4				4
13	SC	Sum of Extension	75			500		575
14		Sum of Qty	3			5		8
15	SW	Sum of Extension	100				140	240
16		Sum of Qty	4				10	14
17	TX	Sum of Extension			2250		406	2656
18		Sum of Qty			45		29	74
19	Total Sum of Extension		2625	211	2250	5800	770	11656
20	Total Sum of Qty		105	7	45	58	55	270

Figure 13-6 Drag the Data field to the right to widen the report

so that it becomes wider and shorter (gains more columns and fewer rows).

I accidentally double-clicked on a cell and new page appeared in my workbook. What's happening?

You have stumbled over a feature in the PivotTable that lets you view the detail that is hidden in any summary. Double-clicking on a cell makes the hidden detail visible in a new table that is stored in a new worksheet in the current workbook.

You can take advantage of this feature by double-clicking to drill down and view the detail that makes up the amounts in your PivotTable.

I double-clicked on a cell and looked at the detail that makes up the number. Now that I'm finished viewing this information, how do I get rid of it?

There's no way to specifically undo this action (such as Edit | Undo), but notice that the detail is presented in a new worksheet. You can delete this new worksheet containing your detailed information by choosing Edit | Delete Sheet. Click OK in the window that appears, and the sheet will be permanently deleted. If you wish to view the detail information again, double-click again on the PivotTable cell, and a new sheet will open containing the detail.

Can I delete an entire PivotTable if I'm done with it?

You can toss away the worksheet that contains the PivotTable. You can also close the file in which you created the PivotTable without saving the changes to the file.

You may also delete the entire PivotTable, but you need to select the whole PivotTable first (including the headers and the Page label). A quick way to select the whole PivotTable is to click in the upper-left cell.

Note that you cannot delete part of a PivotTable. It's all or nothing.

When I click on a row or column header cell in my PivotTable, a whole bunch of cells are selected. What's going on?

You've just met an Excel PivotTable feature called *structured selection*. This is a fast way to select all similar cells at one time. It provides an easy way to highlight a group of similar data or to choose specific cells for formatting. You can turn structured selection off or on by following these steps.

1. While pointing to a particular type of data in your PivotTable, right-click to open the shortcut menu.
2. Choose Select from the shortcut menu.
3. Choose Enable Selection.

You may also tell the structured selection feature whether to select the label and the data, the label only, or the data only. If you prefer (although it might be of limited utility), you can also choose an option to select the entire table.

If Enable is turned on, you can point to the upper or left edge of a data label and wait for the cursor to turn into a small back arrow. When the arrow appears, you can click on

the data label, and all of the data of that type is selected. For example, if you click on the Region field, all of the names of the regions are selected. If you click on a cell that contains the name of a specific region (such as NE), than all of the data rows (or columns) that contain the value of "NE" are selected. If you have defined a PivotTable that shows sales by Product by Region, then clicking on a cell labeled NE immediately selects the performance of every product sold in the Northeast region.

How do I rename the PivotTable column headings?

Sometimes the PivotTable headings seem inappropriate. "Sum of Extension" or "Count of Name" are not very professional-sounding headings for a report that will be viewed by others. You can rename headings quite easily in the PivotTable report. Three methods for changing the heading names exist.

● The fastest way to rename a heading is to double-click on the heading name. A PivotTable Field window will appear showing the field (heading) name, along with information about how the field is computed. Simply type in the new name in the Name area of the window, then click OK. The new name will replace the original one.

● While the PivotTable Wizard is open (you can right-click on the PivotTable at any time and choose Wizard to reopen the wizard if you have already closed it), you can go to the Layout option, double-click on a field name, and then enter the new name in the Name field of the PivotTable Field dialog box.

● You can open the PivotTable Field dialog box at any time by right-clicking and selecting Field Settings from the shortcut menu.

You can save yourself some formatting headaches if you change the names of your fields when you first define them (prior to building the PivotTable). Excel auto-formats the

PivotTable to make the column width correspond to the size of the associated column label. Since the default names of COUNT OF and SUM OF, etc. are so long, your PivotTable tends to use much more space than it needs, which makes it harder for you to see the entire PivotTable at once. If you shorten the field name, Excel shortens the field—but only if the PivotTable does not yet exist.

You can name the fields whatever you wish. One major restriction exists, however. You cannot use the name of an existing field. If you have a field named Sales in your list, and you drag it into the data area of the PivotTable report layout, the default name of the field is probably SUM OF Sales. You cannot name it "Sales," even though that makes the most sense, because the field "Sales" already exists. You can add a space before or after "Sales," although that might be hard to remember, or you could name the field "Sales$," which is probably the best solution.

I changed all of my data labels to shorten the names. How do I get the table to "shrink" to fit the new names?

You can make the column sizes conform to shortened names by choosing Format | AutoFormat. The PivotTable uses the Classic 1 format by default, so selecting it again simply recalculates your column widths.

If you want to change the format of particular groups of cells, you can select the cells, then choose the Format Cells option by right-clicking to see the shortcut menu. Figure 13-7 shows the dialog box.

Sometimes it's easy to overlook the simplest solution. Probably the quickest way to change the width of your PivotTable columns, if the quantity of columns is not overwhelmingly large, is to drag through the column headers (A, B, C, and so on) for each column in the table, then double-click on one of the bars separating the selected columns. Excel will provide you with the best fit for each column.

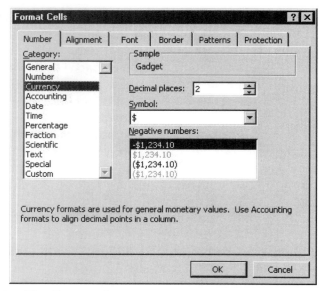

Figure 13-7 The Format Cells dialog box

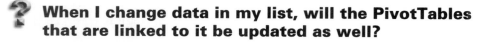 **What happens if I change the text in one cell of the PivotTable and that text is repeated elsewhere in the PivotTable?**

You can change the contents of any cell in the PivotTable. Click on a cell and edit the cell information, just as you would any cell in a worksheet. When you select a label cell to change its name interactively, it doesn't matter whether all similarly named cells are also selected. Changing one label changes them all.

WORKING WITH PIVOTTABLES

When I change data in my list, will the PivotTables that are linked to it be updated as well?

PivotTables are linked to the underlying data, but there is no automatic update process. If you change the linked data, you must select Data | Refresh Data to update it. This is true for both internal and external sources of data.

Refresh data quickly by clicking the Refresh Data button, which looks like an exclamation point, on the PivotTable toolbar. This toolbar appears when you create a PivotTable. If the PivotTable toolbar is not visible, right-click in the toolbar area of your worksheet, and choose PivotTable from the shortcut menu that appears.

I have a list that contains the data of each sale. Is there a way to total the sales by quarter or by other time periods?

You can group the dates into specific chunks of time. For example, assume you have a list that contains fields for all of your investment transactions: Stock, Price, Quantity, Transaction Amount, Date, Transaction Type (Buy or Sell), Stock Category. You want to plot your stock purchases by sale date, but there is too much detail. Each date in the list creates a new column in the report. Instead, you want to group the dates into quarters. To do this, follow these steps:

1. Place your cursor on one of the date cells.

2. Right-click to show the shortcut menu. Choose Group and Outline | Group.

3. In the Group menu, one option allows you to group by quarter. You can also choose to group by months. In addition, you may select a starting and ending quarter. By selecting a start and end range, you place a column for that range into the PivotTable—even if there is no data for that period.

Is there any way to change the sort order for the PivotTable?

By default, the PivotTable sorts data in ascending alphabetical or numeric order. Region 1 always comes before Region 2. Chicago comes before Indianapolis. Many times, you will prefer to view this data in a different order. Often, that order might be by sales amount in descending order (largest sales first).

To change the sort order of your PivotTable, follow these steps:

1. Place your cursor on one of the field cells that you want to change.

2. Right-click to show the shortcut menu. Select Field Settings. In the PivotTable Field dialog box, click on the Advanced button. The dialog box shown in Figure 13-8 appears.

3. Select the Descending radio button in the AutoSort options area of the dialog box.

4. In the Using field box, select the data field that you want to use for sorting (Sum Of Extension is the field to select in this example). This will change your PivotTable so that all of the regions show in order of total sales for that region by category.

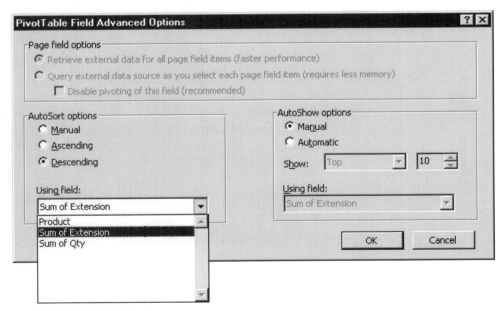

Figure 13-8   The PivotTable Field Advanced Options dialog box

If your report has an extra level of control break—for example, you are viewing sales by customer type broken down by region—each customer type lists the regions in a different order, because the order now reflects the number of sales in that region.

Is there a way to suppress grand totals at the end of the rows of the PivotTable?

You can use the PivotTable Options dialog box to alter the way a number of PivotTable features work. Access this dialog box by right-clicking to show the shortcut menu and then choosing Table Options.

Among the many options in the dialog, you have the option of turning off the grand totals that appear in both the rows and the columns of the PivotTable.

When creating a PivotTable there's an option to create a PivotChart at the same time. But how do I create a PivotChart after the PivotTable is already created?

Create a chart based on your PivotTable data by first selecting the entire PivotTable. To make sure you have the entire PivotTable selected, right-click on the PivotTable itself, then choose Select and Entire Table. The PivotTable toolbar should appear. Click the Chart Wizard button on the toolbar, and a PivotChart will automatically appear on a separate sheet.

Tip: *If the PivotTable toolbar is not visible, you can click the Chart Wizard on the standard toolbar after selecting the PivotTable data, and a PivotChart will be created.*

From this point forward, any changes you make to the PivotTable will affect the PivotChart as well.

Chapter 14

Using Forms in Excel

Answer Topics!

Using Forms in Excel @ a Glance

- **Creating and Using Forms.** Excel is an excellent tool for managing small- to medium-sized databases (called *lists* in Excel). The Data Forms feature of Excel provides an easy way to enter, delete, and search for data entered into a list. This chapter covers creating, using, and validating forms.

- **Data Validation.** The new data validation features help protect your data, so that out-of-range data is kept away from your list—even if inexperienced people are doing the data entry.

- **Templates.** You can standardize the creation of new workbooks and new worksheets by creating templates that can be used again and again.

CREATING FORMS

When I look up *Forms* on Excel Help, I get information for both Templates and Data Forms. What is the difference between them?

A data form and a template are two different things. A template is a blank sheet or workbook that is saved for the sake of consistency so that you will quickly obtain the same structure every time you use the template to begin a new workbook. Excel comes with a number of templates that are predefined for you. You can create your own by simply saving a workbook as a template in the File | Save dialog. Every time you select that template when you create a new file, you'll get the same workbook cells that you originally saved. No matter how you fill it out each time you use it, the template itself is not altered.

A data form uses the structure that you create in a list to make the data entry process faster. When you set up a list (a list is really a flat database), you create a row with column headings (which define the fields) and then enter one row of data per record. A typical list would be a transaction record of

Book1.xls

	A	B	C	D	E	F	G
1	Name	Region	Product	Price	Qty	Extension	Custom
2	Martin, John	NE	Widget	14	4	56	Large
3	Elgin,Mark	TX	Widget	14	6	84	Small
4	Martin, John	NE	Gadget	25	2	50	Large
5	Martin, John	NE	Gadget	25	12	300	Medium
6	Martin, John	NE	Waddle	100	15	1500	Small
7	Elias, Jack	MA	Waddle	100	34	3400	Small
8	Elias, Jack	MA	Gadget	25	23	575	Medium
9	Elias, Jack	MA	Gadget	25	23	575	Medium
10	Elias, Jack	MA	Widget	14	12	168	Large
11	Marley, Jeanne	SC	Gadget	25	3	75	Small
12	Marley, Jeanne	SC	Waddle	100	5	500	Large
13	Wu, Yelana	TX	Twiddle	50	45	2250	Medium
14	Wu, Yelana	TX	Widget	14	23	322	Medium
15	Hunt, Frank	MW	Twaddle	45	3	135	Small
16	Francone, Mark	SW	Gadget	25	4	100	Small
17	Francone, Mark	SW	Widget	14	10	140	Medium
18	Coffee, Marlene	CT	Waddle	100	4	400	Medium
19	Coffee, Marlene	CT	Gadget	25	38	950	Large
20	Kummings, Anita	NW	Twaddle	19	4	76	Medium

Figure 14-1 A list from which you can create a form

each sale by salesperson. It would contain cells for the name, region, product, price, quantity, extended price, and quarter, as shown in Figure 14-1. A data form consists of the field names (cells) that you have included in your list.

What's the difference between a form and a list?

A list is the worksheet representation of a collection of related data. It includes a column for each type of information included in one record, and a single row represents each record in the list.

A form is a fill-in-the-blank window that is a logical data entry device for adding new records to the list. There is a blank area for each piece of information (each column) that is required for the record, and a single record is entered on one form. You can also use a form to edit existing records.

A form is created as a data entry tool for lists.

How is a list created?

Enter a row of titles on your worksheet. This row represents the header row for your list. Records, which include information required by the titles, are entered in rows underneath the header row, one row for each record. For example, if your list is a list of inventory parts, the first two rows of the list might look something like Figure 14-2.

	A	B	C	D	E	F	G
1	Part No.	Description	Weight	Cost	Quantity		
2	158F	Stapler	8 oz	0.79	250		
3							
4							
5							
6							
7							

Figure 14-2 Enter one row of titles on your list, followed by records which provide the information required by the titles

How is a form created?

Position your mouse pointer in a cell that is within the range of the list for which you want to create a form. There must be at least one record in the list, and there must be a distinguishable row of column headings (see the Tip below). There can be no blank rows in the list. Create a data form by choosing the Data | Form command. For the list structure shown in Figure 14-1, you get the form shown in Figure 14-3. It's really that simple. The only requirement is that the first row of the list consists of names and that no blank lines separate the field names from the actual data.

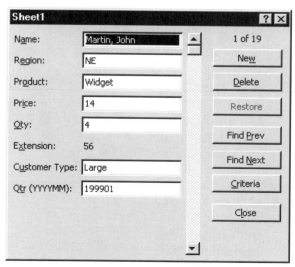

Figure 14-3 The data form for the list shown in Figure 14-1

Tip: *Help Excel figure out which row contains headings for your list by applying some distinguishing characteristic to the heading. For example, use a different font, apply special alignment such as centering, use bold or italics, place a border around it, use color or a pattern, or choose a different capitalization style.*

Can I include a row of pattern or dashes under the field headings to differentiate them from the actual data?

That's not a good idea. The data form won't work properly if there is an extra line that separates it from the actual data. You can, however, format the actual row of field names in any way that you'd like, so long as only that one row is used. See the previous Tip for formatting ideas that make it easy to tell the headings from the data.

If I use a form to enter data, will the program know that it is part of the same list?

Excel 2000 recognizes that a contiguous range of data topped with a row of headings belongs together as a list. No range name is required.

Having said that, you might still want to define a name for your database. If you name your list (Insert | Name | Define) Database, and you use the data form to enter data, Excel automatically extends the range included in the named list Database. Thus, if you have five rows of data plus the heading when you define your list as Database ($A$1:$H$6) and you use the data form to add three more rows (records), the definition of Database will change to become $A$1:$H$9. Naming your list also allows you to use the INDEX() function to dynamically calculate a variety of different types of totals.

Is there ever a time that I don't want use the name Database for my list?

Although this situation is rare, using the name Database can cause a problem on your worksheet if you place a formula in a column so that it shows a value even when the record is blank (for example, formatting an extended price column with price*qty so that all of the rows show a 0 where there is no data in either the price or the quantity columns, as shown in Figure 14-4). If you fill the calculation column with the formula in advance of adding records to the table, you won't be able to use the Data | Form command to add a row to the list; you'll receive an error message instead. If you've used a name other than Database or no name at all, you won't get the error message, and the Data | Form command will work. Unfortunately, the command might also add the new row at the very bottom of the worksheet because it will see that as the first "free" row.

You can avoid this problem altogether by keeping in mind that the data form will apply any calculated formulas to new

	A	B	C	D	E	F	G	H
19	Coffee, Marlene	CT	Gadget	25	38	950	Large	199903
20	Kummings, Anita	NW	Twaddle	19	4	76	Medium	199902
21						0		
22						0		
23						0		
24						0		
25						0		
26						0		
27						0		
28						0		
29						0		
30						0		
31						0		
32						0		
33						0		
34						0		
35						0		
36						0		
37						0		
38						0		
39						0		
40						0		
41						0		
42						0		
43						0		
44						0		
45						0		
46						0		
47						0		
48						0		
49								

Figure 14-4 If you name your list Database, be sure that no formulas produce zeros where no data has been entered

rows that you add, so you don't need to fill entire columns with a formula in advance. If you want to fill the column anyway, make sure that you choose an option that allows you to ignore blanks in the calculation so that the data form works correctly.

USING FORMS

 How can I add a new record to the list using a data form?

Here's how to add a new record to a list with a data form:

1. Place your mouse pointer somewhere in the list to select a cell. It doesn't matter which cell you select.

2. Choose Data | Form.

3. Click on the New button. This clears the form and leaves blank boxes that are ready to receive information about a new record.

4. Type your entries into all of the fields on the form. Press TAB to move from one field to the other, or click on each field where you want to enter information. Don't press the ENTER key until you have finished entering data into all of the fields on the record.

5. When you have finished entering all of the fields, you have three options. Click the Close button if you are finished entering records, scroll up to a previous record if you want to view or edit a previous record, or press the ENTER key to proceed to a new, blank data form on which to enter another new record. All three of these actions will write the data to the list.

 I tried to add a new record with the data form but got an error message saying that the range could not be extended. What does that mean and why is it happening?

The data form won't allow you to overwrite any data in your worksheet. If you have another range of data on your worksheet that is under the list that you created and adding a new record would bump into it, you'll get an error message saying that you cannot extend the list.

If you name your list Database, you are more prone to seeing this problem occur. For example, if you enter some rows of data at the bottom of the list without using the data form, you can no longer use the data form to add new records because the form doesn't know that these rows are part of the Database list. If this happens, just reselect the entire range and redefine the name Database, and you'll be able to use the data form again.

!   ***Caution:***   *Because of the potential problems that can occur when a list is named Database, it is best not to use this term at all when defining a name for your data list.*

Can I see all of the records in my list if I use a data form?

You can scroll through your entire list one record at a time using the data form by clicking on the Find Next or Find Prev buttons. If you have a filter or criteria set, clicking on Find Next or Find Prev takes you to the next or previous record that matches your criteria.

Can I make a change to data if I use the data form?

You can type in any changes that you want in the data form.

1. First, find the record that you need to change by using the Find Next or Find Prev buttons, or by searching for the record using the Criteria button.

2. When you have the correct record in the data form, either tab through the fields until you come to the field that you want to change, or place your mouse pointer directly into that field and click.

3. When you are finished, either scroll to another record or close the data form.

 When I enter or edit data using a data form, none of my calculated fields show up. I can't enter a value and no values seem to be calculated.

Figure 14-5 shows a data form with a record partially entered. Notice that there is no way to enter data into the Extension field, and the result is shown as a blank. That's because the Extension field is a calculated field, and you cannot put data into a calculated field because the formula attached to the field creates the value for you. When you finish entering the record and either close the data form, add another record, or scroll to a different record, Excel calculates the formula and places the result on your list. If you return to the record on the data form using the Find Prev button, you will see that the calculation has been inserted.

Figure 14-6 shows the same record after all of the fields have been entered and the data recorded (as if you had scrolled back to see it again). Now the calculated field displays the correct value. If you edit a record and change the fields that contribute to the calculation, you won't see any

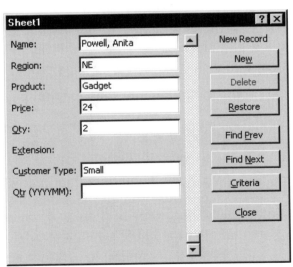

Figure 14-5   The data form doesn't calculate a cell while you are entering the data

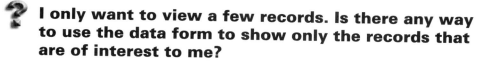

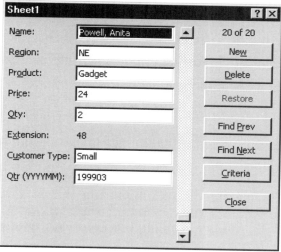

Figure 14-6 The data form calculates a calculated field after the record is stored

change in your calculated total unless you leave the record and scroll back to view it again.

Can I delete a row of a list using the data form?

You can delete any row of data in the list right from the data form. You need to display the unwanted record using the Find Next or Find Prev button or the Criteria command and click on the Delete button. The deletion is permanent. You cannot undo a deleted row if you have used the data form to delete it, so be very careful when you use this feature.

Note that the deletion is permanent only if deleted from the data form. If a row is deleted from the worksheet, you can use Edit Undo to recover data, or, as a fallback, you can close the document without saving and then reopen it to retrieve the data.

I only want to view a few records. Is there any way to use the data form to show only the records that are of interest to me?

You can fill out a Criteria sheet in the data form. The Criteria sheet acts as a filter to your data. It looks just like a

blank record, and it allows you type in the values that you want to use as a filter.

1. Place your mouse pointer in any cell in the list.

2. Choose Data | Form.

3. Click on the Criteria button.

4. Enter the value to search for in the field next to the desired attribute. For example, if you wanted to find all of the salesmen whose region was NW, you would enter NW into the Region field. If you wanted to find all of the records for small companies in the Northwest region, you could also enter **Small** in the Customer Type field. The form assumes a logical AND on multiple criteria fields (see Figure 14-7).

5. Click on the Find Next button to move to the first record that meets the criteria. Or, if you are beginning your search from the end of the list, click Find Prev to move backwards to the first record that meets your criteria. Continue to select Find Next (or Find Prev) until a beep tells you that you've reached the last record.

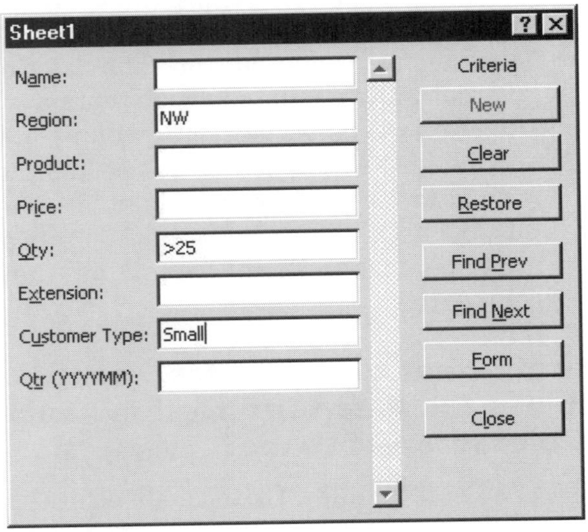

Figure 14-7 You can enter multiple fields as your criteria

You can also use the scroll bars to view the filtered data. Clicking the Form button on the Criteria screen will return you to the data form. As you scroll through the records, only the ones that meet the criteria are displayed.

To see the entire database again, go back to the Criteria form and click the Clear button. Then click the Form button to return to the data form.

You may use any of the normal search criteria that are available elsewhere in Excel. If you want an exact match for text, enclose the text in quotation marks. If you don't, you'll see any records that are partial matches. For example, typing **DAW** into the Name field shows you both Daw and Dawson—or any other names that begin with Daw. If you enter **"DAW"**, you'll see only records for the salesman whose last name is Daw. The Criteria screen is not case sensitive.

The partial name search described above does not apply to numerical searches, however. If you search for 88 in a numerical field, Excel will return all records with an exact match of 88 in that field. Records containing 888 or 88.25 will not be returned.

You may enter numeric values that are exact or you may use the <, >, <=, >=, or <> operators. Unfortunately, there is no way to request, for example, a value that is >5 and <12. You cannot use logical AND or OR within a single field in the data form. If you want to search for values that require the logical AND or OR in your search, close the data form and use the AutoFilter command or an advanced filter. (See Chapter 11 for more information on filtering lists.)

If you enter a Criteria in the data form that is not found, the system still returns one record. However, it beeps to let you know that the record it found is not the record that you wanted.

 ## I know that I have a record that meets my Criteria. Why can't Excel find it in the list?

When you enter criteria, Excel starts looking from your current location in the list to the bottom of the list. If you look at the top of the data form, above the buttons, you'll see your current location (written, for example, as 34 of 1000—wherever the active row is located). If your criteria

points to a record that comes earlier in the list than your current location, Excel won't find it using the Find Next button. It will, however, find it if you click on Find Prev. It's a good technique when searching to make sure that you are always at the first record in your list before you click on the Criteria button to begin a new search.

VALIDATING

 I have a new employee who is going to be maintaining my list. Do I need to protect the list from any mistakes the employee might make?

There are two issues in protecting data. One is to protect the data from erasures and deliberate damage. You can use a password to accomplish this. The other is to try to prevent someone from entering data that is incorrect. The latter process is called *data validation*. Excel 2000 provides some useful features to help you keep incorrect data from being entered into lists.

Data validation is an important part of maintaining a list. The term *GIGO* (garbage in, garbage out) was coined in the early days of computing. If you don't have good data in your system, how can you possibly use it to make good decisions? If your employee enters data for a salesman who works in the Northeast region and enters the region code as NJ instead of NE, then any report that totals the sales for the Northeast region will miss all of this person's records. It is critical that you do everything possible to keep bad data out of a list.

Data validation, explained in the questions below, can only be performed on an actual list, not on a data form.

 How do I decide which fields to validate?

You can add validation to a list by selecting the cell or range of cells to validate and choosing Data | Validation. Figure 14-8 shows the Data Validation dialog box. You can add validation that checks for whole numbers, decimals, text length, lists, dates, and time. You can also write custom validation formulas.

When you validate for whole numbers, decimals, date, time, or text length, you can specify that the entry be

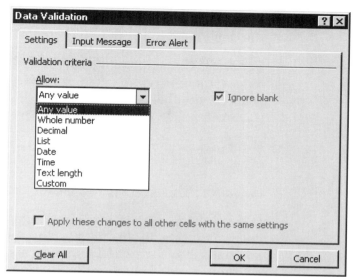

Figure 14-8　The Data Validation dialog box

between or not between two values, or equal, not equal, greater than or equal, less than or equal to a specific value. If you do a list validation, the program checks your source list to see if it can locate the cell value in that list. A custom validation checks the value of the cell against the value of the associated formula.

Although it's easy enough to use the dialog box to specify validation rules, it's a bit trickier to get everything set up properly in your list if your validation is at all complex. Let's use a typical sales list as the example. What kind of validation is needed? Here are the fields:

Salesman's name: It is hard to validate the names unless you want to control the names typed in by choosing them from a list. A list validation would work here.

Region: This should also be a list validation.

Product: This should also be a list validation.

Price: The best way to validate the price is to make this a calculated field that looks up the product in a list and

places the associated price into the price cell. That way, you don't need to validate the field.

Quantity: The quantity should be greater than 0. If it is 0 or less, there is no sale. The only circumstance in which a negative number would be logical is in a return, and, for this example, you can pretend that returns never occur.

Extension: This is a calculated field, so no validation is needed.

Customer: This is a list validation.

Quarter: The validation here is tricky. You can't use a date validation on this field because it doesn't use a standard date format. The quarter uses a 4-digit year and a 2-digit quarter number. You could use a whole number validation between 199901 and 201004 (if you feel that that's a reasonable range), but that wouldn't prevent someone from entering 199907, which is not a correct quarter name. The best solution is to use a list validation and to format the field as text.

How would I validate a numeric field to make sure that only values between 1 and 1000 are accepted?

You need to use the data validation feature that is new to Excel 2000. Here's how.

1. Place your mouse pointer in the cell to be validated, or select a range of cells that need the same validation. The easiest way to apply validation to lists, where many records will be added, is to select the entire column containing the type of cell to be validated.

2. Choose Data | Validation. The Data Validation window will appear.

3. Click on the Allow box drop-down menu and change the default Any Value to Whole Number.

4. In the Data drop-down menu, select Between. Minimum and Maximum value fields appear.

5. Enter **1** in the Minimum value box and enter **100** in the Maximum value box. Note that the minimum and maximum values are included in the allowable entries for this validation.

6. Click on the OK button or specify Input and Error messages.

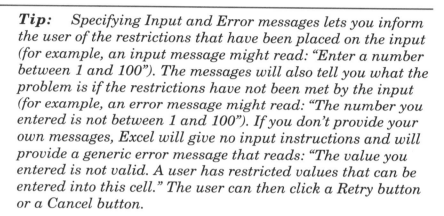

Tip: *Specifying Input and Error messages lets you inform the user of the restrictions that have been placed on the input (for example, an input message might read: "Enter a number between 1 and 100"). The messages will also tell you what the problem is if the restrictions have not been met by the input (for example, an error message might read: "The number you entered is not between 1 and 100"). If you don't provide your own messages, Excel will give no input instructions and will provide a generic error message that reads: "The value you entered is not valid. A user has restricted values that can be entered into this cell." The user can then click a Retry button or a Cancel button.*

7. Try out your validation to make sure it works by entering a negative number, 0, 1, a number in the correct range, 100, 101, and a number that is far out of range. These are the key values needed to test whether your 1–100 validation is working that way it should.

What is a list validation?

A list validation is a type of validation that provides a list of acceptable (valid) entries for the cell. For example, the Job Description column of an employee list might include a list validation that allows a choice of ten available job descriptions. If the user attempts to enter a job description that is not one of the ten on the list, they will receive an error message and be asked to try again.

List validations provide control for data entry so that the user can't misspell an entry, make up an entry, or choose an entry that is not on the allowable list.

 How do I set up a list validation?

A list validation requires some planning. In order to set up a list for the region codes, for example, you need to create a complete list of all the possible region codes somewhere in your workbook or in a linked workbook. A list is best managed when it is the only item on a specific worksheet.

1. On a separate sheet of the workbook, create a list header of REGION. In the cells directly under the title cell, type the acceptable regions (such as NE, MA, SE, or MW). Enter one region code per cell, vertically. Select the entire list and give it a range name such as Region.

2. Return to the main data list. Place your mouse pointer in the cell to be validated, or select a range of cells (such as an entire column) that needs the same validation.

3. Choose Data | Validation.

4. Click on the Allow box drop-down menu and change the default Any Value to List.

5. In the Source field, type the formula **=Region** (or whatever you've named the lookup list). You may also collapse the dialog box and physically select the region list, but using named lists is much easier.

6. Test your validation. Figure 14-9 shows the validation list that drops down when you click on the drop-down box.

 How can I tell the data entry person the range of values that are supposed to be in a specific field?

The Data Validation dialog box contains a tab called Input Message. The dialog box for this tab contains a Title area and a Message area. You can enter text into either part, neither part, or both parts. When someone selects a cell that has validation attached, the message, if there is one, is displayed. If the Office Assistant is visible, your message is displayed in a balloon. The text in the title area is typed in boldface, and the message text is in plain Roman text. If the Office Assistant isn't visible, then the text is displayed in a comment/text box under the selected cell.

	A	B	C	D	E	F	G	H	I
1	Name	Region	Product	Price	Qty	Extension	Customer Type	Qtr (YYYYMM)	
2	Martin, John	NE	Widget	14	4	56	Large	199901	
3	Elgin,Mark	TX	Widget	14	6	84	Small	199902	
4	Martin, John	NE	Gadget	25	2	50	Large	199901	
5	Martin, John	NE	Gadget	25	12	300	Medium	199902	
6	Martin, John	NE	Waddle	100	15	1500	Small	199902	
7	Elias, Jack	MA	Waddle	100	34	3400	Small	199901	
8	Elias, Jack	MA	Gadget	25	23	575	Medium	199902	
9	Elias, Jack	MA	Gadget	25	23	575	Medium	199901	
10	Elias, Jack	MA	Widget	14	12	168	Large	199902	
11	Marley, Jeanne	SC	Gadget	25	3	75	Small	199903	
12	Marley, Jeanne	SC	Waddle	100	5	500	Large	199901	
13	Wu, Yelana	TX	Twiddle	50	45	2250	Medium	199901	
14	Wu, Yelana	TX	Widget	14	23	322	Medium	199903	
15	Hunt, Frank	MW	Waddle	45	3	135	Small	199902	
16		SC							
17		TX	Code						
18		MW	e of the						
19		SW	om this						
20		CT							
21		MT							
22		CA							
		NW							

Figure 14-9 A list validation that shows a list of regions

You can use this Input Message even if you don't choose to validate the field. Do this by selecting the Show input message when cell is selected checkbox. If you have many different people entering data into the list, or if you use the list/form infrequently enough to forget what should go into each type of cell, then you probably should take the time to create input messages even if you don't use the data validation.

What happens when someone types incorrect data into a field that has validation attached?

If a value fails to pass the validation test, Excel displays an error message if the Show error alert after invalid data is entered checkbox is selected. The contents and the specific message depend upon the choices that you have made in the Error Alert tab.

The Error Message entry box again provides you with a choice of Title and Message. If you enter a Title, then your message is displayed in the title bar of the Alert box that appears when an incorrect entry is made. Text entered into the Message area is displayed in the body of the Alert Box in

place of the default message, which is, "The value you entered is not valid. A user has restricted values that can be entered into this cell."

Three levels of alerts exist.

● If you want to stop someone from entering the data if it is incorrect, then select the Stop alert. This offers the user the options of Retry and Cancel on the alert message. If the user elects to Cancel the entry, Excel reverts the cell back to its original value.

● A Warning alert presents the message, "Continue?" The user's options are No (the default), Yes, or Cancel. If the user selects Yes, the incorrect data is allowed in the field. This might be useful when a sales figure is almost always a positive value, but you want to give the user the option of entering a negative return amount in the field.

● An Information alert makes little attempt to stop the incorrect data. It presents the message with the buttons OK and Cancel. OK is the default button, and if selected, lets the incorrect data pass without further comment.

If I assign a Stop alert to my cell, will it keep the bad data out for good?

A Stop alert keeps most of the incorrect data out. However, the data validation scheme is not bulletproof. Attaching data validation to a cell won't prevent a user from pasting in an incorrect value. If the value is entered from the Clipboard, no validation is performed. And if the user enters data with a data form, the validation step is usually sidestepped.

Does data validation work better when I use a data form or when I enter data directly into a list?

Unfortunately, data validation doesn't really work when you enter data using a data form. The results are very inconsistent. Sometimes Excel catches the error and presents the error messages. More often, however, it seems to ignore the fact that you have attached data validation to the cell.

The validation works quite well when you enter data directly into the cells of the list.

I created validation for a group of cells, but not the entire column. Can I copy an existing validation, or do I have to enter this validation all over again?

You can copy validations from one cell to another cell, or a group of cells, by following these steps:

1. Click on the cell containing the validation you wish to copy.

2. Click the Copy button on the Standard toolbar or choose Edit | Copy.

3. Select the cells (or column of cells) to which you wish to copy the validation.

4. Choose Edit | Paste Special. In the Paste Special window that appears, click the Validation option.

5. Click OK to apply the validation to all selected cells.

The restrictions that once applied to a group of cells are no longer necessary. I want to remove the validation. Can I do this?

There may be situations when you no longer need validation. Perhaps you entered a validation on the wrong group of cells and you need to take the restrictions away so that the correct information can be entered. Perhaps the validation you entered when you originally created the list no longer applies, or the users are familiar enough with the requirements of the data list that they no longer need to be reminded of the validation rules.

To remove validation from a cell or group of cells:

1. Place your mouse pointer in the cell for which you wish to remove validation, or select a range of cells for which the validation is no longer necessary.

2. Choose Data | Validation.

3. Click on the Clear All button at the bottom of the dialog box.

One other use for this action is to remove the validation from the header cell when you attach validation to all of the

cells in a column at once. If you plan to attach validation to empty columns, you should select the Ignore Blanks checkbox on the Settings tab.

If I can't use data validation from within a data form, how can I make data entry easy for the people who maintain the list?

Microsoft has almost created a Catch-22 syndrome with the data form and the data validation features. For the moment, if you must do your data entry in Excel, you are probably better off creating a custom form that looks like a traditional paper form and has all of the data validation attached. You can use the Template feature to create a skeleton form that all of your users can open when they need to create a new workbook. This template would contain all of the fields in the list and all of the relevant lookup tables. Special macro or Visual Basic programming is needed to transfer the validated data onto the master worksheet. You could also attempt to use the Template Wizard with Data Tracking add-in, which claims to be able to write the data into another location. If you bravely plan to try this add-in, try it first on something that is both simple and noncritical.

Can I use a template if I don't need to store data into a list?

Templates are very useful because they allow you to create skeleton forms that anyone can use and that don't overwrite the originals. They promote consistency and are tremendous timesavers because you can store any needed calculations in them. Here's one example of a template that is used to calculate a check digit for an invoice.

Picture a company that needs to create invoice numbers but wants to make sure that the invoice number is not easy to transpose (mistype the order of the digits). They want to know that, if numbers are reversed, the invoice number will not be valid. One way to do this is to create an invoice number that checks itself. If you add a single digit to the end of an invoice number in such a way that you can calculate what that extra number should be, then you could also have a

process that validates the number when it is entered into a list. The extra number is called a *check digit*. There are many ways to calculate check digits.

Say, for example, that the company wants to create invoice numbers that are nine digits long and that have a tenth digit as a check digit. The formula to create the check digit is to multiply the first, fourth, and seventh digits in the original 9-digit number by 1, the second, fifth, and eighth digits by 3, and the third, sixth, and ninth digits by 5 (all prime numbers). Then add all of the results together and use the MOD(x,y) function to return the remainder after the number has been divided by 11 (another prime number). Since the largest remainder is 10 (which you can force to 0), you have an easy way to produce a single digit check digit.

To create the template, you would format it any way that you like. You would create nine cells that ask the user to enter a whole number between 0 and 9. In most companies where they use this type of check digit validation, the base number string comes from a pile of cards that contain numbers in order (insurance companies frequently generate policy numbers or claims numbers this way), or the user already knows the last number used.

When the user enters the nine digits, the formulas embedded in the worksheet calculate the new complete invoice number. Each user opens a new copy of the worksheet template for each invoice number generating session. The template that was created and saved (really just a worksheet with formulas, formatting, and no data that was saved as a Template in the Templates folder) makes all of the calculations work the same way.

 ## If I also have Microsoft Access, which program should I use to manage my lists?

Excel contains many excellent features for managing lists, but it does not have anywhere near the capabilities of a "real" database management system. Using Access provides you with many more features for validating and manipulating data.

However, Excel is a good choice if your data is simple and does not need much validation. It is suitable only for relatively small data lists because a worksheet has a fixed size beyond which it cannot grow. If your only list management tool is Excel; it will do a good enough job for lists that aren't too complex.

If you maintain a list in Microsoft Access, you can bring it into Excel whenever you need to perform an analysis on it.

Chapter 15

Excel Macros

Answer Topics!

Excel Macros @ a Glance

Overview. A macro is a program that you record and run to provide a quick and easy way to automate Excel tasks. An Excel macro is like a little robot that lives in your worksheet, executing the same commands effortlessly, again and again, until you ask it to stop. It can be a simple little program that enters a title, like your company name, in a designated cell, or it can be a complex operation that performs interactive calculations based on the results of answers you provide while the macro is running.

Recording Macros. Macros save time by automating repetitious tasks. Record yourself performing a task, then repeat the task over and over by initiating the macro. Use relative rather than absolute references in your macros, and the macro operation will apply to any cell in your worksheet. You can use macros as a quick method of formatting cells, and you can even place macros on your menu.

Debugging Macros. After creating a macro, you can go back and edit it, using easy Visual Basic commands. Use variables in your macros to make them more interactive.

Working with Visual Basic. Learn Visual Basic programming commands by studying existing macros, then create your own advanced macros by writing programming statements.

Other Macro Issues. Transfer macros flawlessly from Excel 97 to Excel 2000. Once created, a macro can be assigned to a button that resides right on your worksheet, making macro access incredibly easy.

RECORDING MACROS

? What is the process for recording a macro?

The basic concept of recording a macro is that you turn on the macro recorder and then perform the steps you wish to record. Excel memorizes your actions and repeats them whenever you ask it to. When you record a macro, keep in mind that every move you make is being recorded. If you

make mistakes or go back over your work, those changes are recorded as well.

Although the process of recording macros is nearly intuitive, there are actually several steps involved. Here is the procedure for recording a macro:

1. Turn on the macro recorder by choosing Tools | Macro | Record New Macro (alternatively, activate the Visual Basic toolbar and click the Record Macro button). The Record Macro window will appear (see Figure 15-1)

2. Enter a name for the macro. Names are limited to 255 characters, with no spaces, and they can't begin with a number.

3. Indicate a desired shortcut key combination for this macro (optional). Note: If the CTRL–*letter* combination you choose is already in use as an Excel command, Excel will replace the existing command with the macro assignment. Excel will not warn you that this is about to occur.

4. Indicate whether you want the macro to be stored in the current workbook (and therefore available only from this workbook) or in your Personal workbook (and available from other workbooks).

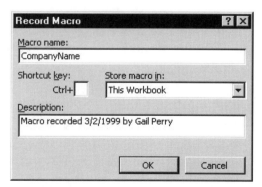

Figure 15-1   The Record Macro window. Designate a name and location for your macro, then click OK to begin recording it

5. Indicate an optional description for the macro. The description you enter will be displayed in the macro window whenever you select a macro.

6. Click OK to turn on the macro recorder. You will note the message, "Recording," at the bottom of the screen, and a tiny toolbar, the Stop Recording toolbar, will appear (see Figure 15-2).

> **Caution:** *If you use the Relative Reference button, you may notice that this button does not reset each time you open the Stop Recording toolbar. The next time you record a macro, if you used the Relative Reference feature and Excel is still open from the last time you recorded, the Relative Reference button will still be turned on.*

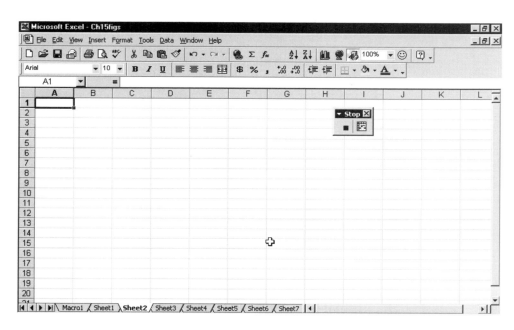

Figure 15-2 Click the Stop Recording button when you have finished recording all the steps of your macro. If this toolbar isn't visible, choose Tools | Macro | Stop Recording to open it

7. Click the Relative Reference button on the Stop Recording toolbar to cause the macro recorder to record your keystrokes in relation to the active cell, as opposed to recording exact cell references.

8. Record your actions.

9. Click the Stop Recording button on the toolbar to stop the recorder.

How do I use a macro once I have recorded it?

Once you have created a macro, you can run (or play back) the macro in one of two ways:

● If you assigned your macro to a key combination, press CTRL and the designated letter.

● Whether or not you assigned your macro to a key combination, you can choose Tools | Macro | Macros, click on the name of the macro you wish to run, and then click the Run button (alternatively, click Run from the Visual Basic toolbar and choose the macro from the resulting list).

I need to enter my company name on every worksheet I create. Is there a quick way to automate this process?

To record your company name in a cell, choose Tools | Macro | Record New Macro. Enter a name for the macro, **CompanyName**, for example, and assign a CTRL+*letter* combination if you'd like. Choose the Personal workbook for the location of this macro, so you will be able access it from any workbook, then enter an optional description. Click OK. Enter the company name and press ENTER. Apply any desired formatting (such as bold, centering, or a special font) to this cell. Stop the recorder.

Test your macro by moving to a different cell or a different worksheet and choosing Tools | Macro | Macros, then clicking on CompanyName and clicking Run (or pressing the chosen key combination). Your company name, with its formatting, will appear in the current cell.

I want to record a macro that runs from the cell I choose, not the cell Excel chooses. How can I control this?

By default, Excel uses a feature called *absolute referencing* when recording macros. This means that any cellpointer movement included in the macro is recorded based on the exact cells you moved to when recording the macro.

For example, if you record your company name and address in cells A1, A2, and A3 and then try to play this macro with your cellpointer beginning in cell B6, the first line of your company name will appear in cell B6, but the macro will return to cells A2 and A3 for the address. This is because the macro recorded you moving to cell A2 and A3. If you would rather have the macro record your company name, then move *down one cell* from the starting point to record the first line of the company address, then move *down one cell* again for the second line of the address, you must specify that you want the macro to record *relative* references instead of the default absolute references.

To do this, when you turn on the macro recorder, before recording any activity, click the Relative Reference button on the macro toolbar so that the button appears depressed. With this feature activated, Excel will record the movement of your cellpointer relative to the surrounding cells, instead of the actual cells to which you move.

Tip: *If the tiny Stop Recording toolbar does not appear when you turn on the macro recorder, right-click on an existing toolbar and choose Stop Recording from the shortcut menu that appears, or choose View | Toolbar | Stop Recording.*

How can I use macros to apply formatting techniques to my worksheets?

If there are formatting styles you use frequently, you can save several formatting features in one macro, saving you the time it will take to apply each feature, one at a time each time you need it. Turn on the macro recorder, give your macro a name (ReportFormat, for example), then apply the formatting features you want to use.

If you want the formatting to apply to cells rather than the entire worksheet, click the Relative Reference button so that it appears depressed before selecting a cell to which you will apply formatting. This way, when you run your macro, you can click on any cell and run the macro to apply the formatting to the selected cell.

Save the macro in your Personal workbook so that it will be accessible from other workbooks.

I have created many macros. It seems there are a lot of steps involved in running macros. Is there an easy way to access my macros from the menu?

One way to easily access all the macros you've created is to add them to your menu. Instead of choosing Tools | Macro | Macros, clicking on a macro from the list that is displayed, and then choosing Run (five steps), you can place a macro right on the Tools menu so you need only click Tools and the name of the macro (two steps).

Note: *For more information about creating a separate menu topic that is completely devoted to your macros, see Chapter 12, "Customizing Excel."*

Place a macro on the Tools menu by following these steps:

1. Choose Tools | Customize. The Customize window will appear.

2. Click the Commands tab and click on Macros in the Categories list.

3. In the Commands box at the right, click on Custom Menu Item, then drag that item onto a menu. The menu will drop down, and you can drag the item to the place where you would like the macro to appear on the list. When you release the mouse button, you will see the text, "Custom menu item," on the displayed menu.

4. Right-click on Custom menu item to display a shortcut menu.

5. In the Name area of the shortcut menu, enter the text that you would like to see displayed on this menu. Use an ampersand (&) symbol to the left of the letter that should be underlined for easy keyboard access to this menu choice, making sure you don't duplicate any other underlined letters on the chosen menu.

6. Choose Assign Macro from the shortcut menu and click on the name of the macro that should be assigned to this menu.

7. Click OK to close the Customize window.

From this point forward, you can execute your macro by clicking on the menu and then clicking on the name you assigned to the menu choice for that macro.

DEBUGGING MACROS

 My macro contains some errors that need to be removed, and I want to add some features to my macro. How do I edit macros?

Use the Visual Basic editor to examine and, if necessary, change your macro. The macro contains coded language for every step you recorded, and you need the Visual Basic editor to view this language.

Choose Tools | Macro | Macros. The list that appears (see Figure 15-3) contains all the macros that are available in the workbooks(s) listed under Macros. Your choices are All Open Workbooks (which includes the personal workbook), This Workbook (the active workbook), or PERSONAL.XLS (the personal worksheet, which contains programming code available to all workbooks).

Click on the name of the macro you want to change, and then click the Edit button. The Visual Basic editor will appear, with the code for your macro displayed (see Figure 15-4).

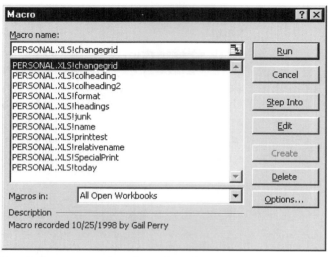

Figure 15-3 Edit a macro by choosing the macro in this window, then clicking the Edit button

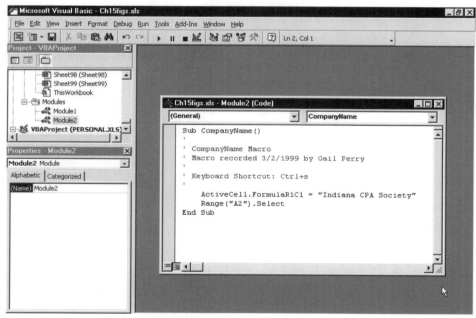

Figure 15-4 Examine the code for your macro in the Visual Basic editor

---

Note: *If you choose to edit a macro in the Personal Macro Workbook on your PERSONAL.XLS worksheet, you may get a message indicating that you need to unhide the workbook by choosing Window | Unhide | Personal and then clicking OK. When you are finished editing and have closed the Visual Basic editor, choose Window | Hide to close the personal workbook. If you go directly to the Visual Basic editor (with ALT-F11 or by choosing Tools | Macro | Visual Basic Editor), the PERSONAL.XLs workbook does not have to be unhidden.*

There are standard features in macro programming:

- Each macro begins with Sub, followed by the macro name, followed by an open and close parenthesis.

- There is a blank line and then the macro title followed by the word *Macro*.

- On the next line, the date on which the macro was recorded and the program user name appears.

- If a keyboard shortcut was assigned to this macro, that key combination appears next.

- All of these introductory lines (under the Sub line, but before the macro code begins) are preceded by an apostrophe, indicating that this is memorandum text and should not be confused with macro code. You can place any textual information in a macro and precede it with an apostrophe at the beginning of the line, and Excel will ignore the text when running the macro.

- Next, you will see the macro code. The code language is typically indented to distinguish it from other parts of the macro.

- End Sub appears on the last line of the macro, indicating that this macro subroutine is completed.

The macro code itself, of course, depends on the steps you took when recording the macro. The more you use this code, the easier it will be to understand. Recreate in your mind the steps you performed onscreen when you were recording the macro, then see how those steps translate into macro language.

You can edit macro language just as you would edit a line of text in your workbook. The backspace and delete keys work, as does the ENTER key. You can select macro information and cut or copy and paste code from one part of the macro to another.

 Is there a way to get back to my original macro if I make a mistake when editing?

If you are uncertain about which lines to change and which lines can be removed, start by making a copy of the macro so that you have a working copy and an unedited copy. Highlight the entire macro (from Sub to End Sub) in the Visual Basic editor, copy the highlighted macro, then paste the macro right beneath the existing macro code. Note: you don't have to place the horizontal line between the two macros—the line appears automatically. You will have two identical macros. Give the second macro a different name so that you can distinguish them (see Figure 15-5). Now you can practice editing one macro and not worry about losing the original one.

After editing your macro, close the editor (either click the "X" in the upper right corner, or choose File | Close and return to Microsoft Excel). Anything you have worked on is automatically saved.

 These Visual Basic commands are overwhelming. Where can I go to figure out what they all mean?

You don't have to travel far to learn about Visual Basic commands. Excel provides an onscreen library of commands for your use. From the Visual Basic editor, choose Microsoft Visual Basic Help (you may be prompted to install this feature, in which case you'll need your Excel disks), where you can find definitions of every Visual Basic command.

There are a number of books on the market that provide reference material for Visual Basic. Try *Visual Basic Programmer's Reference*, *VB from the Ground Up*, and *Visual Basic The Complete Reference*, all published by Osborne/McGraw-Hill. Another good book is *Microsoft Excel 2000 Visual Basic Fundamentals (Step by Step)*, published by Microsoft Press.

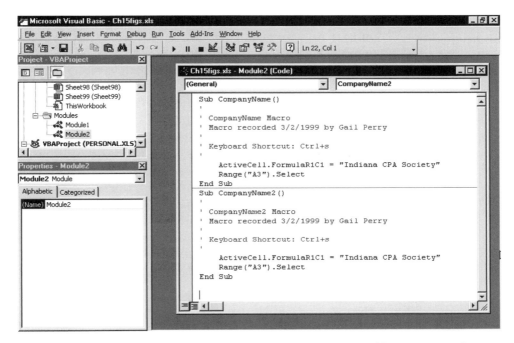

Figure 15-5 Experiment with the macro editor by making a copy of an existing macro

You can also use the Office Assistant to ask questions about Visual Basic. Press F1 to bring up the Office Assistant, then type your question in plain English.

One of the best ways to learn about Visual Basic is to examine existing code. Record macros, then study the code to see which codes have been used.

WORKING WITH VISUAL BASIC

What is a variable and how are variables used in macros?

A variable is a name for a place in your computer's memory that holds information. A variable is used in a macro to hold information while the macro is running. The information is used in the execution of the macro. When the macro is

finished, the variable is no longer needed and therefore no longer contains information. When you run the macro again, you will start over, assigning information to the variable.

For example, a macro that is designed to fill a quantity of cells designated by the user will use a variable that acts as a counter, increasing each time the macro fills a cell, until the designated quantity is reached. If the macro is to fill five cells, the variable will begin with a value of 1, increase to 2 as the macro continues, then 3, 4, and finally 5. When the variable reaches 5, the macro is finished with its execution.

Generally, the existence of a variable is declared at the beginning of the macro using a Dim statement (Dim comes from the word, dimension, a throwback to earlier programming techniques that required programmers to indicate the dimension, or the amount of space, that was to be allocated to a variable). Establish a variable with a line of code like this:

```
Dim Counter as Integer
```

This statement creates a variable called Counter and indicates that the nature of the variable will be an integer.

 ## How can I create a macro that asks the user to provide information, such as the name of a vendor, then places that information in a designated cell in the worksheet?

Some macros just can't be recorded. An example of one is a macro that contains a repeating loop or repeating subroutines. Another example is that of an interactive macro—one that pauses and asks the user for input before continuing. These macros must be created in the Visual Basic editor.

Your macro can request information from the user with the Input Box command. This command allows the macro to communicate with the person using the worksheet. The InputBox command produces a dialog box onscreen and can be used to request specific information, or you can allow the user to make choices from a list of selections.

The InputBox command is created as follows:

```
InputBox("Message"[,"Title"][,Default][,Xpos][,Ypos][Helpfile,Context]}
```

The items in brackets are optional. At a minimum, the InputBox command needs a message. Here is what each item in the command means:

- **Message**   An instruction or informative message that will appear onscreen in the dialog box. The message in the command must appear in quotation marks.

- **Title**   An optional title that will appear at the top of the dialog box. The title must appear in quotation marks.

- **Default**   An optional default answer that will be supplied in the text box area of the dialog box. The text box will be blank if this default is not supplied.

- **Xpos Ypos**   Optional position controls for the horizontal (X) and vertical (Y) position of the dialog box on the screen. The box will appear centered if these controls are not used.

- **Helpfile**   The name of an online help file that accompanies this dialog box. If you enter a help file, you must use the Context option.

- **Context**   Used in conjunction with Helpfile, this is the context ID of the Help topic in the Helpfile.

The response given by the user to the information requested by the input box is stored as a variable. The InputBox command normally appears in this form in a macro:

```
VariableName = InputBox ("Message","Title" [,optional information])
```

The following macro asks the user for the name of a vendor and enters the name in the active cell.

```
Sub NameRequest()
' NameRequest Macro
    Vendor = InputBox("Enter the name of the vendor","Vendor Name")
    ActiveCell.formula = Vendor
End Sub
```

Figure 15-6 shows the window that will appear onscreen when the macro is executed.

The user will enter a name and click OK, and the name will be placed in the active cell of the worksheet.

 I'd like to view the gridlines on my worksheet when I'm working on the sheet, but when I display it for others, I want to turn the gridlines off. Is there an easy way to just click the gridlines on and off?

You can make a little macro that will determine whether the gridlines are turned on or off. The state of the gridlines will become the value of a variable. The macro will reverse the state of the gridlines depending on the value of the variable

You can create some of this macro code by recording yourself turning off the display of gridlines. Record a macro

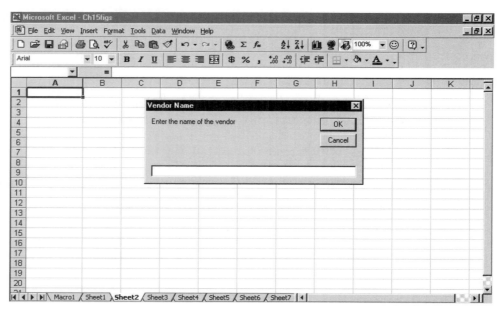

Figure 15-6   The user input box created by your macro

called CHANGEGRID. Turn on the macro recorder, then choose Tools | Options | View | Gridlines, and click OK. Turn off the recorder.

Display the Visual Basic code for this macro by choosing Tools | Macro | Macros, then click on the CHANGEGRID macro and choose Edit. As you can see, the command issued in the macro to turn off the gridlines display is

```
ActiveWindow.DisplayGridlines = False
```

Use the information from this little macro to provide the command you need. You want your macro to create a variable that will capture the status of the ActiveWindow.DisplayGridlines feature. This variable statement will become the first line of your code. The variable, which we will call GridStatus, will be created as follows:

```
GridStatus = ActiveWindow.DisplayGridlines
```

The second line of code asks Excel to reverse the status of the gridlines by executing the opposite of the current gridline status:

```
ActiveWindow.DisplayGridlines = Not GridStatus
```

The final macro code is displayed in Figure 15-7.

To make this macro more accessible, you may want to assign it to a button right on your worksheet—click a button, the gridlines go off; click again, they return. See the question later in this chapter about assigning macros to buttons.

 I use a spreadsheet that contains two large print areas. Can I create a macro that will ask the user which area should be printed and then print that area only?

Use an If/Then/Else routine in your macro, and suddenly your macro can think logically. The process of the macro proceeds in different directions depending on the results of an If command. Just like the IF function in Excel, the If/Then/Else command

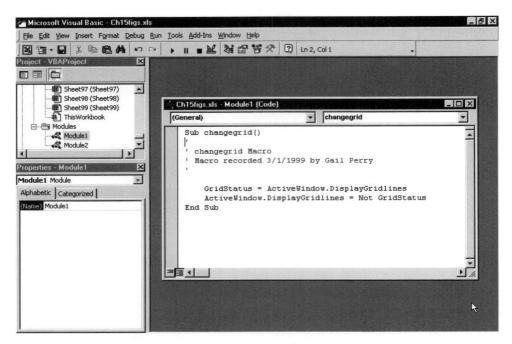

Figure 15-7 This little macro turns the display of gridlines on your worksheet off and on

relies on a logical statement with a true scenario and a false scenario. Here's how to create the requested macro.

First, assign range names to the areas of the worksheet to be printed by naming the areas PrintArea1 and PrintArea2 (use Insert | Name | Define to assign the names). Refer to these areas in the following macro:

```
Sub SpecialPrint()
' SpecialPrint Macro
Report = Inputbox("Enter 1 to print Report 1, Enter 2
to print Report 2")
If Report = 1 Then
    Application.Goto Reference:="PrintArea1"
    Selection.PrintOut Copies:=1
ElseIf Report = 2 Then
    Application.Goto Reference:="PrintArea2"
```

```
        Selection.PrintOut Copies:=1
Else
        Msgbox "No valid entry was made… please try again"
End If
End Sub
```

How are subroutines used in macros?

A subroutine is like a little macro that runs within another macro. The main macro can call a subroutine, and the macro execution will advance to the area of the macro that contains the subroutine. Then the execution will return to the place where the macro left off.

To demonstrate how subroutines work, redo the macro above as follows.

First, create a print macro for each of the areas by naming the areas (assign range names by highlighting the area to be printed, choose Insert | Name | Define)—in this example, call them PrintArea1 and PrintArea2—then requesting the Print command. Here's the Visual Basic code that will print the first print area:

```
Application.Goto Reference:="PrintArea1"
ActiveWindow.SelectedSheets.PrintOut Copies:=1
```

You are going to make these commands to appear as a subroutine in the macro so that if the user wants to print the first print area, these are the commands that will execute. If the user wants to print the second area, another subroutine will execute indicating PrintArea2 instead of PrintArea1.

You will want an InputBox to ask the user which report he wants to print:

```
Report = InputBox("Enter 1 to print Report 1, Enter 2
to print Report 2")
```

The macro needs to contain two print command areas, one for PrintArea1 and one for PrintArea2. Each area should be distinguished with a label (a single word) so that

Excel will know where to go to execute the subroutine. The completed macro:

```
Sub SpecialPrint()
' SpecialPrint Macro
Question:
Report = Inputbox("Enter 1 to print Report 1, Enter 2
to print Report 2")
If Report = 1 Then
    GoTo Print1
ElseIf Report = 2 Then
    GoTo Print2
Else
    GoTo Question
End If
Print1:
    Application.Goto Reference:="PrintArea1"
    Selection.PrintOut Copies:=1
End
Print2:
    Application.Goto Reference:="PrintArea2"
    Selection.PrintOut Copies:=1
End Sub
```

Notice the following things about the macro that contains the If/Then/Else loop:

- Each area of the macro (the main area and the subroutines) begins with a label followed by a colon. The label is used to identify where the macro is to resume executing commands.
- Each subroutine ends with an End command.
- There is no limit to the number of ElseIf commands and related subroutines you can contain in a macro.

As an alternative, the following macro code shows the entire macro using the If/Then/Else feature, without setting aside separate subroutines. This method makes for a simpler macro:

```
Sub SpecialPrint()
' SpecialPrint Macro
Report = Inputbox("Enter 1 to print Report 1, Enter 2
to print Report 2")
```

```
If  Report  =  1  Then
    Application.Goto  Reference:="PrintArea1"
    Selection.PrintOut  Copies:=1
ElseIf  Report  =  2  Then
    Application.Goto  Reference:="PrintArea2"
    Selection.PrintOut  Copies:=1
Else
    Msgbox  "No  valid  entry  was  made…  please  try  again"
End  If
End  Sub
```

OTHER MACRO ISSUES

I plan to upgrade from Excel 97 to Excel 2000. Am I in danger of losing my macros?

Your macros from Excel 97 will work perfectly in Excel 2000, but there is something you need to do before upgrading. Save your PERSONAL.XLS file (which resides in the XLStart folder) before upgrading, then copy this file to your new XLStart folder after you upgrade. All universal macros will be available to you. Any macros saved with individual worksheets will open along with the worksheets when you open those files in Excel 2000.

Choosing Tools | Macro | Macros, picking the macro, then choosing Run is a lot of steps to execute a simple little macro. Is there a way to just click on a button and run a macro?

You can assign a macro button to your toolbar (see Chapter 12, "Customizing Excel"), you can assign a macro to a menu (see the last question in the first section of this chapter, "I have created many macros. It seems there are a lot of steps involved in running macros. Is there an easy way to access my macros from the menu?"), or you can place a button right on your worksheet so the user just has to click on it to run the macro.

Add a button to your worksheet by following these steps:

1. Choose View | Toolbars | Forms. The Forms toolbar will appear (see Figure 15-8).

2. Select the Button icon.

Figure 15-8 Click the Button icon to begin the process of placing a clickable button on your worksheet

3. Drag a rectangle on your worksheet to where you want to locate the button. A Button Box will appear, as will the Assign Macro window (see Figure 15-9).

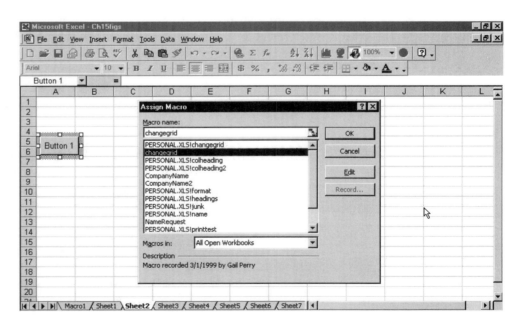

Figure 15-9 After you drag a rectangle for your button, the Assign Macro window appears

4. Click on the macro you want to assign to this button, then click OK.

5. Give the button a name by clicking in the selected button, choosing Edit Text, and replacing the existing text (Button 1) with text appropriate to your macro (see Figure 15-10).

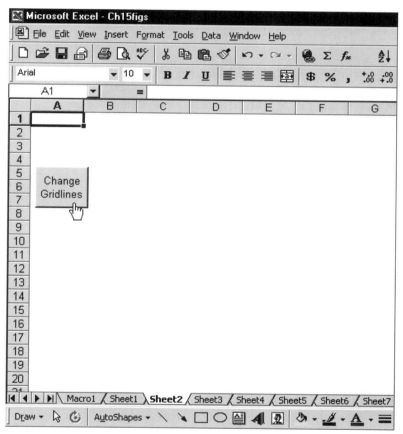

Figure 15-10 From now on, you can click this button (notice that your mouse pointer becomes a pointing finger when poised over the button) to execute your macro

Chapter 16

Excel and Other Applications

Answer Topics!

Excel and Other Applications @ a Glance

Overview. Our world seems to be getting smaller as communication between countries becomes much easier. In a spirit of cooperation, software programs are also finding it much easier to communicate with one another. You can place your Excel worksheet inside of a number of other software programs and expect that you will be able not only to view the file, but to edit it as well. Similarly, you can link an object such as a sound or image file to Excel and launch the original program while staying in Excel. This chapter looks at various ways to make your spreadsheet "talk" to other programs.

Excel and Other Office Applications. Trade information among your Microsoft Office programs with the use of the Windows clipboard. You can cut and paste information from one program to another. You can use the other Office applications to create data, then import the data into Excel for manipulation in a spreadsheet format.

OLE Objects. Exchange live data between your programs using OLE techniques, and maintain a link to the originating program. Placing an OLE object in a file gives the user the ability to not only view the object, but to use the commands in the originating file to control the object. OLE objects are updated immediately in their source location when the originating file is changed. You can place small icons in your file that represent OLE objects, and thus save space in your source file.

Linking to (and from) Other Applications. The process of sharing data doesn't stop with Microsoft programs. You can easily share information between Excel and other Windows programs. Choose clipart, photos, and illustrations from graphic programs to enhance your worksheets. Share information with other spreadsheet programs, such as Lotus 1-2-3. Link directly to an Internet site to obtain the latest information from the Web.

EXCEL AND OTHER OFFICE APPLICATIONS

 ## How can I copy a spreadsheet into a Word document?

You can easily display part or all of your worksheet in a Word document by using the Windows clipboard. Just copy the worksheet to the Windows clipboard and then paste it into Word. This creates a Word table that can be edited in the same way that you edit any other table in Word.

To copy your worksheet into Word:

1. Open the Excel worksheet and select the cells that you want to copy.

 2. Choose Edit | Copy, or click the Copy button on the standard toolbar.

3. Switch to or launch Microsoft Word.

4. Position your cursor at the line where you want to paste the spreadsheet information and choose Edit | Paste, or click the Paste button. The copied cells will appear.

 Tip: *When displaying a pasted worksheet in Word, the table may appear with gray gridlines around the cells. These are nonprinting gridlines. To turn off the gridlines display, choose Table | Hide Gridlines. Turn on the display of gridlines by choosing Table | Show Gridlines.*

5. To make changes to the worksheet, place your cursor where you want to make a change and edit as you normally would.

Any changes you make to the worksheet information that you have placed into Word via the normal Windows clipboard will not affect the worksheet in Excel; the files are not linked in any way. Also, when you paste via the normal Windows clipboard, there is no evidence that the worksheet you pasted did not originate from within Word. It will look, act, and be a normal table within Word, and you can change and format it any way that you want.

How can I copy an Excel chart into a Word document?

Click once on the Excel chart to select it (small square handles will appear around the outside edges of the chart so you'll know it has been selected), then choose Edit | Copy, or click the Copy button on the standard toolbar.

Open the Word document in which you want to place the chart, position your cursor where the chart should appear, and choose Edit | Paste or click the Paste button. The chart will appear at the cursor position in your Word document.

A chart that has been placed in a Word document cannot be edited. If you want to change the chart information, you must return to Excel, make appropriate changes, and copy and paste the revised chart into your Word document (see the next question for information about pasting a link).

How can I make sure that Word always reflects the most current version of the worksheet I copied from Excel?

When you paste a worksheet from Excel into Word, you can choose to paste the worksheet as a *link*, thus preserving the connection between the two programs. If the worksheet changes in Excel, the Word file will be updated. The link does not work in reverse, however; if you link a worksheet from Excel to Word and make changes to the worksheet in the Word file, the changes won't carry back to the Excel file.

Create a link between your Excel worksheet and your Word document by following these steps:

1. Select the worksheet information in Excel that you wish to copy to the Word document.

2. Choose Edit | Copy, or click the Copy button.

3. Open your Word document, or switch to the document if it is already open.

4. Click where you want the worksheet information to appear.

5. Choose Edit | Paste Special. The Paste Special dialog box will appear (see Figure 16-1).

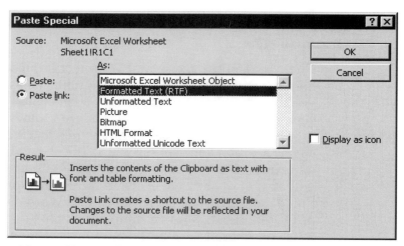

Figure 16-1 Choose Formatted Text to paste your Excel worksheet as a table in Word

6. Click the Paste link button. Choose the format in which you wish the worksheet to appear. The Formatted Text option will put your worksheet information in a table form. See Table 16-1 for a description of all of the Paste Special options.

7. Click OK to create the link.

From this point forward, any changes you make in the worksheet information on your Excel worksheet will be reflected in your Word document. If the Word document is open at the time the changes are made, the changes will occur within a few seconds. If the Word document is closed, the document will be updated the next time you open it.

Option	Result
Microsoft Excel Worksheet Object	The Excel worksheet appears as a picture and cannot be changed from within Word. Double-clicking on the picture opens Excel and the file containing the source information. The linked information is updated when the Excel file changes.

Table 16-1 Paste Special Options for Pasting from Excel into Word

Option	Result
Formatted Text (RTF)	The Excel worksheet appears as text in a Word table and can be formatted and changed within the Word document. The linked information is updated when the Excel file changes.
Unformatted Text	The Excel worksheet appears as unformatted text and can be formatted and changed within the Word document. The linked information is updated when the Excel file changes.
Picture	The Excel worksheet appears as a picture and cannot be changed from within Word. Double-clicking on the picture opens Excel and the file containing the source information. The linked information is updated when the Excel file changes.
Bitmap	The Excel worksheet appears as a bitmap image that retains all formatting from Excel. The image cannot be changed in Word. Double-clicking on the image opens Excel and the file containing the source information. The linked information is updated when the Excel file changes.
Word Hyperlink	The Excel worksheet appears as text in a Word table and can be edited and formatted within Word. Clicking any information in the table produces an immediate hyperlink to Excel and the file containing the source information. Changes in the Excel file do not affect the Word document.
HTML Format	The Excel worksheet appears in HTML format in a Word table and can be formatted and changed within Word. Double-clicking on any information in the table opens Excel and the file containing the source information. The linked information is updated when the Excel file changes.
Unformatted Unicode Text	The Excel worksheet appears as unformatted text in the Word document and can be formatted and changed within Word. The linked information is updated when the Excel file changes.

Table 16-1   Paste Special Options for Pasting from Excel into Word *(continued)*

 I linked information from Excel to Word, but now I want the information to remain independent of my Excel worksheet. How can I break a link?

To break the connection between the original Excel document and the linked information in your Word document, open the Word document containing the link and choose Edit | Links. Click on the linked object for which you no longer want to

maintain a link, then click the Break Link button. Click Yes when asked if you're sure you want to break the selected link, and click OK to close the window. From this point forward, when the linked information in Excel changes, the information in your Word document will remain unchanged.

? Should I put my spreadsheet in a Word document or should I put a Word document in my spreadsheet?

That depends. The most important thing to consider when deciding upon the master application is the final use for the information. If you need to create templates for Excel workbooks and want to maintain the documentation for the templates in Word, then your best solution is to place linked Word files into Excel. Since your users need to create and edit the worksheets as they read the documentation, Excel would be the appropriate place to show the Word files.

If you need to write a report for your management that explains the results you obtained in a worksheet, and your management will see only the paper copy of the report, then you will probably want to paste your spreadsheet into Word. Word has better writing controls and is the easier program in which to format an attractive text-based report.

You can get data from one Office application into another in one of three ways (this is covered in more detail later in this chapter).

- If you paste from the clipboard, use the current application to edit the pasted information.

- If you embed the data, it retains a link to the original application for editing but is independent of the document from which it originated.

- If you link the data, then you cannot edit it at all. Attempting to edit it launches the original source of the data for edit.

Therefore, you need to consider your audience very carefully when you decide which application to use as the controlling application. You need to know what the users will need to do with the document when they receive it. Finally, you need to know which applications the users will be able to access. In order to edit an embedded object, the user must have access to the application. In order to edit a linked document, the user must have the application and the rights to edit the original document. If you are in doubt of either of these two considerations, your best choice is to paste the data directly from the clipboard into the application that is most likely to be used by the person who needs to view or edit the document.

What happens when I use the Paste command to paste something from the clipboard into my spreadsheet? Which cells are affected? Can I change it later?

If you copy a portion of a Word document to the clipboard to paste it into an Excel worksheet, the entire text is pasted into the selected cell. Each paragraph in the pasted text shows up as a single line without any word wrapping on it. Although you can see the text, it isn't a pretty sight. The text is visible on top of the surrounding empty cells.

If you paste the text into a cell, but the nearby cells to the right or down are occupied, the text won't be visible in the worksheet where the occupied cells are located. Even if the adjacent cells are empty when you paste the text, if you later add something to those cells, you obscure the display of your pasted text.

If you need to edit the text, you can do so exactly as you edit the contents of any other cell. Using the Paste command is really only suitable as a shortcut so that you don't need to retype small amounts of text. For longer extracts of text, you simply don't have enough control over the results. It is better to use the Paste Special command (see Table 16-1).

How can I use an external database stored in Access?

Getting Access data into Excel is fairly easy. You cannot link or embed an OLE object from Microsoft Access, but you can Paste or Paste Special the data from an Access file so that it appears with each field in its own cell. You can also export the file directly from Access.

To save the Access table as an Excel worksheet:

1. Launch Microsoft Access and open the Table that you want to export. (You can also export a query, form, or report.)

2. Choose Tools | Office Links | Analyze It With MS Excel. The new worksheet is automatically given the same name as your exported Table, Query, Report, or Form, and it is stored in the current working directory.

3. Launch Excel. Use the File | Open command to locate the saved file (it will have an .XLS extension). You can now work with it as if it were a native Excel worksheet. Nothing that you do to the data in Excel will affect the data stored in your Access table. There is no link between the files at all.

If you prefer to use the clipboard, you have a few more options. You may selectively copy records or fields from the Access database to the clipboard, and then switch to Excel and paste the contents of the clipboard into your worksheet.

1. Launch Access and open the Table from which you want to copy data.

2. If you want to copy the entire Table, click on the first cell at the top of the Table. This highlights the entire Table. To select only a few fields, click on the field header and drag the marquee until all of the fields that you want are selected. In Datasheet View, you can only select adjacent fields. If you want to select a few records, click on the first record that you want to copy and extend the selection with the marquee.

3. Choose Edit | Copy.

4. Switch to Excel. Place your cursor in the cell where you want to place the first record.

5. Choose Edit | Paste or Edit | Paste Special. If you use the Paste command, the field headers are pasted as plain text. You might also need to adjust the column width.

The row height tends to adjust to accommodate word wrap if the data contains spaces that mask a natural break (such as names that contain commas in them).

If you select Paste Special, you have a choice of several different formats. The BIFF format is Excel's native format and that makes it a good choice to use. The field headers retain their shading in the Excel file so that they are easy to recognize. The CVS format (comma delimited) also works well but does not use any special formatting for the field headers.

You can also use an Access file directly when you create a Pivot Table by selecting the database as your external data source.

I want my spreadsheet to be displayed in my PowerPoint presentation, but I need to be able to update without opening PowerPoint. I also need to have the worksheet show the new data the next time that I open my PowerPoint presentation. How do I do that?

You can use the Insert Object command to place your file into the PowerPoint presentation.

1. Launch PowerPoint.

2. Look at your PowerPoint presentation in Slide view. If you are in Outline view, the commands won't work. Add a new slide or position to the existing slide where you want to place the Excel table.

3. Choose Insert | Object. Scroll through the list until you see the Microsoft Excel object option.

4. Select the From File radio button and select the Link check box.

5. Click on Browse and locate the Excel worksheet that you want to embed.

6. Click on OK. The worksheet in the file appears in your slide.

If you want to place only some of the worksheet into your PowerPoint presentation (which is the more likely situation), then follow these steps:

1. Launch Excel.

2. Select the range of data that you want. Choose Edit | Copy.

3. Return to PowerPoint. Look at your PowerPoint presentation in Slide view. Add a new slide if necessary.

4. Choose Edit | Paste Special. Click on the Paste link radio button (see Figure 16-2). Select the Microsoft Excel Worksheet Object option. Click on OK.

5. Position the object where you want it on the form.

Now, although you cannot edit the worksheet in your PowerPoint presentation, you can edit the document either by double-clicking on it in PowerPoint (which launches Excel and loads the original worksheet) or by opening the worksheet directly in Excel. Changing a value in Excel automatically and instantly changes it in PowerPoint. If the PowerPoint presentation is closed when you make the changes, you'll be shown a dialog box asking if you want to update the linked data the next time that you open the presentation.

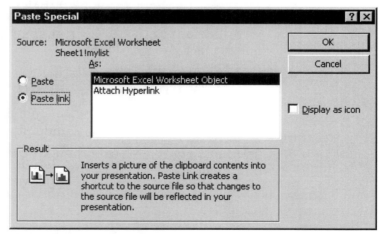

Figure 16-2 You have the choice of linking or embedding your pasted worksheet

OLE OBJECTS

 I've heard about OLE, but I want to know what it's good for.

OLE stands for Object Linking and Embedding. It is a technology developed by Microsoft that allows live data to be exchanged between programs. Data is "live" if the receiving program knows where it came from. For example, if you copy some text from Microsoft Word and paste it into an Adobe Photoshop document, Photoshop sees pixels. It knows nothing about text that can be edited by typing. Therefore, this text is not live. If you use OLE to paste a snippet of text from Word into Excel, Excel knows that you have pasted text and that Word is the program that created the text. Furthermore, when you attempt to edit the text, Excel invokes Word to work as the editor. This text *is* live.

The purpose of OLE is to allow you to use data created in one program in another application. It is a way of sharing information. You might need to show your budget to your management or to create a chart based on an Excel worksheet for a presentation. You might want to attach a Word document that holds instructions for completing an Excel worksheet to your Excel file. You might even want to embed a PowerPoint presentation in your Excel worksheet if the instructions are complex enough that you need a show and tell. There are many, many reasons why sharing data is very helpful. It is the magic of OLE that allows this to happen.

What is the difference between inserting an object and pasting an object?

There are several critical terms to understand when you use the OLE technology. When you place data from one application into another, the placed data is known as an object. Double-clicking on the object allows you to edit it either in the current application with the tool set from the original application, or in the original application itself.

Objects that are placed into other applications can be *linked* or *embedded*. An embedded object is copied into the

document in the application where it is placed. It is not linked to its original document and it can be edited without updating or changing the original file. When you double-click on an embedded object, the original application, if it is part of Microsoft Office or it is a compliant application, sends its tools into the current host application.

For example, if you copy a paragraph of text from a Word document and embed it into an open Excel worksheet, the paragraphs retain their formatting. Unlike the mess that's made if you simply paste the text, the word wrap feature works properly, and the text looks just as it did in Word. If you need to edit the text, you can double-click on the text, and the object will display a Word ruler bar. To stop editing the object, just click on another cell and the Word tools will go away. When you save the Excel document, the text in the object is saved along with the worksheet.

When you create an OLE link object, you only paste the location of the original object into your file. For example, if you want to place a complex graphic from Photoshop into an Excel worksheet but you know that your art department needs to update that graphic, you might want to link rather than embed the file. This makes your file size smaller (because Excel doesn't need to store a large pixel-based graphics file), and allows the art department to do its updates whenever it needs to. You cannot edit the graphic inside of Excel, but double-clicking on the linked object will both open Photoshop and open the original file for editing.

OLE allows you to keep data live by either linking or embedding; the Paste command does not keep data live.

How I can place an OLE object into a file?

You have several ways to place an OLE object. The two relevant commands are Insert | Object and Edit | Paste Special. Both of these commands allow OLE objects to be added to your document.

The Paste Special command uses the Windows clipboard. The technique was shown in an earlier question in this chapter concerning PowerPoint. When you use the Paste Special command, you will usually see the option to link. The As: field in the dialog box shows the applicable formats.

You don't need to have anything on the clipboard when you use the Insert | Object command. The Object dialog box, shown in Figure 16-3, gives you two main choices: to create a new empty container for data of a specific type (e.g., a blank worksheet in a Word document or a blank image file for CorelDraw in Excel), or to create an object from an existing file. If you select the existing file, then you can browse to find the file. The entire file is imported.

What types of objects are available for linking or embedding?

The objects available for linking or embedding depend upon the applications installed on your machine. When you use Paste Special, this is not an issue because you only see options that apply to an object you have placed in the Windows clipboard.

Be very cautious when you use the Create New option to insert an object, especially if you are working on a computer that contains a Microsoft Developers package. You might have a number of controls or objects that can be inserted that do not work without being programmed and which, once inserted, can't be moved, edited, or removed from the

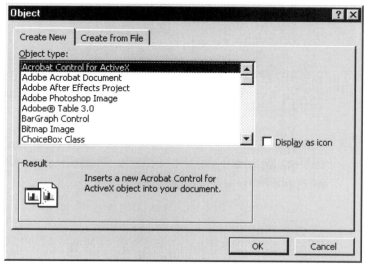

Figure 16-3   Inserting a OLE object

document (Edit | Undo doesn't work on these either). Bottom line: only insert an object from a known application.

You also need to know which programs exist on the machines of others with whom you might plan to share the document. In order to insert, view, or edit an OLE object, you need the correct application and the correct version of the application on your hard drive or network.

 If I insert an object from a file, what happens if I change or delete the original file?

If you make changes to a linked file, you will usually be asked if you want to update your linked object the next time that you open the file that contains it. If the file containing the link is open when the source information is changed, the linked information will change immediately (within seconds). If you have deleted the original file, then the link is no longer valid, and you need to delete the object from your document. You can keep the object in your document, but you might not be able to edit it again.

1. Open the linked file.
2. When asked to update the file, select No.
3. Choose Edit | Links. Change the method from Automatic to Manual.
4. You can also select Tools | Options | Edit and deselect the Ask To Update Automatic Links option.

If you change the location of the linked document, you can restore the link by choosing Edit | Links and updating the location or name of the link.

 I placed a Word document into my worksheet, but it takes up too much room. How can I display something smaller?

You may find that placing an object into Excel takes up too much room. Perhaps the object is a Word file that is nice but not critical for the worksheet users to read. You can place an icon for the file into your worksheet and allow the user to click on it if interested. Clicking on the icon for the Word document launches Word and loads the original document. You can choose to either link to or embed the icon in your document. In either case, Word is called in as the application when the icon is clicked.

1. Select your text in Word (this step is optional if you want to embed an entire document).

2. In Excel, choose either Edit | Paste Special or Insert | Object | From File.

3. Select the Link option if you want to link rather than embed the text.

4. Select the Display as icon check box, as shown in Figure 16-4. Figure 16-5 shows the worksheet with the icon in it.

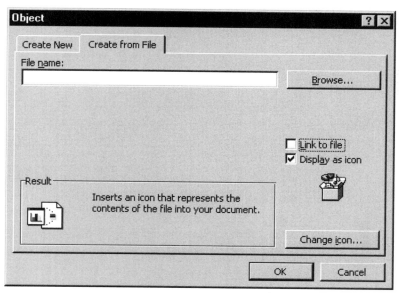

Figure 16-4 Select the Display as icon check box

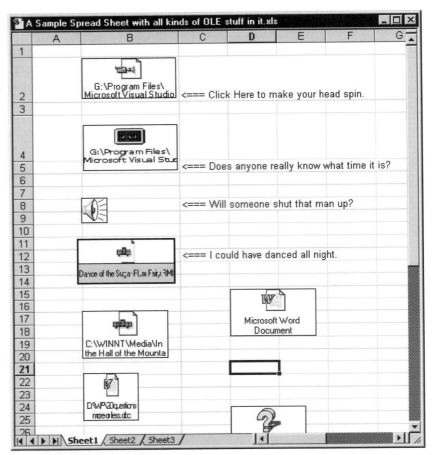

Figure 16-5 The Word icon appears in the worksheet

LINKING TO (AND FROM) OTHER APPLICATIONS

 Can I only exchange data between Excel and other Microsoft applications?

You can paste data into any application that uses the Microsoft clipboard. In addition, many other applications are OLE-aware. You can embed a Photoshop file as an OLE object, for example, and launch Photoshop by double-clicking

on the object in your Excel document. This will allow you to edit the image from Photoshop. CorelDraw is friendlier with Excel than Photoshop. If you embed a CorelDraw or Corel PhotoPaint object and double-click on it, the tools for that program appear in Excel so that you can edit your image in place.

You can also link an Illustrator file to an Excel spreadsheet so that you can maintain data for a graph in Illustrator that depends upon data in an Excel worksheet.

In other words, in addition to the Office Suite of products, many other applications can be hotlinked via OLE.

What kind of neat stuff can I put in my spreadsheet to give it a little pizzazz?

In addition to Word or image files, you can bring in sound, video, or presentation files and embed them in your worksheets using Excel. You can record your voice as a sound file and allow users to hear your message whenever they use the worksheet. You can create a video of office processes (or even of the gang at the office) so that faraway users can experience that personal touch.

In fact, you can add so much pizzazz to your spreadsheet that you forget why you are using it in the first place. Although you can add many types of data to your worksheets, you really need to ask yourself if it will add something to the usability of the worksheet or if the feature is being used merely because it's there. Remember that these objects take up memory and file space and can cause your worksheets to slow down.

Can I import a logo into my worksheet? If so, is there a way to lock it to the worksheet?

Your logo is as easy to import as any other file that you want to embed. Paste the logo into the document using either the Paste Special or Inset Object Form File command, link or embed the file just as you would any other type of object.

If you want to make sure that no one can delete or move the logo:

1. Select the logo (though this isn't really necessary). Selecting the logo places control handles at the corners of the object. These handles disappear as soon as the object is protected, so you have instant conformation that your command was obeyed.

2. Choose Tools | Protection | Protect Sheet.

3. In the Protect Sheet dialog box shown in Figure 16-6, deselect the Contents and Scenarios check boxes. Leave only the Object check box selected.

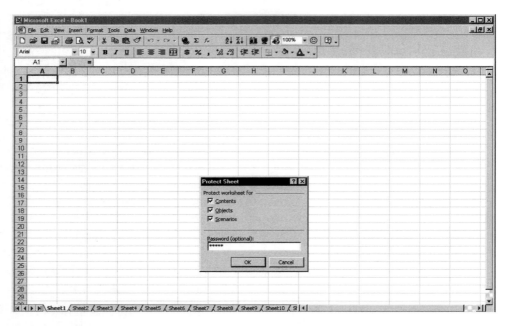

Figure 16-6 Protecting the objects in a worksheet prevents them from being moved or edited

4. Click on OK to exit. The handles around the selected object will disappear and the object can no longer be moved or edited.

How can I convert multiple Lotus 1-2-3 files to Excel format in a single step?

You can use the File Conversion Wizard to convert a batch of Lotus 1-2-3 (or a number of other file formats) to Excel files in one action. You first need to make sure that the menu item Tools | Wizard exists. If it does not, select Tools | Add-Ins. As shown in Figure 16-7, select the File Conversion Wizard check box (if you don't see File Conversion Wizard in the Add-Ins dialog box, then you need to run the Excel setup program to install the wizards). This loads the wizard into Excel. You will then see the Tools | Wizard command

1. Choose Tools | Wizard | File Conversion.

2. The first dialog box asks you to select the file format of the files to be converted and to locate the folder that contains the files. Choose one file of the desired type in the correct location. Click Next to continue.

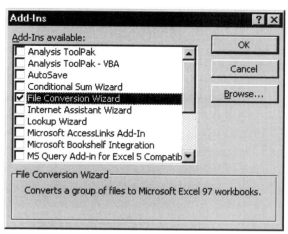

Figure 16-7 From the Add-Ins dialog box, select the File Conversion Wizard

3. The second dialog box in the wizard shows all of the files of the selected type that are located in the selected directory. Select the check boxes of the files that you want to convert. Click on the Next button to continue.

4. The final dialog box asks you to select a location to which to write the converted files. Click on Finish to execute the batch conversion.

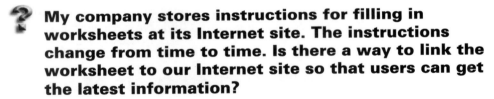

I just imported from Lotus 1-2-3, but my new data shows as zeros. What can I do?

There is a simple fix for this problem.

1. Choose Tools | Options.
2. Click on the Transition Tab.
3. Deselect the Transition Formula Evaluation and Transition Formula check boxes.
4. Click on OK.

My company stores instructions for filling in worksheets at its Internet site. The instructions change from time to time. Is there a way to link the worksheet to our Internet site so that users can get the latest information?

You can insert a Hyperlink object into your worksheet as a link.

1. Choose Insert | Hyperlink.
2. You can then type in the name of the document to which you want to link or browse to find it. You can link to another location in your worksheet or workbook, to another workbook, to a document on your local hard drive or server, or to a document stored on the Internet. Figure 16-8 shows the dialog box.
3. If there is a named range or location within the file to which you want you link, you may also enter it.

4. If you have entered the exact name of the link file, then you can deselect the Use relative path for hyperlink check box.

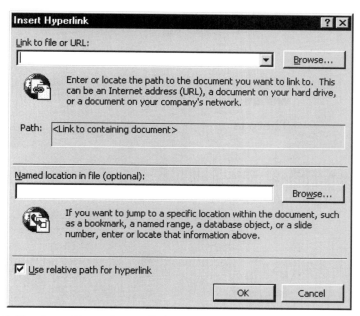

Figure 16-8 Inserting a hyperlink

Chapter 17

Miscellaneous Excel Topics

Answer Topics!

Miscellaneous Excel Topics @ a Glance

- **Overview.** Many features in Excel lend themselves to one or two quick questions but don't necessarily need to take up the space of an entire chapter. The topics covered in this chapter, therefore, have little in common with one another other than the fact that they are all about features in Excel, and they are all questions that have come up again and again.

- **Excel Odds and Ends.** Excel's miscellaneous features include audit tracing tools, WordArt letter-drawing, cell comments, retrieval of corrupt data, text boxes, sheet separators, and rotation tools. This chapter wraps up with a discussion of Excel resources on the Web.

EXCEL ODDS AND ENDS

I just received a spreadsheet file that is full of complicated formulas. Is there an easy way to figure out the source of all the numbers for these formulas?

You can easily trace the source of calculations in your worksheet. Use Excel's auditing commands to get a visual display of the numbers being used in formulas and which cells are being referenced in different areas of the worksheet.

Open the Auditing Toolbar by choosing Tools | Auditing, Show Auditing Toolbar:

A precedent, in spreadsheet terms, is a cell that provides data for another cell. If cell C7 equals the sum of cells A7 and B7, A7 and B7 are precedents for C7. Click on a formula on your worksheet, then choose Trace Precedents from the Auditing toolbar to display blue arrows pointing from the cells that feed into the formula (see Figure 17-1).

A dependent, according to Excel, is a cell that contains a formula which is dependent on the information in another cell. Using the same example as above, if cell C7 equals the sum of cells A7 and B7, then C7 is dependent on A7. Click on a cell, then choose Trace Dependents from the Auditing toolbar. Excel will display blue arrows showing which cells are dependent on the one you selected (see Figure 17-2).

Remove these blue arrows when you are finished analyzing the cell contents by clicking the Remove All Arrows

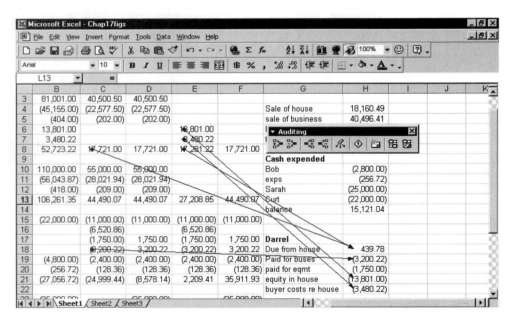

Figure 17-1 Click on a cell, then choose Trace Precedents and find out which cells in the worksheet provide information for the selected cell

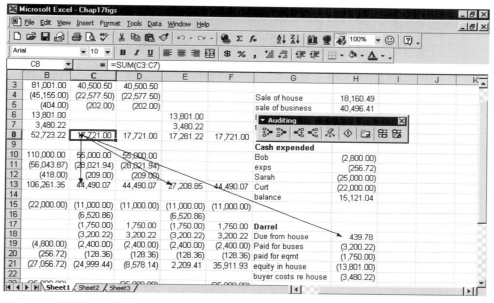

Figure 17-2 Click on a cell, then choose Trace Dependents to find out which cells in the worksheet get their data from this selected cell

button on the Auditing Toolbar. Click the "X" in the upper-right corner of the toolbar to make it go away.

I love all the drawing features, and I'm the worst artist I know. Can you offer some advice for quick and easy art techniques to spruce up my worksheets?

I recommend WordArt as the answer to gussying up a worksheet with the minimum of artistic ability necessary. Choose Insert | Picture | WordArt, and the WordArt Gallery will appear, displaying a collection of text styles (see Figure 17-3). Double-click on a style, and the Edit WordArt Text window will appear with "Your Text Here," emblazoned across the window. Replace the sample text with your own words of wisdom. Edit the font and size choices, indicate if you want to apply bold or italic, then click OK to place your text on the worksheet (see Figure 17-4).

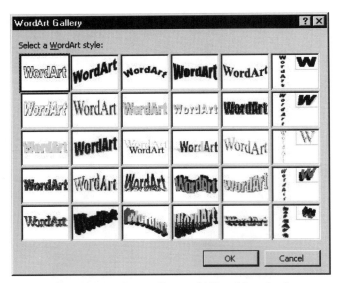

Figure 17-3 Choose from the gallery of WordArt designs

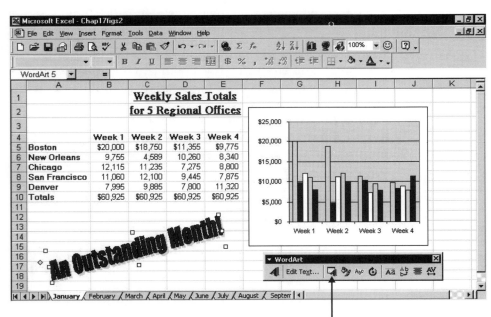

The WordArt toolbar appears whenever you select a WordArt object on screen

Figure 17-4 Use the WordArt toolbar tools to rotate, change the color (format), and change the style of your WordArt object. Click off the object, and the toolbar disappears

Resize your WordArt objects to make them larger or smaller by dragging one of the handles on the outside edge of the object. To keep the object proportional while resizing so that it won't look stretched or squished, follow theses rules:

To resize WordArt in this manner	Do this
To resize proportionally from a corner	Press SHFT while dragging a comer handle.
To resize vertically, horizontally, or diagonally from the center	Press CTRL while dragging a handle.
To resize proportionally from the center	Press CTRL-SHIFT while dragging a corner.

You can rotate your WordArt object by clicking the Rotate button on the WordArt toolbar, then placing your mouse pointer over any of the handles on the corners of the object. You can drag the object to a new location by placing your mouse pointer directly in the middle of the object and dragging.

How can I display my worksheet without the little red dots that represent comments?

The presentation of the comment dots is controlled in the Options dialog box. Choose Tools | Options, then click the View tab (see Figure 17-5). In the Comments section, choose None, and the comment dots will disappear.

Note: *Hiding the little red dots effectively hides the comments as well. The comments are still saved with your worksheet, but if the dots are not visible, you will not be able to read the comments.*

To redisplay comments and their associated red dots, choose View | Comments.

I am unable to open one particular Excel file but my other Excel files open without a problem. Is there a way to access my data in the corrupted file?

You may get an illegal operation error when you try to open an Excel file that has been corrupted. The error may read

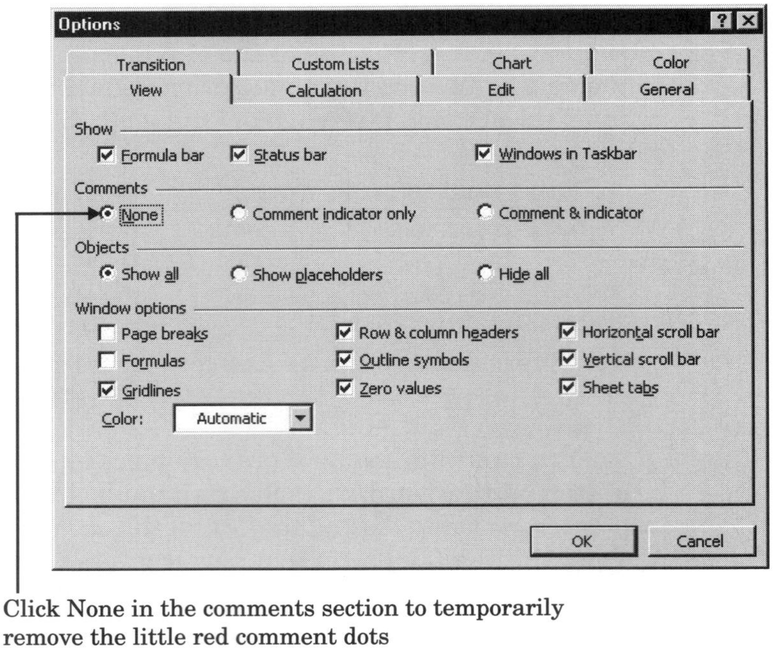

Click None in the comments section to temporarily
remove the little red comment dots

Figure 17-5   You can control the display of comment indicators in the
Options dialog box

something like, "Excel caused an invalid page fault in
Excel.exe." You can still get access to the data in the file by
opening the file in Word, then copying and pasting the
information onto a new Excel worksheet.

Follow these steps to retrieve your data:

1. Open Microsoft Word.

2. Choose File | Open.

3. Change the Look in location to the folder where the
   problem file is located.

4. Change the Files of type box to read All Files.

5. Locate the corrupted Excel file and double-click on the
   file name.

 Note: *You may get a message indicating that a feature isn't installed. If you receive this message, insert your Word CD as requested and install the feature, then continue.*

6. An Open Workbook screen will appear that will be set to Entire Workbook (see Figure 17-6). You can specify a particular sheet from the workbook on this screen. Once you select the desired options, click OK. The spreadsheet will open in Word.

7. Highlight the area you want copy to Excel, or choose Edit | Select All.

8. Choose Edit | Copy.

9. Open a new Excel workbook and choose Edit | Paste.

When I right-click on a text box and choose Copy, then click on a different location in the worksheet and choose Paste, the text box is not pasted. How does one paste a text box?

To paste a text box, you must first position the cursor over the border of the text box, as opposed to in the center of the box (see Figure 17-7). Then right-click and choose Copy. Right-click elsewhere on the worksheet or on another worksheet and choose Paste. Now the text box will be pasted.

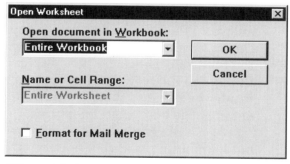

Figure 17-6 When this box appears, choose Entire Worksheet or select a particular screen (you may only select one), to restore your corrupted file

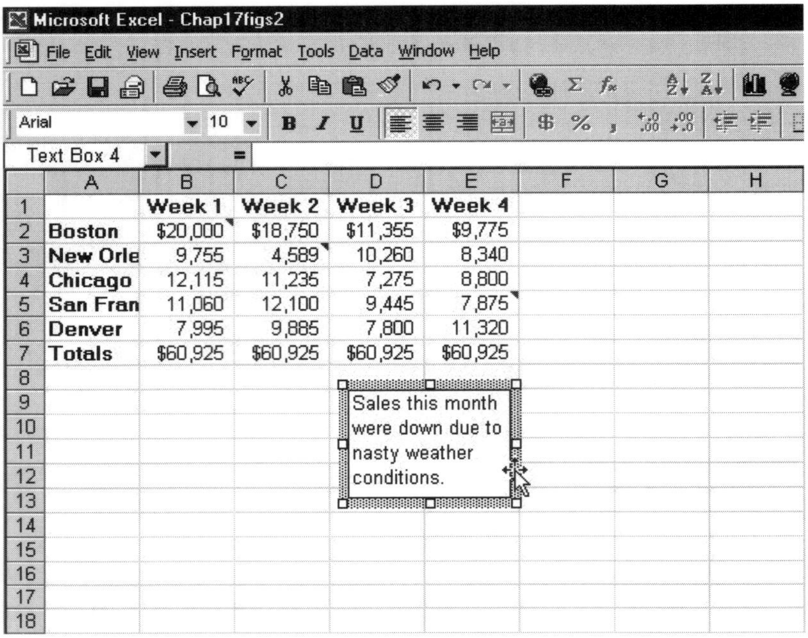

	A	B	C	D	E	F	G	H
1		Week 1	Week 2	Week 3	Week 4			
2	Boston	$20,000	$18,750	$11,355	$9,775			
3	New Orle	9,755	4,589	10,260	8,340			
4	Chicago	12,115	11,235	7,275	8,800			
5	San Fran	11,060	12,100	9,445	7,875			
6	Denver	7,995	9,885	7,800	11,320			
7	Totals	$60,925	$60,925	$60,925	$60,925			

Sales this month were down due to nasty weather conditions.

Figure 17-7 Right-click on the border of a text box, or the Copy and Paste functions won't work

When I right-click on a text box and choose Format, I only get the Font tab. Where are the rest of the formatting options?

The answer to this question is the same as the previous answer. When you right-click on the inside of a text box and choose Format text box, the window that opens contains only the Font tab. This is because you are clicking on the inside of the box, and Excel assumes you are referring to the text inside the box, not the box itself. Thus, the features you see are only the text-related features.

To see the entire Format window, right-click on the border of a text box, choose Format Text Box, and the window that appears will be complete with all the formatting tabs (see Figure 17-8).

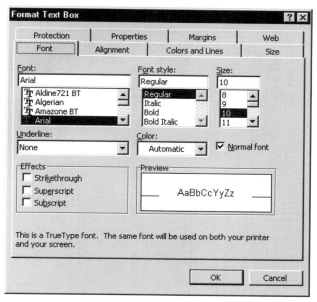

Figure 17-8 The full formatting selections are only available if you right-click on the edge of a text box

I work with really large worksheets and need to be able to see different areas in a hurry. Is there a way to view more than one area of a worksheet at once?

You can view multiple areas of your worksheet simultaneously by using Excel's split screen option. Drag the horizontal and/or vertical split bars to view up to four sections of your worksheet simultaneously, each section becoming a scrollable area independent of the other sections (see Figure 17-9).

Another technique for viewing multiple areas of your worksheet is to display the worksheet in two completely separate Excel windows. Choose Window | New Window to create a second window, and then use Window | Arrange | Tile if you want two or three horizontal or vertical views. This process takes up a bit more room but sometimes offers a different view than split can.

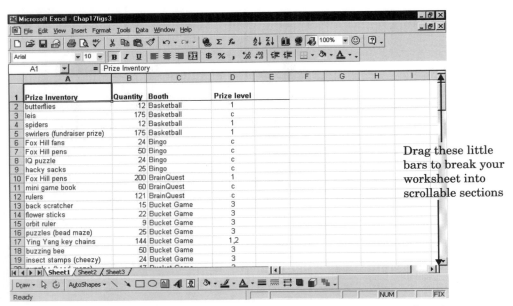

Drag these little bars to break your worksheet into scrollable sections

Figure 17-9 View different areas of a worksheet at the same time by using Excel's split bars. Remove a split by double-clicking on the bar

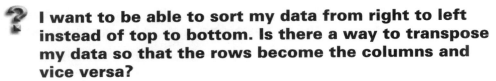

I want to be able to sort my data from right to left instead of top to bottom. Is there a way to transpose my data so that the rows become the columns and vice versa?

There are a couple of ways to accomplish this task. You can reorganize your data so that the rows actually become the columns and the columns the rows. Do this by selecting the data, choosing Edit | Copy, then clicking on a blank area of the worksheet or a new sheet and choosing Edit | Paste Special. In the Paste Special window that appears (see Figure 17-10), click the Transpose button, then click OK. The data rows and columns will be reversed.

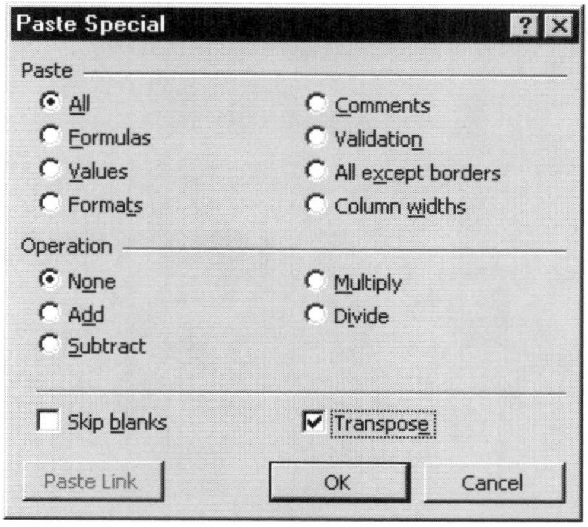

Figure 17-10   Click Transpose if you want to reorganize your data rows and columns

Make sure you have plenty of available room when you convert from a vertical list to a horizontal list. Remember that each row in the list is going to need a separate column. You might find it a good idea to use a blank sheet to receive your transposed data.

If it's only a sort you want and you don't need to actually change the status of rows and columns, you can perform the row sort by following these steps:

1. Click anywhere in the data area.

2. Choose Data | Sort. The Sort window will appear.

3. Click the Options button. The Sort Options window will appear (see Figure 17-11).

4. Select the Sort left to right option, then click OK and click OK again. The sort will occur without having to change the row/column status of your data.

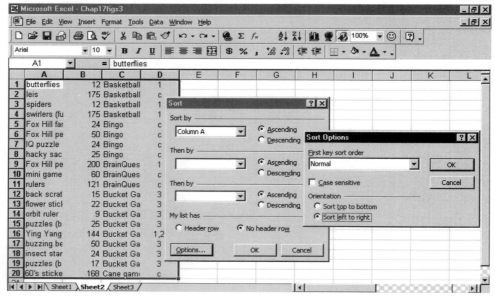

Figure 17-11   Choose Sort left to right to perform a sort of your rows instead of your columns

 What does the Internet have to offer to Excel users?

Head for www.microsoft.com for the latest information about Excel software, including downloadable updates and add-ins (see Figure 17-12).

Choose support options, including lists of frequently asked questions and a support screen where you can enter your own questions in plain English. Microsoft will sift through its archives of similar questions and provide you with detailed information in answer to your question. Support options are at www.support.microsoft.com (see Figure 17-13).

Another Web location to explore is the Stream site at www.stream.com (see Figure 17-14). Stream provides technical support for all Microsoft products and provided us with many of the questions answered in this book.

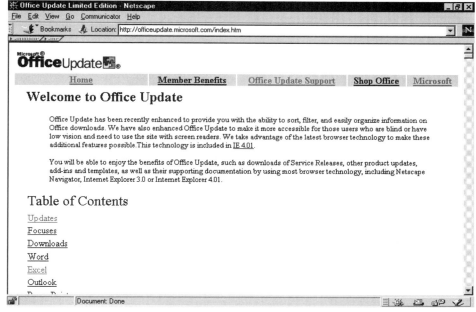

Figure 17-12 Get the latest program updates and read up on Microsoft software developments at the Microsoft Web site

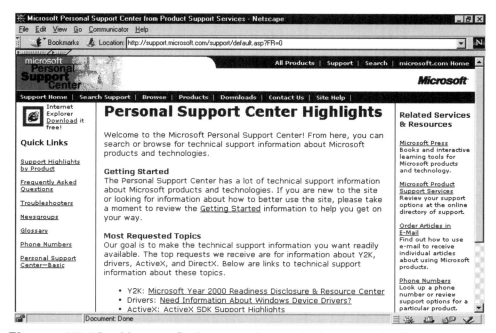

Figure 17-13 You can find top notch technical support for free at Microsoft's support site

Figure 17-14 Check out the frequently asked questions on Stream's Web site

Index

AVERAGE function, nonadjacent cells, 64-65
averaging
 array formulas and, 111-112
 nonadjacent cells via functions, 64-65

B

backgrounds, Sheet Background window, 133
BACKSPACE key, editing data, 35
backward compatibility of worksheets, 1
bar charts, described, *161*
black and white option, printing charts, 194-195, *196*
blank cells, zero values as, 85-86
borders
 printing gridlines without, 190
 worksheet design, 81-83
breaking links, Microsoft Office applications and worksheets, 317-318
breaks
 See also subtotals
 control break reports, 249, *250*
bubble charts, described, *161*
built-in functions. *See* functions
Button Editor, creating toolbar buttons, 234-236, *237*
buttons
 adding graphics to toolbar, 234
 adding to toolbars, 233
 creating macro, 309-311
 removing from toolbars, 233-234

C

calculated fields, data forms, 274-275
case of letters
 fonts, 83-84
 functions, 65-67
cellpointer
 ENTER key and, 32
 locked, 29
 multiple columns and, 33-34
cells
 borders, 81-83

checkmarks, 84-85
combining with concatenation symbol (&), 55-56
converting from formulas to results, 58
copying and locking formulas, 107-108
copying and moving contents, 23-26
error values in, 72
formatting. *See* Format Cells dialog box
formating specific letters within, 86
formatting nonadjacent, 19-20
global PivotTable changes, 262
moving contents of, 25-26
multiple AutoFormat to groups of, 87-88
named ranges, 138-157
nonadjacent. *See* nonadjacent cells
referencing without typing, 56-57
selecting, 18-22
selecting nonadjacent in charts, 162-163
summing from multiple worksheets, 127-128
zero values appearing blank, 85-86
Center button, aligning worksheets, 91
centering, Merge and Center feature, 76, *77*
Change Source button, linking formulas, *105*
CHANGEGRID macro, gridlines toggle, 305, *306*
characters
 naming worksheets and restricted, 136
 versus numbers in columns, 96
Chart Wizard, 160-161, 163
 printing charts, 193-194
charts, 158-176
 Chart Title field, 167-168, *169*
 color options, 173
 copying into Word documents, 315

To **speak to the support experts** who handle more than one million technical issues every month, call **Stream's** Microsoft® Excel® answer line! Trained specialists will answer your Microsoft® Excel® questions including built-in functions, formatting, charts and printing.

Have all your questions been answered?

1-800-477-7614 $29.95 per problem (Charge to a major credit card.)

1-900-555-2006 $29.95 per problem (Charge to your phone bill.)

Visit our web site at www.stream.com.

We help people use technology!